2020

£2.50

29/7/24

The Book of
WINE
ANTIQUES

Robin Butler &
Gillian Walkling

Antique Collectors' Club

© 1986 Robin Butler and Gillian Walkling
World copyright reserved
First published in hardback 1986
Reprinted 1987
Published in paperback 1993
Published in laminated paperboard 1995

ISBN 1 85149 227 5

British Library Cataloguing-in-Publication Data
A catalogue record for this book is available from the British Library

The authors and publishers are greatly indebted to
Harveys of Bristol for their generous support in the subsidising of
the photographic contents of this book.

Printed in England on Consort Royal Satin paper from Donside Mills, Aberdeen,
by the Antique Collectors' Club, Woodbridge, Suffolk IP12 1DS

PREFACE

During the winter of 1976 the British Antique Dealers' Association called upon members to produce a nationwide festival of exhibitions in their own premises to celebrate its Diamond Jubilee. In an attempt to avoid the obvious commercial cliché of staging a 'recent acquisitions' show, I looked for an exhibition subject which would cut across the boundaries of the disciplines to which most students of the decorative arts are bound, namely those of silver, porcelain, glass, pictures, etc. Noticing a pleasant pair of decanters and a wine cooler in my stock, the subject of wine antiques seemed a promising one, particularly in view of my enjoyment of wine. During the ensuing eighteen months I collected a large quantity of mostly British antiques which had something to do with the storage, serving or consumption of wine. When it happened, the exhibition was a modest commercial success, at least to the extent that I resolved to maintain this area of my business as a permanent feature. However, from a personal point of view, the greatest joy of the exhibition was learning about disciplines other than furniture (my original area of study), in particular glass and silver. Understanding, for example, how a drinking glass was made or how a silver wine cooler was manufactured, was not the only pleasure. I was also fascinated by the study of objects such as corkscrews, which are not contained within any of the standard categories.

After a while I was able to dictate my thoughts on the subject. These thoughts were ramshackle, brief and far from complete, but they were sufficient to suggest that a book should be forthcoming. My problem was that business commitments left little time for such an immense undertaking. Fortunately at this point I met, at a meeting of the Furniture History Society, a friend of long-standing whose young and expanding family made her temporarily reluctant to commit herself to writing a book on her own, but who was very happy to share the burden of this one. With two books, numerous magazine articles and seven years museum experience behind her, Gillian appeared to me to be a well-qualified collaborator. She has since proved to be so and has edited and rearranged many hundreds of pages of typescript, has rewritten many paragraphs and has researched and written certain sections of her own. She has shared the immense task of gathering together the 350 or so photographs and has done much letter writing and form filling regarding reproduction rights and fees. She has been the perfect foil to my disorganised and erratic style.

My long-suffering assistant Rosemary Prosser deserves much credit for transcribing all the original text from tapes and has been a constant source of support. My family too have been uncomplaining and encouraging.

A very substantial number of people have been forthcoming with help and advice, letting us have photographs to illustrate this book, and their names are listed in the Photographic Acknowledgements. Museums and private individuals alike have been most generous of their time and effort and to them we are very grateful. However, particular thanks must go to

Christopher Sykes who provided not only pictures, but captions, for the chapter on corkscrews, spending much time and effort to ensure accuracy. Peter Williams of Jonathan Horne Antiques, Robert Luck of Stair & Company, Jeanette Hayhurst and Brian Beet, and the Brothers Kern of Hotspur Ltd. have all lent a hand where most needed. My brother Roderick has also put up with many demands on his time. Karin Walton at the Bristol City Museum and Art Gallery has gone to much trouble to make items available for photography and has provided valuable information. We are particularly indebted to Brand Inglis for kindly reading through the entire text and coming up with valuable suggestions where silver is concerned. Martin Mortimer of Delomosne & Son Ltd. repeated this procedure for glass and not only put right several minor errors, but correctly suggested that we re-organise an entire chapter. The book would be much the worse without his help We would also like to thank Captain Sir Thomas Barlow Bt. D.S.C., D.L., R.N. Rtd., for his welcome advice on the Wine Labels chapter.

Throughout the writing of this book the proximity of Harveys Wine Museum and its staff have been a constant support. Not only have they contributed towards the cost of the photographs, which has resulted in a vastly increased number of both colour and black and white plates, but they have also made the services of their museum free to us. Robin Frost and Mike Corbett have given us every possible encouragement and the book owes much to them.

I should also like to thank those who have suggested possible titles for this book, perhaps the greatest enigma we have encountered. There appears to be no adjective in the English language meaning 'pertaining to wine' and notwithstanding good suggestions such as *The Mechanicks of Drinking* and *Bacchus at Home,* we finally plumped for *The Book of Wine Antiques,* the suggestion of Mary Berry whose works sell volumes. We rather thought the direct message matched our style. Our thanks to all who bent their minds to this knotty problem.

May I add our thanks to two photographers, Ian Blantern and Tom Brydon, whose photographic skills adorn many pages of the book, and with whom it has been a pleasure to work. Sharon Baker has transferred the whole text onto a word processor, a long and onerous task which has saved countless re-typings and irritations. To her both I, and particularly Gillian, are very thankful. Samantha Taylor has made a valuable contribution at the last minute by undertaking the tedious job of indexing. Finally Liz Watson has cheerfully given so much of her valued time and expertise.

In conclusion we would like to thank you, the reader, without whom this book would not have been worth writing. We can only hope that it repays your investment with enhanced enjoyment of wine antiques.

Robin Butler
Clifton, Bristol, 1986

PHOTOGRAPHIC ACKNOWLEDGEMENTS

The authors are particularly grateful to the people, businesses and institutions who have kindly supplied, or allowed them to take, photographs for reproduction in this book. A few individuals have preferred to remain anonymous.

INDIVIDUALS
His Grace the Duke of Atholl, Colour plate 22; The Marquess of Bath, Longleat House, Colour plate 46; His Grace the Duke of Beaufort, Colour plate 21; in the collection of the Duke of Buccleuch & Queensberry K.T., at Boughton House, Kettering 266; His Grace the Duke of Devonshire, 149; Trustee of the will of the late Earl of Berkeley, 152, 153; the Earl of Harewood, Colour plate 45; Miss Rosemary Prosser 203; J.P. Smith Esq., 120.

BUSINESSES
Asprey plc, Colour plate 42, Plate 88; Brian Beet, London, 278, 281; Tony Bingham, London, 279; Blairman & Sons Ltd., London, 111; Robin Butler Antiques: Colour plates 1, 4, 5, 19, 24, 33, 34, 35, 50 and 51, Plates 1, 3, 4, 24, 29, 33, 51, 56, 66, 67, 91, 97, 99, 101, 104, 136, 143, 146, 150, 173, 174, 175, 177, 182, 183, 184, 187, 188, 189, 190, 195, 203, 209, 218, 219, 239, 240, 241, 243, 245, 250, 254, 259, 262, 263, 274, 282, 292, 294, 302, 306; Roderick Butler, Honiton, Colour Plate 2, Plates 145, 223, 242, 249; Christie's, London, 2, 106, 110, 113, 148, 185, 193, 233, 269; Corney & Barrow, London, 25; Andrew Dando, Bath, 114; Delomosne & Son Ltd., London, 90, 115, 125, 127, 129, 130, 131, 132, 133, 134, 141, 142, 147, 154, 155, 156, 157, 197, 199, 200, 202, 205, 207, 208, 211, 212, 216, 217, 247, 272, 291, 295, 305; Eliot Antiques, Stanford Bingley, Colour plates 26, 27; Ferneyhough Antiques, Henley in Arden, 108, 109; David Gibbins, Woodbridge, Colour plate 37; Grants of St. James, Colour plate 14; John Harvey & Sons Ltd., Bristol, 40, 86, 210; Jeanette Hayhurst (Fine Glass), London, 137, 138, 140, 151, 221; Jonathan Horne, London, Colour plate 43, Plates 6, 251, 298; Hotspur Ltd., London, Colour Plate 23, Plate 103; Brand Inglis Ltd., London, Colour plate 44, Plates 41, 42, 89, 100, 144, 159, 160, 161, 179, 180, 192, 224, 225, 226, 227, 252, 257, 261, 264, 270, 287, 300, 303, 304; Laymont & Shaw Ltd., Truro, 176; Charles Lumb & Sons Ltd., Harrogate, 112; Thomas Lumley Ltd., London, 180, 181, 271; E.P. Mallory & Son Ltd., Bath, 119; Phillips of Hitchin (Antiques) Ltd., 236, 237; Ernest Quinton, Bath, 246; Racal-Chubb Ltd., 283; Sotheby's, London, 178, 244; Stair & Co. Ltd., London, 102, 105, 231, 267; Ston Easton Park, near Bath, Colour plate 16; Christopher Sykes Antiques Woburn, 62, 63, 68, 69, 70, 71, 72, 73, 74, 75, 76, 77, 78, 79, 80, 81, 82, 83, 84, 85; B. & T. Thorn & Son, Budleigh Salterton, 93; Charles Toller, Datchet, 289; C.J. Vander (Antiques) Ltd., London, 254; Peter Willis, Nailsworth, 30, 38.

CONTENTS

COLOUR PLATES

Introduction

Who could deny that the drinking of wine and the collecting of antiques are among the most pleasurable of pursuits? It may well be said that the two activities combined may give more than twice the pleasure. This book concentrates on the many British artefacts which have been made in the past to assist in the storage, serving and consumption of wine and the aim has been to produce a volume with sufficient information to interest both the collector and drinker alike.

A very wide variety of wares, either simply utilitarian or very highly crafted, can be covered by this single title, and not just such objects as decanters which spring immediately to mind. Indeed, it is such a broad canvas that limitations of space have made it necessary to make a few carefully considered omissions. Ecclesiastical and ceremonial vessels for example have only been given a brief mention and Continental wine antiques, although developing on similar lines, have only been included where relevant to the design of those made in this country. References to sixteenth century Venetian glass have necessarily been made in the preamble to the subject of drinking glasses, but we have not considered say, French decanters or Portuguese coasters, nor the very large subject of nineteenth century Bohemian glass. Neither have we concerned ourselves with beer, ale, cider or spirits unless, as they occasionally do, the subjects overlap. An eighteenth century ale glass for example, is an excellent vessel from which to drink champagne today and a study of decanters would be incomplete without consideration of those made to hold spirits.

There are areas in which this book breaks fresh ground, although in a large measure the book is a collation of existing knowledge rather than the first publication of extensive original research. Some chapters have already been the subject of substantial monographs, such as Dumbrell's book on bottles or the book on corkscrews by Dr. Bernard Watney and while much praiseworthy writing has been published about wine glasses, the subject of decanters has not yet been adequately covered by a single volume. The majority of these monographs, plus references to those subjects which have sadly been omitted, can be found in the bibliography at the end of this book.

It will be seen that in many chapters suppositions have been made which are, as far as we know, unsupported by tangible proof, but which would appear to be the logical result of surviving evidence. Also, throughout the book we have suggested that certain things do not exist. By this we mean that having studied the subject for many years we have not to date come across an example. We will of course be only too pleased if the reader can plug the gaps in our knowledge.

Plate 1. A group of miscellaneous wine antiques. In the glass punch bowl is a silver ladle with the bowl in the form of a shell, while in the foreground are two 17th century two-handled dishes which may, or may not, be wine tasters (see Chapter 6). Next to the magnum carafe is a pretty silver measure made by Hempston & Prince, the York silversmiths.

When studying antiques it is customary to do so by medium, thereby concentrating on, say, furniture or silver or glass. In this book there are many objects which cross these barriers and the chapters have therefore been arranged according to the use of each object and the order in which they assisted the wine on its journey from the vineyard to the table.

It is perhaps surprising that so many wine-related objects made in a non-wine-producing country have survived dating from the eighteenth and nineteenth century. This can best be accounted for by the high esteem in which wine was then held. Good wine has always been a precious commodity. There have been many times during the history of the British Isles when we have been at war with wine-producing countries in Europe and at such times the already valuable liquid became less accessible and correspondingly more prized. It was not consumed, as eventually was tea,

14

by the working majority, but by the monied minority and it was this group, and the aristocracy, who laid down the rules of etiquette associated with its drinking and demanded that precious materials be lavished on the paraphernalia required in the process.

It will be noted throughout the book that only a few items date from the period immediately following the restoration of King Charles II to the throne in 1660. The substantial bulk of material derives from the second half of the eighteenth century and later. This situation can quite simply be attributed to supply and demand. As improved vinification methods and better handling resulted in better wines, and an enlarged merchant navy was able to carry larger cargoes to this country, so consumption increased and with it a corresponding demand for drinking glasses, decanters, coasters, wine coolers and so on. These products of the eighteenth and nineteenth centuries are worthy of consideration because, in the first instance, many are very beautiful or charming, and in the second, their raison d'être is as valid today as it was when they were made. From the point of view of practicality many old designs have never been improved and it is merely the changing notions of fashion which have dictated alterations.

At this point it may be helpful for those who are not familiar with the decorative arts to discuss the general evolution of design in Europe, and in Britain in particular, from the mediaeval period onwards. Reference is made continually in the book to various design styles such as 'Gothic' or 'Neo-classical'. These can roughly be summarised as follows: the Gothic evolved in France in the middle of the twelfth century and was an elegant contrast to the severe forms of the Romanesque style which preceded it. In architecture the most obvious features were the pointed arch, the ribbed vault and the flying buttress. An infill of the arch was often achieved with trefoil or quatrefoil tracery. The Gothic art form was revived in the decorative arts in Britain during the 1750s and 1760s, for a short while around 1800-1802 and then on a larger and more dramatic scale during the 1830s and 1840s. In its original form it died out in Southern Europe in the fifteenth century and in Northern Europe approximately a century later.

The Gothic style was succeeded by the Renaissance which originated in Italy and represented a growing quest for knowledge and a precise understanding of Roman antiquity. The Renaissance style is characterised by strapwork, masks, cherubs and arabesque scrolling foliage on outlines of monumental and rectilinear form, though arches and other architectural features were put to decorative effect. Repetitive motifs such as 'egg and dart' and 'bead and reel' decoration, usually associated with Neo-classicism, were also used.

The Renaissance then developed into the Mannerist style which is characterised by particularly elongated forms and frequently incorporates figures, both animal and human. Both the Renaissance and Mannerist

Plate 2. A sarcophagus-shaped wine cooler in the full-blown Regency taste. The X-frame base is in the form of an ancient piece of furniture, a clear allusion to Classicism.

movements were revived in the nineteenth century. An example of true Renaissance decoration can be found on the tigerware jugs mentioned in the chapter on decanters, while in its revival form can be seen on Victorian claret jugs.

The Baroque style, which followed Mannerism, was typified by symmetrical outlines of a curvilinear type. Baroque items are typically heavy in concept and in this book examples may be found in late seventeenth and early eighteenth century silver. Just as Mannerism had grown out of the Renaissance, so too Rococo sprang from the dying years of the Baroque. This was an altogether happier, lighter style and was characterised by a lack of symmetry and abundant decoration in the form of acanthus leaves, rock work (from which the name derives), S and C scrolls and icicles. In England the Rococo style enjoyed popularity from about 1740 to about 1765 although a few pieces are to be found from a slightly later date. It was later revived briefly in the 1820s. Eighteenth

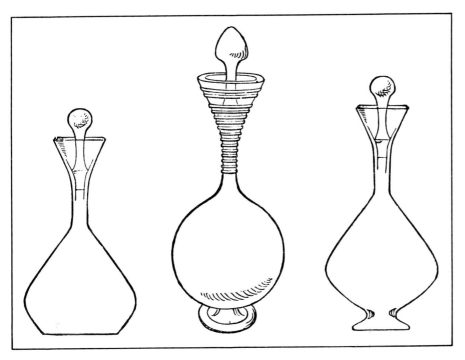

Plate 3. Three designs from The Principles of Decorative Design *by Dr. Christopher Dresser, 1873. Their stark simplicity and functionalism contrasted strongly with preceding fussy Victorian designs.*

century examples in this book are pierced silver coasters and enamelled Beilby drinking glasses. Often incorporated in the Rococo style, although originally fashionable during the seventeenth century, was chinoiserie, a form of decoration inspired by the trading activities of the East India Company with the Orient. Thomas Chippendale, of course, is famous for his use of chinoiserie designs, either on their own, or combined with Rococo, for his furniture of the 1750s and 1760s.

Neo-classicism in the decorative arts enjoyed popularity in Britain in the 1760s having been fashionable in Continental Europe a few years earlier. It was in every way in sharp contrast to the extravagant, asymmetrical frivolity of Rococo. Forms were greatly simplified and a clean-cut symmetry emerged. Dainty swags of formalised flowers, ribbon-tied or pendant from rams' heads, were interspersed with fluting and reeding, paterae and vase shapes. Neo-classicism flourished for a surprisingly long time, from the 1770s to the 1790s, and reappeared in a modified form some hundred years later. Numerous objects mentioned in this book were made in this style, particularly those of silver such as wine labels and coasters.

In 1797 Admiral Lord Nelson defeated the French at the Battle of the Nile and patriotic Englishmen took the Egyptian theme very much to heart. Decorative objects in Egyptian style abounded and nowhere was the style more clearly demonstrated than in the sarcophagus-shaped wine coolers popular for the first thirty years or so of the nineteenth century. The remainder of the century was primarily taken with a succession of revival styles (as just recorded), some of them popular concurrently. Objects made in these revival styles were pastiches, not direct copies, and

Plate 4. Three silver wine coasters. The two left-hand examples are neatly fretted in a style which vaguely echoes the Gothic taste, while the right-hand one has simple wire mouldings.

were in no way intended to be fakes. Rather they represented a newly awakened interest in past history. Their proportions usually differ noticeably from the original prototypes.

The last quarter of the nineteenth century was dominated by the Arts and Crafts movement which advocated a return to natural materials and straightforward methods of construction. At the same time Christopher Dresser and others were producing designs based on Japanese principles and their fresh thinking and totally new approach was laying the foundations for the modern movement of the twentieth century. Amazingly, the stark simplicity of Dresser's work was simultaneously popular with rather clumsy, revived neo-classical designs and the totally different sinuous, plastic curves and 'natural' forms of Continental Art Nouveau. Although subsequent developments in fundamental art forms are of course important, they are not generally applicable to any categories of items in this book, most modern examples of which are reproductions of earlier types.

In various chapters of this book mention is made both of silver and of glass and an understanding of the basic principles of their manufacture is more than desirable. There are many techniques which a silversmith may employ. A large number of objects are made by 'raising' them to the desired shape from a flat sheet of silver by a process of hammering and beating. Other pieces may be made by casting, that is, by pouring molten metal into a mould. When making more elaborate items both these techniques may be employed, the main body of the piece being raised and the other parts first cast and then attached by hard soldering (i.e. with silver as opposed to lead which is used for 'soft' soldering). As far as decoration is concerned various techniques may be used. The surface of the metal may be hammered with punches, either from inside or outside, to produce indentations in the required pattern. When executed from the outside surface this process is known as 'chasing' or 'flat chasing' and is

Colour plate 1. An interesting assortment of antiques, most of which are connected with
wine. In the centre there is a tôle peint verrière with better-than-usual gilt decoration.
In the foreground there is a glass wine funnel with a cranked spout and also a wine
label for champagne, spelled incorrectly. The large amethyst glass punch bowl in the
background was unfortunately broken in the post soon after this photograph was taken.
Opposite it is a very fine turned wooden decanter, an example of an art form known
as treen.

Colour plate 2. Detail of a drawer front from a small cabinet which is divided into
panels indicating the months of the year. Here, in the month of October, the barrels
are being filled, the grapes are being trodden and the men are making themselves ill
with greed.

characterised by the pattern being seen in reverse on the inside. Some fine detail may be achieved in this way. When the decoration is hammered from the inside surface so that it stands out from the general line of the piece it is said to be 'embossed'. Generally embossing is further chiselled up to produce a finer finish by more working from the outside, a technique known as 'repoussé' work.

Another quite different form of decoration on silver is engraving. This requires the use of a tool called a 'graver', a sharp instrument which gouges out pieces of metal to leave behind the desired pattern. The gravers, and consequently the grooves, can of course be of a variety of different shapes to produce different designs. A particular variety of engraving on silver is 'bright cut' where the graver is brightly burnished to give a glittering effect. During the seventeenth century many silver items had 'pricked' decoration whereby initials, cyphers and dates were formed of numerous lightly struck pinpricks.

Many silver objects described in this book are fretted or pierced. This can be achieved either by drilling a hole and then inserting a saw blade to cut out the desired pattern, or the hole may be stamped out with a press. Pieces could be made from lengths of silver wire of various cross-sections which were purchased by the yard and used by silversmiths as required.

Since the Middle Ages by far the largest majority of silver objects made in Britain have by law been stamped with the silversmith's own peculiar device. Each individual maker's mark was registered with the appropriate assay office (the place where silver was officially tested). The mark was made with a steel punch after the maker had roughly shaped his object and added any applied mounts, but before any engraving, chasing or piercing was executed. It was also at this point in its making that the object was sent to the assay office for hallmarking. Before any hallmarks were punched or stamped a scraping was taken by the assay office and analysed. If the piece was in more than one part, for example a wine funnel, then both sections would be tested. As precious metals were a major form of investment it was considered necessary to protect the public from unscrupulous craftsmen by setting a legal standard of fineness of silver for all wrought plate. It should, at this point, be explained that 'plate' is a term used to embrace all silver, gold and silver gilt; it should not be confused with the word 'plated' which implies the deposit of one metal (usually precious) upon another. Between 1300, when hallmarking was first introduced, and 1697 the proportion of pure silver to the base metal alloy necessary to harden it sufficiently for use, was $92\frac{1}{2}\%$ to $7\frac{1}{2}\%$. This standard, known as Sterling and not incidentally to be confused with silver manufactured in the Scottish town of Stirling, was the same as that set for coinage which enabled plate to be easily converted to coinage when required by the Government. By the end of the seventeenth century demand for silver wares was so great that the reverse process was found to be in operation on a large scale and an Act

Colour plate 3. A selection of glasses demonstrating the versatility of the wine glass maker. Cutting and wheel engraving are shown, as are opaque and colour twist stems. The coloured glass contrasts sharply with the elegant baluster stem glass on the right-hand side.

of Parliament was introduced in 1697 setting a higher standard of fineness containing 3.3% more silver. This was known as the Britannia Standard because the figure of Britannia was used as a hallmark. Also at this date makers were instructed to mark their wares with the first two letters of their surname as opposed to the variety of letters and symbols previously used. The Britannia Standard was enforced until 1720 when an optional return to the Sterling Standard was allowed and almost universally adopted. It was accompanied by a duty payable on the weight of wrought silver. Many silversmiths endeavoured to avoid this new levy by simply retailing their wares without marking them, but such pieces were (and still are) illegal and are commonly known as 'duty dodgers'. Makers' marks on post 1720 sterling standard silver comprise their initials.

As well as the maker's mark, which is not strictly speaking a hallmark, one should find at least three marks on most silver. Apart from items not being retailed, the only pieces legally exempted from hallmarking were items weighing less than ten pennyweights made before 1790 and those weighing less than five pennyweights made after that date. (Wine labels incidentally fell within the former category.) A pennyweight (dwt) is equal to one twentieth of an ounce. In the first instance there should be the assay mark of the town in which the silversmith is registered. For London it will be the leopard's head, crowned before 1820, uncrowned after. For

Plate 5. A page from Diderot's Encyclopedie, *1762, showing a working glasshouse. The furnaces are in operation and the various procedures — blowing, the working of vessels on a pontil rod, and marvering — can be seen.*

Birmingham there will be an anchor, for Sheffield a crown, and so on. While the Britannia Standard was in operation the London leopard's head without a crown was changed to look sideways and was cut off at the neck. Heraldically this is called a 'leopard's head erased'. Following this there will be a date letter. By varying the form of the alphabet and by using upper and lower case letters, various cycles of letters enable almost all English plate to be accurately dated to within a year. The date letters usually run for one year and the starting and finishing points may differ from town to town. In London, for example, the year begins on May 19th and ends on the following May 18th. The former is the saint's day of St. Dunstan, the patron saint of silversmiths.

The next mark to be found will be that which indicates that the standard of silver has been verified. This will either be the Britannia figure or a lion passant representing the Sterling Standard.

On many pieces of silver, an additional mark will be found called the duty mark which indicates that the various taxes levied by Acts of Parliament on the weight of silver have been paid. This was introduced in 1784 and finally abandoned in 1890 and took the form of the heads of the monarchs George III, George IV, William IV and Queen Victoria. Several books of tables of marks are freely available, some with more

Plate 6. A rather amusing Wedgwood creamware teapot, enamelled in black and red by Robinson and Rhodes. It depicts three gentlemen and a cleric smoking and drinking and it dates from about 1765.

detailed information than given above, and they make the identification of most British plate a simple matter.

A very large number of items included in this book were made of glass. The basic constituent of glass is silica in one of its various forms, either sand, flint or quartz. To this is added a flux which reduces its melting point and makes it workable. Flux is either composed of burnt vegetation or 'potash', or of naturally occurring minerals such as carbonate of soda. When potash is used the glass tends to have a greenish hue, whereas soda glass is naturally clearer and resembles rock crystal. In the past various other additions have been made to produce different effects. Lime was often added to make a harder product and in England specifically lead oxide was included to produce the 'lead glass' with which this country has been long associated.

Soda glass is not only light in weight, volume for volume, but has a property which makes glass blowers want to blow it thinly, producing a correspondingly 'light' style. The colour and other properties of lead glass by contrast mean that it can be worked in one of two ways to best advantage. It may either be blown or moulded into heavy, almost sculptural forms and left plain, or it may be cut deeply to reflect the light from its many facets. Just as gem cutters learned to cut precious stones in such a way as to maximise their colour and refractivity so too glass cutters devised many patterns with which to decorate their wares.

Rather confusingly the term 'metal' is used to describe the substance of glass. In its making the various ingredients are first heated to produce a molten sticky mess known as the 'melt'. The melt is then collected in a blob

Colour plate 4. A fine group of wine-related treen. On the left is the decanter already shown, while next to it is a large barrel-shaped wine cistern made of lignum vitae. Apart from the goblet and coasters, which are shown elsewhere in the book, there is a very fine early 18th century spice grinder with an oval body.

or 'gather' on the end of a long, metal tube. This tube can either be used to blow the glass to produce a hollow vessel (a technique invented by the Romans) or it can be used to hold the gather while it is stretched and cut with pliers and shears to produce a solid object. When making a rounded piece the tube will be rolled to and fro to ensure that the vessel retains its regular shape on a special glass maker's chair, an ordinary chair but for its long, flat arms placed horizontally to the ground. A variety of other tools and more complicated procedures are then employed to work the glass to the required shapes.

When making a decanter for instance, the leader of the team of makers will first take a gather on the end of the blow pipe and blow a bubble to the required size. Naturally blown, the glass would assume a bladder shape and other shapes are therefore achieved by shaping the bubble with a pair of blades (in the past made of pearwood and today of steel). Then a solid pontil rod is heated and attached to the end of the melt furthest away from the pipe. The blow pipe is then cut away and the nascent decanter rotated on the pontil rod while its neck is formed at the newly cut end. Neck rings and any other applied mouldings will be added at this point. As the glass is cooling the rod is broken away leaving the characteristic mark in the middle of the decanter's base. The object is then transferred to an oven where the cooling rate is carefully controlled to prevent the glass from cracking. Any cut decoration will be added at a later stage.

Colour plate 5. Another group of unusual wine antiques which includes a ribbed papier mâché coaster and a Leeds creamware example. The four-bottle carrier is of an uncommon form and the decanting machine in the centre is modern.

Where drinking glasses are concerned, a slightly different story obtains. First the leader of the team will blow a small bubble to form the bowl of the glass. Meanwhile another member will be making the stem (at first a solid rod) while a third is busy making the domed foot. Next the three sections are joined and a hot pontil rod attached to the underside of the foot. As with the decanter the bubble will be cut free from the blowing rod and paddles will be used to shape the bowl. (The striations which are frequently found on old drinking glasses are occasioned by the wood grain of the paddles used in their making and are one of the features which have

Plate 7. An early engraving depicting Bacchus wantonly pouring wine into a goblet while in the background, in front of the tent, a flagon and pilgrim bottle sit in a wine cooler.

given old glasses so much of their character.) While the bowl is being shaped pincers and other tools will be applied to the stem to produce the required knops. The glass will naturally cool while this process is in hand and it may be necessary to return the glass to the hot oven several times before the final effect is achieved. Clearly the entire operation demands a fair degree of coordination and sympathy within the team and great skill is required to achieve perfection.

Not all glass was free-blown in this manner. In the eighteenth century and later glass was also moulded as will be explained in the chapter on wine bottles. Decoration could be applied to both forms in a variety of ways. It could be cut, as already mentioned, by bringing the cooled glass into contact with rotating wheels of different shapes or it could be engraved, either by a selection of copper wheels motivated by a small treadle-operated lathe, or by free-hand cutting with a fine diamond-point tool. The most sophisticated form was diamond point stipple engraving whereby the surface of the glass was lightly tapped with the diamond point many times rather than cut in lines. The pattern was formed by areas of light or shade according to the density of the dots and is only clearly visible under bright light against a dark background. This very exacting technique was pioneered by Frans Greenwood, a Dutchman of English extraction, in the early eighteenth century. Its principal exponent however, was David Wolff who was working during the second half of the century. It has been, until now, generally assumed that much of the Dutch engraving of the period was carried out on English glasses imported from Newcastle. Current opinion refutes this and many so-called Newcastle glasses may well be shown to have been made, albeit of lead glass, in the Low Countries. A certain amount of glass was enamelled in various colours and/or gilded. The brother and sister team of William and Mary Beilby in Newcastle were famous for this technique. During the nineteenth century in particular, some glass was etched, a technique whereby vessels were dipped in wax and decorated with a fine steel point, first by hand, but later mechanically. Subsequent immersion in hydrofluoric acid fixed the pattern and the wax could then be removed.

Although many of the objects in this book are made of these two major materials many others will be found executed in earthenware, porcelain, tin and wood. The latter, usually categorised as 'treen', were frequently made in lignum vitae, a particularly dense wood with a close and wild grain which was admirably suited to turning. (By 'wild' it is meant that the pores of the timber do not run in parallel lines, but rather twist and turn, not only giving the wood a more interesting figure, but also giving greater stability when turned on the lathe.) Lignum vitae comes from the West Indies and the Central American mainland, areas where British colonial influence was very strong. Originally only prime timbers were used and centuries-old wood enabled items to be turned up to twenty inches in diameter. As the supply of these ran out, the width of pieces was reduced, but such items were no less highly esteemed. Some lignum vitae pieces were embellished with turned ivory. Other woods commonly used were mahogany, pear and other fruitwoods, and sycamore.

A fair number of the items described in the book are made of earthenware or porcelain. During the seventeenth century the most popular medium for ceramic pieces was delftware, a form of tin-glazed earthenware with an opaque white glaze which had first been developed by Dutch potters in Delft to simulate Oriental porcelain. The chief centres for its production in England were Lambeth, Southwark and Bristol. In the eighteenth century delftware was largely replaced by a stronger cream-coloured earthenware appropriately named 'creamware'. This was mostly produced in the Staffordshire area which, by the middle of the century, had become the centre of the pottery industry. One of the most important makers, who experimented widely with various clays and glazes, was Josiah Wedgwood.

Surprisingly, although porcelain was made in France at the end of the seventeenth century and at Meissen in Saxony early in the eighteenth, it was not manufactured in England until 1745. Once the secrets of its making had been discovered however, it very quickly replaced earthenware as the most sought after medium and was produced in vast quantities by the larger factories of Chelsea, Bow, Derby and Worcester and amongst many others the smaller factories of Liverpool, Newhall and Lowestoft.

Throughout the book frequent mention is made of toleware (tôle peint) or japanned tin. Japanning, or imitation lacquerwork, was first executed in the late seventeenth century when imported Chinese and Japanese lacquer was highly prized. The technique was at first applied to wood and plaster, but by about 1730 the japanned metal industry was well established. Tin was not the only metal used as a base; iron and copper were also employed. One of the best makers, Edward Allgood, was based in Pontypool in Monmouthshire and the quality of his work was so high that 'Pontypool' has become a generic name for much eighteenth and nineteenth century japanned metalware. Early pieces were usually decorated with chinoiserie designs in emulation of imported lacquerwork, but later pieces had a variety of decoration in line with prevailing fashions. A small number of pieces were painted rather than japanned.

During the 1770s some toleware makers began experimenting with papier mâché or paperware in an attempt to find a cheaper alternative to metal. The most successful producer was Henry Clay in Birmingham. (Moulded paper was already known of course, and had previously been used in place of wood and plaster for moulded ceilings and for mirror frames and girandoles.) In 1816 Clay's business was purchased by Jennens & Bettridge and it is with their name that papier mâché is popularly associated. In 1825 they patented their distinctive form of mother-of-pearl decoration in which shell was inlaid in the layered paper and overlaid with coloured varnishes and other painted or gilt decoration. Although this material was at the height of its popularity between 1825 and 1850, the earlier work of Henry Clay is often of higher quality and far more sophisticated in design. Decoration was largely confined to simple gilt neo-classical borders and the larger areas of a piece were left plain, showing off what must originally have been a highly glossy lacquered finish.

Variety in this book is not confined to medium, design or type of object. There is also a great variance to be seen in quality. It is our intention to give as much advice to collectors as we can, either as the book develops or more particularly in the final chapter where we attempt to explain the modern relevance of these objects to today's world. Those already familiar with this subject will know only too well that many objects, due either to their superb quality or simply to their scarcity, are financially beyond the reach of but a handful of people. The novice collector, however, should not be dismayed by the high prices such pieces command; not everything is expensive and there should be something to suit everybody's taste and pocket.

CHAPTER 1
The History of Wine Drinking

It is generally believed that wine was first made during the fourth millenium B.C. in the countries of the Ancient Middle East — Egypt, Syria, Palestine, Persia and Mesopotamia. Although there are many legends regarding its discovery (interestingly nearly always attributing it to a woman), a lady of the harem of the mythological Persian King Jemsheed (Jamshid) is generally held responsible. Being inordinately fond of grapes, the king had them stored in jars for gradual consumption during the year and one day, on finding a jarful had fermented and no longer tasted sweet, had the container labelled *Poison*. The lady, distraught with a nervous headache and determined to end her suffering by suicide, drank some of the liquid and on awakening free from her troubles quickly consumed the remainder of the drink. She later admitted her secret to Jemsheed who tried the liquid himself and liking it, introduced this new beverage to his court.

Whatever the mythological content of the story may be, in essence it can not be far from the truth. Presumably it was not uncommon for the stored juice of fresh grapes or raisins to run, and under the right circumstances, to ferment. At some time complete fermentation must have taken place and someone must have discovered that the resulting liquid was drinkable.

Colour plate 6. A painting from the tomb of Kha-Amwese of Thebes dating from the 12th century B.C. showing various aspects of the grape harvest. The grapes are being gathered and stored and then transported by ship in large pottery amphorae.

Plate 8. A Roman amphora showing signs of encrustation following excavation from the sea bed. These two-handled, pointed-bottomed storage vessels were used in Ancient Greece, Egypt and Italy.

Despite its uncertain origins there is no doubt that in Egypt the cultivation of vines for the express purpose of wine making was well established by the end of the third dynasty (c.2600 B.C.). Many agricultural vineyards were purely commercial, producing grapes for fresh consumption as well as for the wine press, but in the upper echelons of Egyptian society large 'leisure vineyards' were highly esteemed. These were formally laid out gardens with open walkways, shady loggia and secluded resting places. The vines provided decoration and shade as well as grapes for eating, and at some stage, for drinking. Often close by or attached to the garden were orchard vineyards specifically for wine making.

Nevertheless it was in Ancient Greece that viticulture first became a widespread professional occupation and the drinking of wine a national pastime. Whether the expertise of the Greeks was acquired from the Egyptians or from the nearby Minoan civilisation of Crete with which Egypt had devoloped close links, we shall probably never know. In the *Odyssey* (written it is believed in the ninth century B.C.) Homer describes in the city of the Phaeacians a picture of well-organised and cultivated orchards and gardens. In the Palace of King Alcinous 'with a hedge running down on either side, lies a large orchard of four acres where trees hang their greenery on high…Their fruit never fails nor runs short…it comes at all seasons of the year…so that pear after pear, apple after apple, cluster on cluster of grapes and fig upon fig are always coming to perfection. In the same enclosure there is a fruitful vineyard, in one part of which is a warm patch of level ground, where some of the grapes are drying in the sun, while others are gathered or being trodden, and on the foremost rows hang unripe bunches that have just cast their blossom or show the first faint tinge of purple.'

Wine was stored and transported in Greece in large pottery amphorae — tall, slender, pointed containers with two handles at the top end. The majority were sealed with pitch or plaster (or both) and sometimes the sealings were tied with cords. Although a wine jug discovered in Athens and dating probably from the fifth century B.C. has a cork stopper, corks are not known to have been used as long term sealers, but, as in this case, presumably acted merely as temporary stoppers. Most amphorae were unglazed, but some were coated internally with pitch or resin or were smeared with oil. A few vineyards appear to have had their own kilns and amphorae are occasionally found stamped with the name of the wine they contained. In shops and houses they were often stored horizontally in wooden racks and while in use were simply leant against the wall, slotted into a hole in the ground or fitted in to a stand or tripod. The latter could be quite elaborate. The wine was poured into smaller vessels prior to serving.

The majority of wines consumed by the Greeks were the produce of local

Plate 9. A Greek 'krater' or mixing bowl dating from about 450-440 B.C. in which the wine was diluted with water. It is appropriately decorated with scenes of a 'symposium' in progress, showing two men reclining on couches while drinking wine and beng entertained by a flute girl. Note the two-handled 'cylix' in the hand of the man on the left.

Plate 10. A Greek 'rhyton' or drinking cup in the form of a seated sphinx. This rather grand Athenian drinking vessel, dating from about 470-460 B.C., has gilt enrichments and is attributed to the Sotades painter.

vineyards and few wines were allowed to mature. Flavour was enhanced (or disguised) by blending or the addition of 'perfume' (in the form of herbs and spices), resin and even in some areas, sea water. The existence of resinated wines, still of course popular in Greece, is sometimes attributed to the resin-coated linings of amphorae. Although this may have been their origin there is plenty of evidence to show that in many areas it was an intended additive. It was sometimes thought to extend the life of the wine as well as to add a certain piquancy to its flavour.

An important feature of Greek social life was the symposium. Supposedly an opportunity for indulgence in metaphysical discussion, symposia were more often straightforward drinking parties. In classical times houses of any importance were equipped with an *andron* or 'room for the men' in which couches were arranged around the walls for the men to recline on. A symposium usually began with a meal accompanied by wine during which a libation was made to the good spirit of the house. When

Colour plate 7. This is a detail of a late 16th century banquet and masque at the house of Sir Henry Unton by an unknown artist in about 1596. Note the absence of cutlery and drinking vessels on the table and the presence of a buffet of plate on the rear left-hand side of the room.

the meal was over three further libations were poured, one to the gods, one to departed heroes and the third to Zeus. A hymn was sung and garlands handed round before the serious drinking began. Women were excluded from the proceedings with the exception of a number of flute girls who provided musical, and evidently at times, other forms of entertainment. Further amusements included the composition of *scolia* or short songs and the game of *kottabos* in which participants flicked wine dregs from their cups into a distant target.

Colour plate 8. An oil painting by Gawen Hamilton entitled 'The Brothers Clarke with other Gentlemen taking Wine'. It was painted in the early 1730s. Note particularly the shaft and globe bottles on the table and a decanter which almost matches them in shape. In use is a set of glasses which appear on close examination to have funnel bowls and light baluster stems. On the left two servants are busying themselves at a marble-topped table with a wine cistern beneath, apparently made of terracotta, a medium not encountered elsewhere.

Wine was always drunk diluted with water (even in the common drinking taverns) and was usually strained, either through muslin or through pierced metal strainers. In warm weather it was served chilled. Dilution took place in a large *krater* or mixing bowl and was transferred to the wine cups in a 'ladle', usually a jug of ewer form. The most common wine cup was the *cylix*, a shallow two-handled bowl on a short stem. Other types included the *cantharos*, a vase-like cup on a long stem with twin handles curving up above the rim of the bowl, the self-explanatory drinking horn and the *rhyton*, a vessel in the form of an animal or mythological creature. Simple beakers were also used. The majority of drinking vessels, whether for daily or ceremonial use, were pottery, although silver and gold versions were the most highly prized. It has been suggested that the black and terracotta colour of these pottery vessels emulated those in parcel-gilt silver, Greek silver being intentionally blackened by oxidisation.

The Greek wine trade flourished from about the eighth century B.C. onwards when colonies were established in various parts of the Central

Plate 11. In Italy wine was consumed either neat or diluted with water as in Greece. This Etruscan bronze mixing vessel, dating from the 4th century B.C., is decorated with satyr masks beneath the handles and the inscription 'Larisal Hafrenies Suthina' around the rim.

Mediterranean. Greek merchants also found their way south to Egypt and northwards to Turkey and the Crimea. The presumed introduction of Greek vines and efficient methods of viticulture to other countries via the colonies inevitably brought competition, particularly from Sicily and Southern Italy. In France vineyards were established in the area around Massilia (now Marseilles). The great wine regions of Central and Northern France were founded later by the Romans and indeed, were so successful, producing wines far better than those of Italy, that during the first century A.D. the Emperor Domitian banned planting in Gaul and dictated that half the existing vineyards should be destroyed.

Wine making in Northern and Central Italy is thought to have been initiated by the Etruscans in about 800 B.C. but did not begin on any substantial scale until the Roman Empire was fully established. Throughout the Empire were merchants dealing in wine alongside other commodities. Like the Greeks, Italian wine growers stored and transported

Plate 12. A silver drinking set composed of a cup, a jug, a ladle and a pierced strainer, one of the earliest finds of Roman silver. It dates from about 100 B.C. and was found at Arcisate near Lake Como.

wine in amphorae, albeit heavier and fatter than their Greek counterparts. Many were marked with the name of the presiding Consul, thus providing an indication of the vintage. Evidence exists to show that flat-binning (or horizontal storage) in wooden racks was not unknown. A large amount of Italian wine was sold locally direct from shops attached to vineyard villas, although in the towns and cities bars and taverns of varying degrees of sophistication and quality abounded.

Wealthy Romans had evidently well-developed palates and appreciated the importance of maturing wines. They also eagerly imported the better wines from Greece and Spain and even from Egypt. They drank neat as well as watered wines and were careful in the matter of decanting and straining, the latter being done through a linen *saccus* or a metal colander called a *colum*. Cooling was also common practice.

As in Greece blending and additives in the form of honey, herbs, salt and resin were widespread, the latter again performing the dual purpose of preservation and piquancy. A process peculiar to Italy was the artificial maturing of wines by the action of smoke and heat and some 'smoked' wines were evidently considered a luxury. The most highly prized vessels for the serving and consumption of wine were silver. Indeed, one of the earliest finds of Roman silver, dating from about 100 B.C., is a drinking set consisting of a cup, a strainer, a jug and a ladle. Jugs were usually of ewer form, strainers were punched with geometric patterns and drinking cups were frequently made in two sections, the inner cup being plain and the outer, two-handled cup standing on a stem and foot, being highly ornamented. Similar items were also made in bronze. Again beakers, in a variety of materials, were also used.

Although the Romans influenced the Britons in most areas of their culture they never succeeded in making Britain a wine drinking nation.

Colour plate 9. The outer cover for a late 19th century song sheet entitled the 'Sparkling Moselle Galop' by C. Godfrey Junior.

Wine had been imported in pre-Roman times, probably from Gaul, and was primarily consumed at tribal feasts and other entertainments, but beer still remained the principal beverage. Imports obviously increased with the influx of Roman troops, officials and traders, and indeed, a rough wine called *posca* was included in the army ration. Amongst the more educated though, a distinct preference was shown for French wines.

There is of course evidence of vine growing being undertaken in Southern parts of Britain at the time of the Empire, but climatic conditions must have rendered such vineyards commercially unprofitable. It has been argued that the Christian religion was largely responsible for their continued existence after the Romans' departure. Christianity was first introduced to Britain by Gaulish traders and Roman soldiers and dignitaries during the 1st century, but remained a subversive cult until the Emperor Constantine made it the official religion of the Empire in 312 A.D. By the end of the fourth century it had become the country's principal religion. The symbolic significance of red wine as the blood of Christ and its consumption during the service of communion has been used as a logical explanation for the existence of the vineyards so frequently attached to monasteries. Some of the wine was undoubtedly destined for the communion table, but there is ample evidence to prove that much wine produced by monasteries was intended for the pleasure and refreshment of the monks and their visitors. Those religious communities who had neither

Plate 13. Four from a larger set of silver wine cups, one plain, two with chased Bacchic motifs and one with cast decoration of vines and olives. These may have been exported from Italy to Britain, perhaps via Gaul, during the period of about 30 B.C. to A.D. 20 as part of the general expansion of trade. They may alternatively have been imported at the time of the Roman Conquest in A.D. 43. They were found at Hockwold in Norfolk in 1962.

the knowledge nor the means to cultivate a vineyard presumably relied largely on donations of wine from the wealthy faithful, a common form of religious offering.

By the early Middle Ages vine-growing was fairly widespread in England, but suddenly declined after the marriage of Prince Henry to Eleanor of Aquitaine in 1152. Her dowry included some of the most prosperous wine-making areas of France and before long vast quantities of Bordeaux wine were being traded for grain and English cloth. In 1273 imports amounted to 8,846 tuns of wine (about 10 million bottles in today's terms).

Despite legislation to control the price and quality of wine, much of that imported was probably undrinkable straight from the cask and as secure corking and the addition of sugar to fortify the wine were unknown, its life was short. Throughout the Middle Ages there was a preference for 'cooked' or spiced wines, usually called *piments* after *Pigmentarii*, dealers in drugs and spices. Recipes of course varied considerably although the most common added ingredients were honey (or sugar), ginger and cloves. Herbs could also be used. The most popular drinks appear to have been *Hippocras*, *Clarre* and *Gariofilatum*, although numerous others, with equally appealing names, have been recorded.

Owing to its price, wine was of course consumed largely by the aristocracy and their households and the growing merchant middle class, beer and ale remaining the drink of the labouring classes. The ritual involved in the serving and eating of meals in a great mediaeval household and a description of the plate and drinking vessels required is complex; suffice it to say that the display of gold and silver plate was an important indication of the wealth and status of its owner and consequently many elaborately decorated vessels were intended primarily for show, not for actual use. This attitude was not considered the least bit vulgar. Plate also provided a suitably portable method of investment in a geographically mobile society and right up until the nineteenth century, show-plate was converted into bullion when finance was required.

In Shakespearian times it seems that French wines were still available, although the most popular were the Mediterranean wines *Malmsey*, and more particularly, *Sack*. The latter seems to have been a generic name for a number of strong, rather heavy, sweet wines of varying provenances which were probably equivalent in effect to today's spirits.

Until the advent of pottery flasks in the mid-seventeenth century and of bin and wine labels in the 1730s and 1740s, reliance for what was drunk must be placed entirely in the hands of those who wrote, a state of affairs which can be very confusing, for, apart from the fact that so few of the wines we know and drink today are mentioned, the nature of wine was very different and generic terms were largely used. Nevertheless, it is probably safe to say that until the middle of the seventeenth century when competition arrived first from spirits and later from coffee, tea and

Plate 14. A buff-coloured earthenware pitcher stamped with shields in relief bearing the arms of Clare. This mediaeval jug was found in a well on the site of the Palace of the Bishops of Ely in Holborn, London. It stands 15ins. high.

chocolate, the general preference for Mediterranean wines remained unaltered. Sack is an oft-quoted beverage and is also found on earthenware wine jugs made between the 1630s and 1670s. A great many ideas have been put forward concerning the origin of the name; its closeness to *sec* or *secco*, meaning dry, is tempting, but many other suggestions have equal plausibility. (See plate 45, page 65.)

The most substantial change in drinking habits occurred during the last part of the century with the manufacture of glass bottles and, more importantly, the introduction of permanent cork stoppers. A paper presented to the Royal Society in 1662 entitled *The Mysterie of Vintners* described the 'various sicknesses of Wines, and their respective Remedies' and recommended that the best way to ensure that a wine was palatable was to drink it very young before it had time to go off. The importance of the introduction of cork as a stoppering cannot be over-emphasized; it enabled wine to be kept for prolonged periods thus realising its potential which was not possible previously.

At the same time political discussions were affecting the types of wines consumed. The Whigs had been responsible for bringing the Protestant William III to the throne in place of the Papist James II and were anti-French on most counts. Between 1688 and 1703, when the Methuen Treaty was signed between Britain and Portugal, the duty on wine increased fourfold. The Methuen Treaty diminished the tax on Portuguese wines by one third compared with those from France, a differential which existed until well after the First World War and which accounts for the substantial number of Portuguese and Portuguese-controlled wines to be found on eighteenth and early nineteenth century wine labels and the relative paucity of French names.

A wine which must be mentioned at this point which was, as it is today, a luxury, is champagne. Tradition has led us to believe that this drink was discovered by Dom Perignon, cellarer at the Benedictine Abbey at Hautvilliers, though this cannot be substantiated. Champagne is certainly recorded before that worthy man joined the order at Hautvilliers in 1668 and indeed some 'Shampaigne' wine was entered in the cellar accounts of the Duke of Bedford at Woburn Abbey in 1665. Nevertheless Dom Perignon must still be credited with greatly improving the wine and increasing its popularity and consequently its distribution. In England it was possibly introduced by Charles II and his followers on their return from exile in France, though it seems it was not widely stocked by vintners. This was mostly because of the very high duties and it therefore took some time to receive widespread acclaim. Another drink reputedly made fashionable at court as a result of the marriage of Catherine of Braganza to the King was Madeira, a wine fortified with brandy from the Portuguese island of that name. The Queen apparently established the vogue for ladies to take a glass of Madeira as a mid-morning refreshment.

Plate 15. A six-compartment spice box. Although it is silver it is not hallmarked, but the presence of the Royal Tudor arms suggests that it was made in London in about 1560. Spices were a necessary addition to food and drink to disguise unpleasant flavours. This is possibly the earliest surviving example.

THE COFFEE-HOUSE.

Plate 16. 'The Coffee-House', an etching by William Dickinson (1746-1821). This is a caricature of patriots, amongst them John Wilkes, receiving with dismay the news of the capture of the island of St. Eustacius. Not only coffee, but food and alcohol, were available at such establishments, as can clearly be seen here.

One of the most frequently occurring names in seventeenth century records is *Port*. This may refer to Portuguese wines generally or specifically to wines shipped from Oporto. Port as we know it today, which is made by the addition of grape brandy to the fermenting must, was not invented until the eighteenth century. Initially it was a very coarse wine and did not find favour with British consumers. Undoubtedly some so-called Port was in fact French wine deliberately shipped via Oporto under false appellation to avoid the duties. Despite the prohibitions to trade instituted by war with France, French wines were still highly sought after and a large number of bottles were smuggled into the country, at times quite openly. Cargoes of French wine which had been captured by naval ships or privateers could sometimes be purchased, though at a cost, at auctions held in the by now popular coffee houses. The difficulties encountered in obtaining these wines encouraged many deceits in the form of English-made 'faked' wine.

Changes too occurred during the seventeenth century in the procedure for serving both food and wine at the tables of large houses. The communal meals eaten at long refectory tables in the Great Chambers of mediaeval houses, which had been such an important feature of the households' life, had been gradually replaced with more intimate meals taken only by the immediate family and their guests. The servants and other members of the household retinue dined separately in rooms allocated according to their status. At Ham House in Petersham, Surrey which was substantially extended and lavishly refurbished in the very latest fashion during the 1670s, the Duke and Duchess of Lauderdale ate in a small dining room on the ground floor, while the gentlemen residing in the house took their meals in their own dining room on the same floor, but separated from the private apartments. The servants ate in their quarters in the basement. For state occasions and formal entertaining the grander eating room on the first floor, where the sequence of rooms forming the State Apartments were situated, would have been used. Dining tables had become correspondingly smaller and were typically oval with two folding flaps or leaves. They were large enough to seat between four and ten people, their diameter seldom being more than six feet. When more guests were present than could be accommodated at a single table further tables were brought in. When not in use the tables were folded up and stored in a corridor outside the dining room and the dining chairs were placed against the walls of the room to present a more formal atmosphere. This custom prevailed until the end of the eighteenth century. The food and wine were served from side tables under the supervision of the butler and the plates and glasses carried to and from the table by footmen.

In the eighteenth century, for the most part, the first meal of the day in a well-to-do household was taken in the bedchamber. Though wine may have been consumed, it was more likely to have been beer or ale. The principal meal of the day was dinner, which at the beginning of the century was served between one and half past two in the afternoon. As the century progressed the time of this meal was gradually delayed until by 1800 between five and six in the afternoon had become the norm. Most houses had a comfortable parlour, which was used daily by the family for eating as well as other occupations, and a quite separate room for more formal meals. At these there was a strict pattern of service. As guests took their places at the table(s), which were incidentally always covered with a tablecloth, the dishes were placed by servants on the main table and the major joint put in front of the host to carve. A diner might politely have taken a small portion of food from the dishes closest to him, otherwise footmen catered for the individual's wants by taking his or her plate to the other dishes on the serving tables. As before, the butler presided over the wine at a separate side table and footmen would bring charged glasses to each diner as required. Wine glasses were of small capacity and immediately the contents were consumed, the footman would remove the glass and recharge it or wait for a further request. Toasts were often made during the dinner which involved the entire table in drinking to the health of some person or cause, or sometimes one diner enjoined another in a

Plate 18. *A print by Robert and George Cruikshank entitled 'Cribb's Parlour, Tom introducing Jerry and Logic to the Champion of England'. Portraits of pugilists adorn the walls and on the table can be seen a punch bowl, glasses, a triple-ring neck decanter sitting in a coaster and other drinking accessories.*

Plate 17. *A political cartoon by James Gillray referring to Pitt's speech on the Defence Bill on March 6th 1805. Many of the characters and jokes are lost on a modern audience, but such cartoons were exceedingly popular in their day.*

personal toast. In either case the footmen would bring each person concerned a charged glass for the occasion. Cisterns were on hand for rinsing, not only glasses, but also plates and cutlery. When a course was finished the servants removed the remaining food, plates and cutlery and the next course was laid. Eventually the entire table was 'desserted', that is, all the contents, including the tablecloth, were removed, a procedure which has given rise to the modern term 'dessert'. After this the sweetmeats were eaten. It was at this point that the servants were dismissed, anything further that might be required being placed on a 'dumb waiter' for the host to pass around. This was also the time when the ladies 'withdrew' while the men continued to drink and talk, often holding conversations of a bawdy or political nature, but at any rate of one which was considered unsuitable for the ladies to hear. In winter it was customary for the men to gather around the fire to consume their port in warmth and comfort. This period of segregation of the sexes (which does not obtain in any other country in the same manner) gradually increased in length, but eventually, provided that they were still fit to do so, the men would join the ladies in the drawing room for tea, which the lady of the house would serve herself. After tea the party would socialise, dance or play cards according to the occasion.

The eighteenth century is often quoted as being the great age of drinking. Certainly by the end of the century alcoholism had become a problem amongst the poor, particularly in the inner urban areas, but in general the reputed heavy drinking of more fashionable society has probably been exaggerated. There were undoubtedly many rowdy

Plate 19. Another cartoon by James Gillray entitled 'A Decent Story'. This illustrates that drinking was not a male preserve, but in polite society was undertaken by ladies also. Note the decanter with its wine label, and glasses with ovoid bowls.

Plate 20. 'The Brilliants', signed and dated by Thomas Rowlandson in 1798 and published by Ackermann in 1801. 'The Brilliants' was a club in London's Covent Garden for actors and journalists, the sole purpose of which was excessive consumption of alcohol. Those who failed to comply with this rule were fined.

Plate 21. A 19th century dining room showing a dinner of the Dilettante Society at the Thatched House Club. Close examination reveals a profusion of decanters both on the table itself and on the various side tables around the room. A toast is being proposed by one of the diners, while servants are busy filling decanters and one (on the right hand side) is about to attend to the contents of a wine cooler. The absence of cutlery on the table should be noted.

Plate 22. A picture entitled 'My First Season. The Dinner Party. A Middle Aged MP took me in'. Here the service 'à la Russe' is indicated with serried rows of cutlery clearly showing the number of courses to be eaten. The large number of wine glasses give a similar indication in that quarter. Each guest is provided with a menu card and clearly a long and sumptuous evening will be enjoyed.

drinking parties, such as those so cleverly satirised at the time by George Cruikshank and others and indeed there were many drinking clubs, most notably in London and often of dubious intent, at which excess consumption of alcohol played an important part.

A less bawdy, but probably no less spirited, form of drinking took place in the growing number of public and coffee houses. One of the most popular beverages for such convivial consumption was punch, initially made with a rum base, but later with brandy. According to the diarist James Boswell, four bowls of punch consumed by him and his friends once made him 'merry to a high degree...of what passed I have no recollection with any accuracy'. It is interesting to note that his cure for a hangover was a glass of brandy.

Also common was *negus*, a beverage devised by a Colonel Francis Negus and originally concocted of wine, water, sugar, lemon and nutmeg. Before long the name came to refer to a similar hot drink made specifically with port wine as the base. Beaten eggs were sometimes added to the mixture.

For table wines claret was undoubtedly preferred, particularly during the early part of the century, but its consumption was restricted to those who could afford its high price. The majority of the populace had to remain content with wines of Iberian origin, in particular port. Although port had had such unpromising beginnings, it was soon discovered that its flavour

Plate 23. A menu card for a Saintsbury Club Committee luncheon held on the 9th October 1934 at Harveys of Bristol. The quality of wine reflects the discerning tastes of those attending the function. The Saintsbury Club was founded in 1931 in memory of George Saintsbury, a noted oenophile and gourmet. Although the club usually met at the Vintners' Hall, they also visited notable restaurants elsewhere.

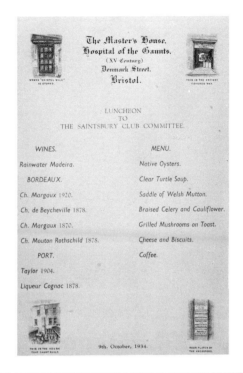

The Master's House.
Hospital of the Gaunts.
(XV Century)
Denmark Street.
Bristol.

LUNCHEON
TO
THE SAINTSBURY CLUB COMMITTEE.

WINES.	MENU.
Rainwater Madeira.	Native Oysters.
BORDEAUX.	Clear Turtle Soup.
Ch. Margaux 1920.	Saddle of Welsh Mutton.
Ch. de Beycheville 1878.	Braised Celery and Cauliflower.
Ch. Margaux 1870.	Grilled Mushrooms on Toast.
Ch. Mouton Rothschild 1878.	Cheese and Biscuits.
PORT.	Coffee.
Taylor 1904.	
Liqueur Cognac 1878.	

9th. October, 1934.

CLARETS—ENGLISH BOTTLED

St. Emilion	—	14/-	7/9
Ch. La Cottière	1966	14/3	7/9
Dom. de L'ile Margaux	1966	15/-	8/3
Ch. Macay	1964	15/6	8/6
Ch. Le Gardera	1962	16/9	9/-
Ch. Font Guilhem, Bourg	1964	16/9	9/-
Dom. Du Romefort, Calvet	1961	17/9	9/6
Ch. Calon, Calvet, St. Emilion	1964	18/-	9/9
Ch. Labrède	1961	18/3	9/9
Ch. Franquet Lamarque	1955	19/6	—
Ch. Latour Camblanes	1961/62	20/3	10/9
Ch. La Rose, Pauillac	1964	20/6	11/-
Ch. Léoville Lascases, St. Julien 2nd Crû	1963	21/3	11/6
Ch. Beau Site, St. Estèphe	1959	21/3	—
Ch. La Fleur, Lde de Pomerol	1959	21/6	—
Dom. de L'Eglise, Pomerol	1962	22/-	11/9
Ch. Batailley, 5th Crû, Pauillac	1962	24/3	12/9
Ch. Moulinet, Pomerol	1964	24/3	12/9
Ch. Boyd Cantenac, 3rd Crû	1964	24/3	12/9
Ch. Pontet Canet, 5th Crû, Pauillac	1960	24/9	—
Ch. Cos D'Estournel, 2nd Crû, St. Estèphe	1960	24/9	—
Ch. Montrose, 2nd Crû, St. Estèphe	1962	26/9	14/-
Ch. Talbot, 4th Crû, St. Julien	1959	29/6	—
Ch. Talbot, 4th Crû, St. Julien	1962	29/9	15/6
Ch. Gruaud Larose, 2nd Crû, St. Julien	1962	29/9	15/6

CLARETS—CHATEAU BOTTLED

Ch. des Templiers	1961	18/6	—
Ch. Haut Mazeris, Fronsac	1961	19/9	—
Ch. Font Guilhem, Bourg	1964	20/3	11/-
Ch. Calon Ségur, 3rd Crû, St. Estèphe	1963	23/3	12/6
Ch. Léoville Lascases, 2nd Crû St. Julien	1963	23/9	12/9
Ch. Canon la Gaffelière, St. Emilion	1962	26/-	—
Ch. Haut Batailley, 5th Crû Pauillac	1959	27/3	14/6
Ch. Malescot St. Exupéry, 3rd Crû, Margaux	1962	28/6	—
Ch. Cos D'Estournel, 2nd Crû St. Estèphe	1960	29/9	—
Ch. Calon Ségur, 3rd Crû St. Estèphe	1960	30/3	—
Ch. Latour à Pomerol, Pomerol	1959	31/-	—
Ch. Les Carmes Haut Brion, Pessac	1959	35/9	—
Ch. Montrose, 2nd Crû, St. Estèphe	1959	35/9	—
Ch. Margaux, 1st Crû, Margaux	1958	43/-	—
Ch. Mouton Rothschild, 2nd Crû, Pauillac	1960	47/-	24/6
Ch. Lafite Rothschild, 1st Crû Pauillac	1960	49/3	25/6

The above is a very small selection of wines, now ready for drinking, taken from our full list of over 275 Clarets of vintages 1954 to 1967. The full list will be found in the Handbook of Wines. We also have magnums of some 50 different Clarets and we will gladly give you full particulars on request.

Plate 24. A portion of a wine list from a reputable wine merchant dated 1969. A lack of description of any of the wines and the fact that more than half of them were bottled in England, makes a sharp contrast to present day marketing techniques.

52	1	Château de Montdespic,			65	2	Château Latour à Pomerol	1976	90.00
		Côtes de Castillon	1975	42.00	66	2	Château Mouton Rothschild	1976	300.00
53	2	Château Puy Blanquet, St. Emilion	1975	85.00	67	3	Château Beychevelle		
54	1	Château Cantemerle, 5e Macau	1975	90.00			(Magnums only)	1977	77.00
55	2	Château de Sales, Pomerol	1975	85.00	68	150	Château Bel Air,		
56	8	Château Rauzan Gassies	1975	120.00			Bordeaux Supérieur	1978	37.00
57	1	Château Brane Cantenac	1975	140.00	69	150	Château de Montdespic,		
58	1	Château Mouton Rothschild					Côtes de Castillon	1978	39.00
		(Magnums only)	1975	500.00	70	47	Château Bertin, Montagne St. Emilion		
59	14	Château Bel Air Bordeaux (Halves only)	1976	32.00			(Halves only)	1978	45.00
60	1	Château St. Gerome, Graves	1976	37.00	71	150	Château Macquin St. Georges,		
61	16	Château Sainte Colombe, Bordeaux	1976	38.00			St. Georges St. Emilion	1978	49.00
62	100	Château Lartigue,			72	1	Château Latour St. Bonnet, Médoc	1978	50.00
		Bordeaux Supérieur	1976	40.00	73	10	Château Gruaud Larose	1978	124.00
63	1	Château Latour de By, Bégadan	1976	60.00	74	150	Château de Montdespic,		
64	2	Château Plaisance, St. Emilion	1976	60.00			Côtes de Castillon	1979	38.00

Plate 25. A small section of a Christmas 1983 bin end list showing an almost total lack of English-bottled wines. The quantity of each vintage, and indeed the prices, are an interesting reflection of today's connoisseur tastes. Earlier in the year this wine merchant produced a list in the form of a book with a full description of all the wines.

improved greatly with age and by the end of the century it had become a favourite tipple, especially for after-dinner drinking.

Also by this time arrangements for entertaining in the dining room had begun to change. Guests were seated around a single table, much larger in size than previously. At first this was of necessity supported on a great many legs, but later on a pedestal arrangement. Extra leaves could be inserted or removed depending on the number of diners present. Early in the nineteenth century it became customary to leave the dining room set with its tables and chairs, as has remained the fashion until today. The sideboard, a more complicated piece of furniture than its predecessor the simple side or serving table, had become a necessary feature of the dining room and was still the butler's province, the footmen serving the guests under his watchful eye as before.

By the mid-nineteenth century a fresh development in the dining room had occurred — the service *à la Russe*. This dispensed with the various 'removes' or course changes and although the main joint was still carved by the host, the servants circulated the vegetables and side dishes around the table serving each guest in turn. Whereas it was previously necessary to have a servant for every diner, one servant per three or four was now considered sufficient. It was at this stage that the dinner setting with which we are now familiar first emerged, with serried ranks of cutlery placed either side of the plate and a large assortment of different glasses (for the various wines) arranged at the top right hand corner. Decanter wagons enabled wine to circulate around the table on top of the tablecloth and although the servants were on hand to assist the guests if required, the latter were able to fill their own glasses if they wished.

Dinner was served at a still later time, at about 7.30 in the evening. To fill the long interval following breakfast 'luncheon' had been introduced and was already becoming fashionable. By the 1840s it was also customary for society ladies to entertain one another during the afternoon with biscuits or cake and a glass of port or madeira (or sometimes home-made wines such as elderberry or cowslip). Before long the wine was replaced by tea and the 'afternoon' tea for which the English are famous was born.

During Victoria's reign wine generally found a wider market as a result of increased wealth, particularly amongst the expanding middle class, although society as a whole, reflecting more prudish social attitudes, was becoming more temperate in its drinking habits. To most middle class households wine meant port or sherry and these wines were served at towards the end of, and after dinner. Negus and punch were served at parties and consumed by those who patronised the growing number and variety of public eating houses.

For the upper classes French wines were yet still preferred, most particularly claret. Imports of all French wine increased dramatically after 1860 when Gladstone considerably reduced the British duties. Port and sherry were also served at fashionable tables. At a dinner and dance at Goodwood on Christmas Eve 1847, for seventeen guests two bottles of port, one of claret and ten bottles of sherry were apparently brought up from the cellar. In 1876 Mrs Beeton, in her *Complete Etiquette for Gentlemen*, confirmed that 'sherry is the dinner wine'. Nineteenth century sherries were on the whole medium to sweet in taste and to our palates would be a rather rich accompaniment to a large meal. The concept of the aperitif had of course not yet arrived. In late Victorian times sherry was joined by champagne as a dinner wine which was correctly followed only by a good claret. The nineteenth century generally saw a greater interest in the classification of wines and a more widespread understanding of individual vintages. Connoisseurship consequently increased. In response to expanded and more knowledgable demand the European wine industry flourished until the fatal year 1879 in which the tiny mite phylloxera began to ravage the vineyards and to cause damage so great that the industry did not fully recover until the 1950s.

This misfortune affected quality rather than availability and wine continued to be consumed in growing quantities. In Edwardian times there were normally four meals taken each day, breakfast, luncheon, tea and dinner, late-night supper having finally been abandoned apart from after-theatre dining. It would in fact be hard to imagine that a diner could find room for a further morsel of food if contemporary menus are to be believed. The average meal in an upper class home, be it breakfast, lunch or dinner, seems to have been more in the order of a gourmet's feast than a provider of basic sustenance. A simple luncheon hamper for four which was offered for sale by the Army & Navy Stores in 1902, included four bottles of champagne, one of whisky and sherry, two of claret and six of mineral water. The food incidentally consisted of 'veal and ham pie, roast lamb with mint sauce, roast fowl, cut ham, salad and dressing, bread, butter, cheese, cake, pastry and condiments'. Generally a large assortment of wines were served with dinner, now appearing with the first course and continuing throughout the meal. Pre-dinner cocktails and aperitifs had arrived and were already beginning to gain acceptance. The combination of wines (and spirits) may seem strange, even unpleasant, to modern palates. For example, whisky mixed with mineral waters was sometimes served with the soup following white wine with the hors d'oevres. This in turn was followed by champagne for the fish and main courses and claret with the dessert. On the whole the general trend was for more champagne and less sherry and claret. Port began to replace the latter as the dessert wine.

During the 1890s the first stirrings of women's liberation were being felt and large numbers of educated women and girls were respectably employed, particularly in shops and offices. The large variety of coffee shops and public and other eating houses had always been solely a male province and to cater for the new demands the tea shop made its first appearance. By 1900 it was also acceptable for women to dine in some, but still *only* some, restaurants. Some of the most famous and luxurious of these were the Trocadero and those of the Savoy Hotel and Claridges.

The splendid and extravagant lifestyle of the Edwardian rich was soon tempered by two world wars and the intervening depression, which exaggerated the effects of fewer servants and produced a heartfelt need to avoid former excesses. The twentieth century has since seen a gradual diminishing of formality and a slow trend towards simplicity. The almost complete disappearance of servants from the dining room, a reduction in the number of courses and corresponding wines and a general abandonment of the table cloth are all features of this trend. The past twenty years have probably seen the greatest changes in social habits. The formal dinner party, with strict table setting and serving procedures, has diminished in popularity in modern homes, a surprising fact in view of the considerably increased affluence of the younger, professional sections of society. Drinking habits too have changed and wine has found a wider market than at any previous time. The supermarket has done much to extend its popularity, and although true connoisseurs might balk at the thought of stocking their cellars from such establishments, plenty do so. The cardboard box and plastic cup may be far removed from a cut glass decanter or a silver-gilt goblet, but no doubt in time they too will be seen as representative of their age. Fortunately we are no longer bound by so many conventions, nor very often by lack of choice, and we can indulge our preferences as we so wish. We are perhaps most fortunate in having today a superb choice of wine itself, with vintages available from all parts of the world and of every quality and price. Modern technology and research have enabled the industry of today to produce wines which would have been considered impossible even only thirty years ago. This has produced not only a new level of excellence in wines and food, but men and women with palates to match — a heady spiral with no apparent vortex.

CHAPTER 2
From Vineyard to Vintner

The raw ingredient of wine is of course the juice of the grape although certain chemical additives, whether man-made or naturally occurring, are sometimes used to clarify and purify it and to improve its lasting qualities. It follows therefore that the first objects one encounters when tracing its passage from the vine to the table are the tools used for its cultivation. While there is now a growing band of individuals seeking such items, on the whole these tools do not concern the collector of antiques but a good assortment can usually be seen by those who are interested, in museums associated with wine making.

The vine grows in climates ranging within the year from sub-equatorial to almost sub-arctic conditions, and so requires careful tending to produce the best results. The ground in which vines are planted is now tilled with specially designed tractors which straddle the long rows of posts and wires. Formerly ordinary spades and forks were used. Shears and secateurs are employed to prune and train the vines to ensure maximum yields and they must also be regularly sprayed to prevent damage by the many fungi, pests and diseases to which they are prone. Even in these days of automation most of the tasks involved in vine growing have to be performed manually and many of the tools required have seen little change over the centuries in their basic design.

The first object grapes are likely to encounter on their journey to the table which is designed specifically for the vineyard is the grape carrier. Typically this is constructed of copper (though occasionally brass) and stands between two and three feet tall. It is of approximately conical outline, truncated at the point and with the open end of uneven configuration, one side being taller than the other. The taller side is often flattened along its entirety. It might be described as hod-shaped. The grape carrier is worn on the back of the harvester and is attached by a leather harness running through various rings or lugs. Most examples are entirely plain, although embossed decoration was fashionable during the nineteenth century. It is possible that some grape carriers surviving from the eighteenth century may be of English origin, but this seems unlikely as English copper at that date was joined or seamed in a different manner to that employed on the Continent and no examples of grape carriers seem to show that particular type. Grape carriers were also made of lightweight wood of coopered construction.

After the grapes are harvested they are pressed to extract the juice. Like many other agricultural devices the wine press is hardly a suitable subject for collection, being far too large to accommodate in the average house. A traditional method of pressing wine was for men to tread it with their bare

Plate 26. A plate from Defehrt's book on agriculture, showing some of the tools and methods of training vines employed in viticulture.

Plate 27. An old engraving of 'October' showing the grape harvest. On the left is a press very similar to the one shown in the next plate, while in the foreground variously sized examples of the cooper's art are shown. Immediately behind the central column is a coopered grape carrier as worn by the two figures on the right.

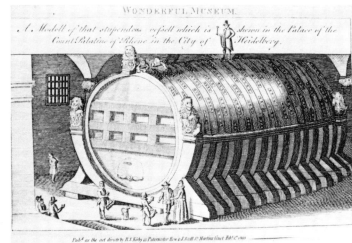

Plate 28. *A typical old Continental wine press. This example is in fact German, but could easily be mistaken for one from pretty well any other European country.*

Plate 29. *'The Heidelberg Tun', made in 1751 by Jakob Engler and still at Heidelberg Castle. This print of it was published by Kirby and Scott in 1803.*

feet in a large vat and this method still obtains in rural areas of Portugal and elsewhere. An alternative method was to exert force on the grapes by rotation of an out-sized screw held in a gantry or frame. Indeed this operation was used by the ancient Greeks and is recorded on an ancient marble tablet. Modern methods are still based on the screw principle though horizontal Archimedian screws are now used.

Also to be encountered from the pressing stage are the special boots sometimes worn by Spanish treaders. These can be identified by the pointed studs or hobnails covering the sole and heel which prevent the pips from being squashed and broken releasing detrimental pectins and tannins into the grape juice. Once the juice has been separated from the solid residue or 'must' it is collected and poured into a vat, cask or barrel.

The art of coopering was known to the Romans and is a craft requiring great skill. The best casks are made of oak and for centuries the bands which hold the coopered staves of the barrel together have been made of riveted mild steel. Early and rustic examples were bound with bands of wattle or bent hazelwood. Being essentially utilitarian, barrels are normally completely undecorated, although some decorative barrels were made, particularly in Middle and Eastern Europe and mostly during the sixteenth and seventeenth centuries. These masterpieces were of mammoth proportions, the largest known having a capacity of over a quarter of a million litres of wine. Their purpose was quite straightforward. The prince or landlord of a vast estate would be accorded a tithe from every grower which was collected in a large vat for distribution among all servants and staff (including both the officers and ranks of a prince's personal army) as part of their wages. It is perhaps interesting to note that in England casks were made for a similar purpose, but of totally opposite proportions. Tiny barrels called 'firkins,' which were as little as six to eight inches long, were

Plate 30. A late 19th century engraving of a cellar in Bordeaux. This idealised view goes out of its way to show the different processes employed prior to bottling.

made in large numbers during the seventeenth, eighteenth and nineteenth centuries. They were though, filled with cider or ale rather than wine and were a daily ration for all agricultural workers. Some barrels of normal size were made as gifts or for ceremonial use, as testified by inscriptions, and these were often decorated on the flat sections at either end with carving, painting or gilding (or occasionally all three).

Until the introduction of the stainless steel vats usually used today, it was accepted that a quantity of wine would be lost during storage, some through seepage and the rest through evaporation. It is important that the ullage (the air space left above the surface of the wine in both the cask and bottle) is kept to a minimum and it was therefore necessary to top up each barrel from time to time from a cask specifically set aside for the purpose. This entailed employment of a set of apparatus composed of various containers and funnels, most of which would be made of copper and plated with tin on the inside. A barrel normally has two apertures, a hole at its widest diameter which may be bunged or corked, and a second aperture positioned at the bottom of one end into which may be inserted a spigot or tap. In general it may be said that the first hole was for filling the barrel, while the second was for emptying it. Barrel taps were occasionally, though not often, decorated.

While the wine is maturing in its cask (and this it may do for a period of weeks or years depending on the type of wine), it may be subjected to a number of tests. At this point in its making it would be undesirable to broach the barrel by inserting a spigot and so testing is done by drawing off a small quantity in a pipette through the bunged aperture. This pipette, similar to those used in any laboratory, is often known as a 'thief'.

Once removed from the cask the wine is tasted in a special taster or *tastevin* (see Chapter 7). In addition to knowing how his wine is tasting a

Plate 31. While a pipette, in some form or other, is used to draw wine from a barrel in most wine-producing areas, sherry is sampled in its own traditonal way, the wine being gathered in a small cup at the end of a long stick, which is then theatrically poured into sherry's traditional wine glass, the 'copita'.

grower, buyer, shipper or vintner will want to assess its other qualities. Of particular importance is its strength. Apart from the various flavouring elements, the bulk of the wine is composed of water and alcohol. These two liquids have different specific gravities and by measuring their proportions one may ascertain the alcoholic strength. This may be expressed either as a percentage of alcohol or in degrees of 'proof' spirit. The latter term, which is principally used in Britain, is analogous with the proofing of a gun. If alcohol is mixed with gunpowder it explodes, or at least self-ignites, while water has the opposite effect. 100 degrees proof spirit is the minimum combination of water and alcohol at which self-ignition will occur if tested in this way. This rather dramatic though haphazard and dangerous method tends to be inaccurate and currently proof spirit is defined as approximately 49½% alcohol by weight or 57¼% by volume. Today consumer protection demands that every bottle is marked with its alcohol content although this is primarily important to the Customs and Excise authorities who levy taxes or duties according to its level.

The most common instrument used to measure alcoholic strength is the hydrometer. This was invented by the great seventeenth century physician, Robert Boyle. It is simply composed of a floating ball through which is passed a rod with various weights attached. The weights are pre-

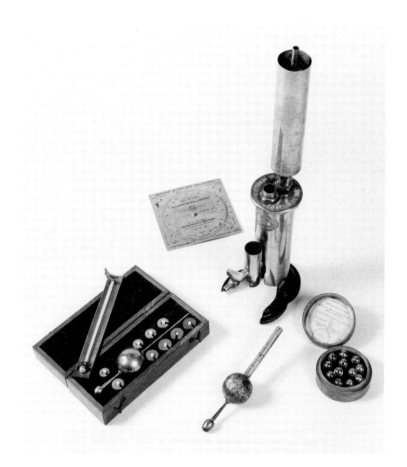

Plate 32. A selection of instruments used for the testing of alcoholic strength. Clockwise from the top: an ebulliometer, a box of Wilson's beads, a crude hydrometer and a Sikes's hydrometer. The ebulliometer is a 20th century invention allowing greater accuracy than hitherto. In order to use the Sikes's hydrometer a set of tables is necessary.

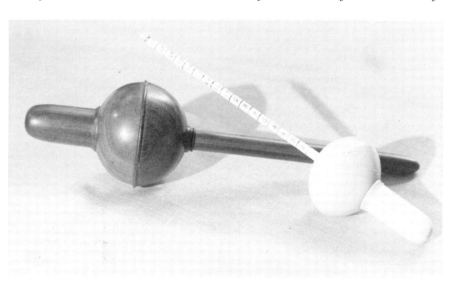

Plate 33. A mid-18th century ivory hydrometer in its original treen case. Such a piece, while having much charm and being very collectable, is a rather crude measuring instrument.

Left. Plate 34. Four dipsticks used for measuring the contents of different sized barrels. The far left hand one is incorporated in a walking stick.

Plate 35. Equipment used in the bottling of wine and a corking machine. Such items tend to fall outside the general sphere of domestic collecting.

Plate 36. On the left is a mid-19th century seal with interchangeable heads for the impressing of wax capsules. On the right is a group of cork branding irons somewhat later in date.

balanced to enable a specific gravity to be computed from an accompanying table when the apparatus floats to a particular level. One problem encountered during this procedure is that specific gravity alters according to the temperature of the liquid and so a thermometer and a table of conversion are also necessary. In response to demands for greater accuracy, numerous improvements were made to Boyle's 1675 invention by a Mr Clark in the 1730s and later by Atkins, Jones, Beck and others. However, by far the most common variety is Sikes's hydrometer which was in use from the late eighteenth century until only recently. On these the float, stem and weights are made of brass and the whole piece is commonly encased in a mahogany case seven to nine inches long with a thermometer

Plate 37. A travelling salesman's boxed set of cork samples. Corks can vary in length, density and porosity and come in many different qualities. The standard of finish and presentation clearly indicates that the salesman was working in a commercial and competitive market.

Plate 38. Three bills from wine and spirit merchants. Such documents, while not being of great aesthetic merit, give an interesting insight into the pricing and availability of wines and spirits over a prolonged period of time. In addition they show what sort of people were drinking what sorts of beverages, information which can provide a valuable record for social history.

with ivorine scales. Countless thousands of hydrometers were produced in a wide variety of sizes and finishes.

An alternative and rather amusing method of measuring a wine's specific gravity is that employing 'Wilson's beads'. These comprise a set of calibrated and engraved glass bubbles, each with a slightly varying density according to the amount of air trapped within. The entire set is thrown into the liquid in which some will float and some will sink. If one bead is in equilibrium it will prove to have the same specific gravity as the wine; otherwise it will be somewhere between the heaviest floating bead and the lightest sinking one. Other instruments have been used, mostly in Europe, which take into account not only variations caused by temperature, but also by barometric pressure and altitude.

An interesting area for collectors at this pre-bottling stage is that of measuring instruments such as barrel dipsticks. These are frequently calibrated with a plethora of measurements which will tell not only if the barrel is full or totally empty, but will indicate any level in between, whether the cask is held on its side, or upright, or at an angle. These rulers are usually made in boxwood as this wood is almost impervious to dampness and will neither swell nor contract along its length. To protect the ends it will be encased in a brass ferule, usually canted on one side to enable the tip to reach into the very corner of the vessel. Measurements will often be marked in barrels, hogsheads, kilderkins or firkins as well as imperial pints and gallons, bushels or simple inches. Some early examples

Colour plate 10. A group of coopering tools, including planes, mallets, writhing irons, spoke-shaves, and beneath the adze, a completed firkin or small barrel.

are calibrated only with brass or other metal studs and would have depended on the expertise of their operator for their efficacy. Some charming examples are disguised to look like walking sticks, the barrel being hollow to accommodate the ruler. Travelling vintners sometimes had folding measures.

An alternative but less accurate method of measurement, was to tap the cask with a special wooden mallet, though these mallets must have had many other uses in the cellar as well.

When a buyer visits a cellar where wine is being made he will first need answers to a number of important questions before he can assess its potential value. He will need to consider what volume he will be buying, what the alcoholic strength of the wine is, what it tastes like, which vineyard the grapes have come from and exactly which variety of grape has been used. He will also want to know which additives have been included. Until the 1960s a very substantial proportion of wine was purchased in casks and bottled on arrival in Britain. One has only to look at a wine list of the 1920s or even 1950s to see that only a small percentage of wines are noted as chateau-bottled or, in the case of German wines, estate-bottled. However, since the 1960s many growers have realised that they can achieve a higher price for their wines if they are prepared to do their own bottling and this procedure is now the norm. It is because of the earlier system that a great many now obsolete bottling and corking machines can now be found, not very often from domestic cellars, but from those of the vintner. Some hand corking machines were made for private use, but these are rare. Before 1860, when a patent was granted to C. Bossalaer for 'An Improved Apparatus for Corking Bottles, Jars and other Vessels' most bottles were corked with a pair of wooden tongs rather like a pair of nutcrackers. Depending on its diameter, the cork was held in one of three variously sized apertures and hammered into the bottle with a wooden mallet. The bottle itself was sometimes held firmly between the knees of the bottler in a 'bottle boot', a leather receptacle which, according to Mrs Beeton's *Book of Household Management,* 1861, was buckled to the knee with a leather strap. The name 'Boot and Flogger' is still apparently seen on some inn signs.

Another tool which many vintners have is a cork branding machine or iron. Before the days of good, modern adhesives, bottles were apt to become parted from their labels and at times the only way to identify a bottle's contents was to examine its cork on which the name was normally branded. This practice still continues today. Harveys Wine Museum have a rather amusing case of cork samples dating from the 1920s and presumably left behind by a travelling cork salesman!

Once a wine has been bottled and corked it is normal procedure today to cover the cork with a lead or plastic capsule, usually embossed and decorated with the name of the wine it covers. Previously, with the introduction of cork stoppering, the neck of the bottle was immersed in molten wax which was then stamped with a seal to indicate the contents. The seals used for this operation were not unlike those used to seal letters, but it was normal for each seal to be detachable from its handle so that a battery of alternative names could be substituted (see plate 36, page 55).

Under perfect conditions wine should be stored in a cellar below ground where the temperature remains constant. Ideally this should be between 11 and 14 degrees centigrade though the precision of the temperature is less important than its constancy. To keep a check on this special cellar thermometers are made which indicate ideal temperatures for the storing and serving of wines and spirits.

An item to be found in any wine cellar of repute is a cellar book. In a professional cellar this will be a detailed log of incoming and outgoing wines and a separate tasting book will be kept in the vintner's office. Early ledgers, and cellar books provide an interesting insight into the wine drinking habits of former days and give us an indication not only of which wines were available and in approximately what proportions, but also of the numbers and types of people who preferred them.

CHAPTER 3
Bottles

The Romans were adept at the manufacture of glass and numerous glass bottles made during the period of the Empire have been excavated. As wine was also produced in Ancient Rome such bottles were presumably sometimes used as wine containers. However, for many centuries Roman glass making skills were forgotten and although a very few pieces of mediaeval glass have been found, glass was little used for domestic purposes until the sixteenth century and even then was often decorative rather than utilitarian.

Plate 39. A flask-shaped bottle (i.e. one of oval section) with some of its original contents. It is reputed to have been given to Queen Anne by the Persian ambassador in 1708 and it has an interesting spiral applied to the neck.

Plate 40. A salt-glazed stoneware jug with a wide-bellied body and narrow neck with a handle. When impressed with a mask head, as this one is, such items are known as bellarmines. This one has a single area of impressed decoration on the body; some have none, while others are profusely impressed. The quality of these, together with the quality of the glaze, dictate their desirability. They were made from the 16th century onwards in the Rhineland. This example is 17th century.

Colour plate 11. A very good example of a wine bottle jug, an onion-shaped bottle with a handle and thumbpiece. Opposite the handle is a prunt bearing the legend 'Ric^d Wight 1703'. Note also the high kick-in of the base.

Colour plate 12. A group of modern bottles showing classic shapes and colours. From left to right: for red Burgundy, Hock, Moselle, Champagne, white Bordeaux (Sauterne), red Bordeaux (Claret), white Burgundy, a fancy modern shape (for Beaumes de Venise), Alsace. Other classic shapes not shown are flasks, spirit bottles and those wanded with raffia.

Colour plate 13. Two interesting bottles. On the left an onion-shaped bottle engraved all over in diamond point with rustic floral motifs and a drinking scene on the reverse. It is inscribed 'John Littler 1739', although the bottle dates from some 15-20 years earlier. On the right is a half bottle with the gilded inscription 'Success to the John Blackwell' which dates from about 1800.

Colour plate 14. The marketing of wines and spirits has undergone certain changes in recent years as this group of modern products shows. Extruded aluminium cans, screw-on bottle tops and wine 'boxes' are now ubiquitous.

The glass wine bottle as we know it today, intended specifically for the storage of wine, first emerged in this country during the 1660s. Prior to that date earthenware and stoneware jugs had been employed which were general purpose vessels used for the storing and dispensing of wine, ale and many other beverages. During the late sixteenth and early seventeenth centuries these were in large measure the product of the Rhineland. They were of a muddy brown colour and were potted to a balloon shape with a small foot and a narrow, ribbed neck. Their handles were also small and of horizontal cross-section. They were usually decorated with a salt glaze which gave them a mottled appearance. Their most peculiar feature was a moulded mask of a man with a beard which was placed opposite the

Plate 41. A tigerware jug with a glaze superior to the bellarmine in plate 40. The mounts are silver-gilt, engraved and embossed, and are prototypes for the Victorian claret jug made some three hundred years later. This piece was made in about 1560.

Plate 42. A Sieburg jug with fine repoussé and chased mounts. Note the superior workmanship accorded to a more esteemed form of pottery.

handle. This was a representation of Cardinal Roberto Bellarmino (1542-1621) who was an excessively enthusiastic Counter-Reformationist and therefore detested in northern Europe. These jugs, which survive in large numbers, are now consequently known as 'bellarmines' (see plate 40, page 59). These are sometimes potted in a grey-blue colour which has given rise to an alternative name, 'greybeards'. Bellarmines are often additionally decorated with seals and coats of arms. Particularly good quality versions had refined glazes and no bellarmine mask and because of their mottled appearance are known as 'tigerware' jugs. Like imported Chinese and Persian ceramics of the period, they were often mounted in the late sixteenth century in silver or silver-gilt and were highly prized. Jugs (or livery pots) were also made in silver at this time, or more usually, in silver-gilt.

Plate 43. A Chinese blue and white porcelain wine jug (Wanli 1573-1619) with fine silver-gilt mounts hallmarked for 1585-6. The maker's mark is three trefoils in a shaped shield. This maker appears to have specialised in mounting imported porcelain and stoneware.

Plate 44. A travelling stoneware drinking flask of the 17th century, flanked by two leather serving vessels. The pan top of the right hand example bears a close resemblance to its contemporary Ravenscroft decanter jugs.

Colour plate 15. An oil painting by an imitator of Jean-Baptist Chardin. A still-life showing a bottle of wine, a glass and a loaf of bread on a newspaper, which perhaps proves that not only collectors believe bottles have artistic merit.

In about 1630 another type of pottery container was introduced which was intended exclusively for the storage of wine. This was a globular pottery vessel with a neck, the latter part commonly having an upstanding moulding which allowed a cork or bung to be tied in position. Attached to the body and neck was a handle of thin horizontal cross-section. Its most notable feature was its overall white tin-oxide glaze. On the body, opposite the handle, was written in underglaze blue the name of the contents, most commonly claret, sherry or sack, with the date underneath. (These were in fact the only wine receptacles which named their contents until decanters revived the practice a hundred years later.) The only decoration common to all was a looped flourish below the date. Their capacity varied from one half to two pints. These objects were made in large quantities for approximately forty years and there can be little doubt that their demise was due to the more widespread use of glass and the consequent emergence of the true wine bottle during the 1660s.

It should be said at this point that a clear distinction between early glass bottles (which were for storing wine) and some varieties of early decanters (which were for pouring) cannot easily be made. The earliest form of glass serving vessel, which is depicted often in contemporary paintings, was actually an ordinary bottle encased in osierwork. Another vessel which could be included in either category, is a particular type of pale green bottle bearing a prunt and sometimes a handle. These have survived only in

Plate 45. Before the advent of glass wine was stored and served from earthenware wine bottles. This particular form was popular from the 1630s to the early 1670s. These, in sizes, for sack are a rare group. It may be that 'sack' derives from the Spanish word 'sacar' meaning to export. Other frequently encountered names on such bottles are 'Claret' and 'Whit'.

small numbers. Similar to these are dark green bottles with handles as illustrated in colour plate 11, page 60. Both forms are referred to as serving bottles and have been much reproduced in the twentieth century.

With the exception of bladder-shaped bottles which are difficult to date, and polygonal ones which are probably Dutch or at least European in origin, the evolution of the wine bottle is briefly outlined in the following paragraphs.

The very earliest type of glass bottle which concerns us here dates from the middle of the seventeenth century, has a spherical body and a long, parallel neck. This is a true 'shaft and globe' bottle. Some way down from the lip is the string ring or rim which held the string anchoring the cork or bung. The underside of the bottle has a very shallow kick-in, that is, a slight depression formed when the pontil rod was pushed in during its making while the glass was still molten and slightly plastic. The metal of early bottles was palish green and fairly lightweight. As the seventeenth century progressed the body was slightly compressed and the neck developed a taper, being narrow at the lip and wide at the body. The string rim also became closer to the lip and the colour of the glass darker. By the end of the century this was often almost black. In addition, by this date the entire proportion of the bottle had altered, the neck being shorter and the body swollen in size. The bulbous bodies were sometimes marvered (that is, they were rolled upon a flat, steel surface in the glass-making workshop) to give the lower side of the body a distinctly conical outline, tapering in towards the base. By 1700 a typical bottle would have had a very short tapered neck and a wide bulbous body. The string rim would be very near the lip and the underside would have a very distinct kick-in. The shaft and globe had now become the onion-shaped bottle.

During the first two decades of the eighteenth century the onion shape became exaggerated with the body becoming wider and wider in relation to the height, so that by about 1715 it sometimes exceeded it. By 1720 however, bottles were suddenly once again having marvered sides. At first these straight sides tapered out towards the base to produce a true mallet shape.

Plate 46. A selection of bottles explaining the evolution of bottle shapes from about 1660 until 1820. The shapes progress from the shaft and globe, through the onion and mallet, to the cylindrical shape required when binning became common after the 1740s.

This was accompanied by a slight elongation of the neck. Over the following twenty years the straight sides gradually became less canted until they were perpendicular and the first truly cylindrical-sided bottle had emerged.

At first the width and height of the body were very similar with, if anything, the former exceeding the latter. Gradually this proportion changed, the bottle becoming taller and narrower, until, by the last decade of the eighteenth century, a bottle not dissimilar to that used today had evolved. Throughout this period the kick-in of the base was pronounced. One particular feature of eighteenth century cylindrical bottles, which results from their being handmade, is a slight swelling near the base caused by sagging when the bottle was placed in an upright position to cool. During the second half of the century many bottles were made in cylindrical earthenware (and later metal) moulds, but nevertheless remained hand-blown and when removed from their moulds to cool, still acquired this sagging outline. In the 1820s the metal moulding machines patented by the Bristol glass makers Ricketts, in which the entire shaping process could be carried out, finally did away with the 'sagging' which gave the bottle so much of its charm and individuality and for the first time made it possible to produce a bottle of standard capacity and form. Ricketts' bottles can easily be identified by 'Patent' moulded in the

Plate 47. A late 18th century plain wine bottle showing the sagging which occurred when it was cooled in an upright position. Note the contrast with the bottle in the next plate which was made in a mould.

Plate 48. A wine bottle sealed 'W. Leman, Chard 1771'. This common sealed bottle is something of an enigma as it was made (and impressed) by Ricketts of Bristol after 1821. W. Leman was a brewer.

shoulder and the impression on their underside 'H Ricketts and Co, Glassworks, Bristol'.

Around the turn of the eighteenth century substantial alterations were made to the design of the rim of the bottle. In general it may be said that many bottles were fitted with enlarged string rims of complex cross-section, a development necessitated by improving corking methods which required bottles to have much stronger necks.

The origin of the present day cylindrical shaped bottle lies in experiments made by Portuguese wine makers in the years following the

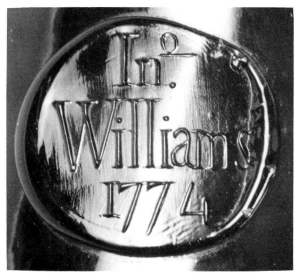

Plate 50. A typical bottle seal for John Williams, 1774. Such seals add greatly to the value of the bottle and are avidly collected.

Plate 49. Two bottles made in steel moulds by Ricketts and Company of Bristol. Such bottles have the word 'patent' in raised letters on the shoulder, a cylindrical body and an impression of the maker's name on the underside.

Methuen Treaty of 1703 which gave their exports precedence in England over those of France. Despite this distinct advantage Portuguese wine on the whole did not find favour with British buyers, lacking the quality and finesse of French wines and being deemed less able to withstand travelling by sea. It was soon realised that wine which had a small amount of brandy added travelled considerably better and it is very likely that in this way the fortified wine we know as port was first discovered. Furthermore it was found that the longer the wine was stored (within certain limits) the greater was the improvement. However, once the cork had dried out and allowed air to reach the wine, the flavour was spoiled and it was recognised that in order to keep the cork moist long enough for the wine to mature, the bottle had to be stored on its side. For obvious reasons globular bottles did not store conveniently in this position (although they were sometimes laid on the floor in a bed of sand) and breakage was likely if more than one row were stored together. The problem was simply overcome by making the bodies of the bottles cylindrical. It was then possible to stack several rows of bottles one on top of another in a horizontal position and within a confined space. This practice was known as binning and its beginnings can safely be assumed to have coincided with the emergence of the cylindrical bottle during 1730s and 1740s. Binning was not an overnight phenomenon however, and the transition from the onion to the cylindrical-shaped bottle took place over a period of ten to fifteen years.

Since earliest times it has been recognised that light should be kept from wine while it is maturing. The cellar itself, where most wine bottles are stored, is usually below ground and ill-lit, even while being visited. However, there are numerous occasions when bottles which are not to be opened immediately will be in daylight and during this period the wine itself must be protected. It is principally for this reason that wine bottles are usually of a dark colour. Today wine bottles are produced in a variety of shades and specific areas of wine producing regions have bottles of a particular shape and colour. For example, in Germany hocks are always bottled in brown glass and mosels in green. It is common practice to have dark green claret bottles, although sweet white wines from the same region are bottled in almost clear glass. Today's bottle capacities and shapes also vary from region to region. For example, burgundy (pale green) has gently sloping shoulders, as opposed to claret (dark green) which has definitely pronounced shoulders. In the nineteenth century and before, bottle glass was almost universally dark olive green and was ideally suited to the long term storage of wine. The colour was usually achieved by the addition of iron oxide to the melt, although it could also be accidentally produced by naturally occurring impurities.

In a later chapter various aspects of wine antiques are discussed from the point of view of collectability, an area in which bottles play a considerable part. Collectors will want to have in their collections all the representative shapes demonstrating the bottle's evolution, but without a doubt the prime target is the 'sealed' bottle. These have been avidly discussed elsewhere and were the subject of an exhibition in Truro Musuem in July/September 1976. From the seventeenth century onwards it was common practice to affix to the bottle an additional blob of glass which was then impressed with the owner's seal in much the same way that a hard wax is used to seal a letter. The blob, or more correctly the 'prunt', was placed on the shoulder or body of the bottle and after impression was generally about 1 ½ inches in diameter. The most common impressions were coats of arms, initials or crests of the owner, whether individual, corporate or commercial. Thus one will find, say, 'IC' for Sir John Church, or 'ASCR' for All Souls Common Room, All Souls College, Oxford. The complete name of the owner is sometimes found and frequently encountered is the date. Therefore one might see 'John Holme 1721' or 'AD 1714'. Far less common is the owner's profession. Various symbols might indicate a business premises, hence a bunch of grapes for the 'Vine Tavern'. (The term 'tavern' originally meant a cellar, but later a tap room where wine, as opposed to beer and ale, was retailed.) Coats of arms often refer to a tavern rather than an individual and a substantial percentage of the relatively small number of surviving seventeenth century bottles sealed in this way belonged to taverns. As bottles were a reusable commodity and could hold a variety of different wines over a period of several years, sealed bottles are not found impressed with the names of individual wines.

After 1636 wine was only sold straight from the cask, its sale by the bottle (or flask) having been prohibited by law in an attempt to protect the customer from being short-served. (It was of course not possible at that time to produce vessels of standard capacity.) Consequently the sealed bottle became an essential part of the wine connoisseur's equipage. Wine could be bought by the barrel and bottled for the owner on his own or the vintner's premises, usually under his own personal supervision to avoid watering or adulteration of the wine. Samuel Pepys' diary entry for October 23rd 1663 relates 'to Mr. Rawlinson's and saw my new bottles, made with my crest upon it, filled with wine, about five or six dozen of them'.

Examples of dated seals have been recorded for most years of the eighteenth century, although seventeenth century examples are seldom encountered. During the nineteenth century the practice of sealing bottles diminished and apart from those made for the Peak family of Rousdon to celebrate Queen Victoria's Jubilee in 1887, post-1850 examples are rarely encountered.

Not all dated, sealed bottles are quite what they seem. A not uncommon seal, 'J. Leman, Chard 1771', appears on bottles made by Ricketts glass works in a steel mould, a process which positively dates the bottles as post-1822. As Mr. Leman was a brewer we can surmise that these bottles marked a celebratory year. Another bottle, illustrated in colour plate 13, page 61, quite clearly dates from about 1720 yet is engraved with the date 1739. It is only conjecture, but one can suppose that the artistic engraving may have been accomplished by a guest artist in the house when the wine was actually consumed many years after it was bottled, as a mark of appreciation of a good vintage.

In recent years bottles have in some cases been replaced by other forms of packaging. In the early 1960s some South African sherries were being sold in plastic bags contained within cardboard boxes (see colour plate 14, page 61). These were fitted with a tap in the same manner as barrels. This method has the advantage that, as the wine is drawn out, the bag collapses and no air can reach the wine to oxidise it. This method failed to catch on immediately and has only been re-adopted since the late 1970s. Boxes of wine are now quite a common sight, particularly at parties. Presumably in an attempt to attract the casual wine drinker some wine is now being sold in cans made from extruded aluminium with a capacity of a quarter to a third of a litre, although some are of a half bottle capacity. While no doubt this may prove to be a successful financial venture there surely cannot be a single reader of this book who would prefer to buy his wine that way!

CHAPTER 4
Bin Labels

It has already been described how, by the 1740s, the practice of binning had become popular to improve the quality and flavour of wine. Also by this time houses were fashionably being built with cellars specifically designed to accommodate the storage of wine and other drinkables. Then, as today, it was the practice to divide a cellar wall into compartments, shallow brick divisions deep enough to hold a bottle and between two and three feet square, thus enabling the storage of between two and five dozen bottles, each stacked on its side. A pigeon-hole of this type is known as a 'bin'.

While wine was still in its cask or barrel, it was perfectly easy to mark the barrel with chalk, ink or paint to indicate its contents. Glass, though, presented a different problem as it does not mark easily and requires a good adhesive to retain a paper label for any length of time. The wines bottled from a single cask were therefore placed in one or more bins and each bin was marked with a single 'bin label' denoting the contents of the bottles.

Although earlier examples do exist, the general commercial practice of gluing paper labels to individual bottles dates from 1860 when the *Grocers' Licences Act* enormously increased the sale of single bottles. There are now collectors of this type of label and while the selection available is a specialist subject, those commissioned each year from famous artists by Baron Philippe for Chateau Mouton Rothschild are a particularly interesting and very collectable recent series.

The earliest known bin labels were of pottery, although other media such as parchment, paper and wood were sometimes employed, but have failed to survive due to the impermanent nature of their composition. An interesting rarity is a set of white-painted lead labels discovered in the cellars of Knole at Sevenoaks. They are of semi-circular form with a humped cresting. Also rare are slate labels which were of rectangular form and which one may presume were made for commercial rather than domestic use when it would have been necessary to rewrite the contents of the bin at regular intervals. Polychrome faience bin labels of Continental provenance are also known, but are rare in this country.

In outline early pottery labels were in the form of shields or escutcheons, although their popularity seems to have been short-lived and surviving examples are extremely rare. Soon after the middle of the century the so-called 'coathanger' pattern appeared and this has remained a popular form ever since, albeit with some variations. Most coathanger labels were between 4½ and 6 inches in width although, during the latter part of the

Plate 51. Two from a set of five cellar keys of typical 18th or early 19th century form. They have turned shanks and kidney shaped bows. On these examples the bows are in-filled with a brass plate which is engraved appropriately.

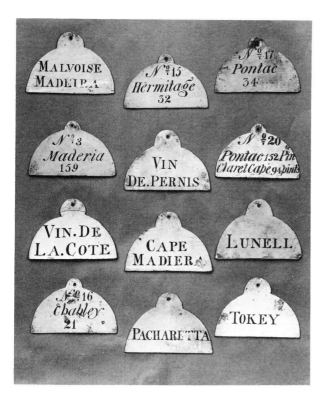

Plates 52 and 53. A highly unusual collection of bin labels from Knole, Sevenoaks. They are particularly interesting because they are made of white painted lead and they display unusual names, sometimes quaintly spelled. Note the paucity of French wines.

nineteenth century, they were sometimes made in a smaller standard 3 inch width. Circular labels of 3 to 4 inches diameter were also made.

A great rarity once encountered was a set of three leaf-shaped labels with a brown glaze and yellow slipware calligraphy. They are thought to have been made in Sussex and the style of writing suggests a late eighteenth century date.

Early bin labels were made in delftware with a beigy-brown pottery base and an overall blueish-white glaze. The lettering is either blue or, more commonly magenta, the latter varying in hue from pale to almost black. By the end of the eighteenth century the majority were made in creamware, a more robust and relatively inexpensive earthenware made from a pale Devon clay. On these the lettering was almost invariably black. The earlier angled shoulders had given way to curves and the body was generally thinner. All the leading potteries manufactured labels — Minton, Spode, Copeland, Davenport and, most particularly, Wedgwood. They often bear their manufacturer's mark on the reverse and many examples (especially those made by Wedgwood) also bear the name of the retailer. Noted names are 'Farrow & Jackson of London and Paris', 'W.J. Burrow of London and Malvern' and 'T. Rolfe, wine cooper etc., of 10 Great St. Helens'. The names of the wines were either painted or stencilled, the latter being a later feature, across the broader part of the coathanger shape. Generally capital letters were used (more or less based on the Roman alphabet), although occasionally at the end of the century,

Colour plate 16. A corner of an old cellar showing the brick divisions called 'bins' with bottles stored on their sides.

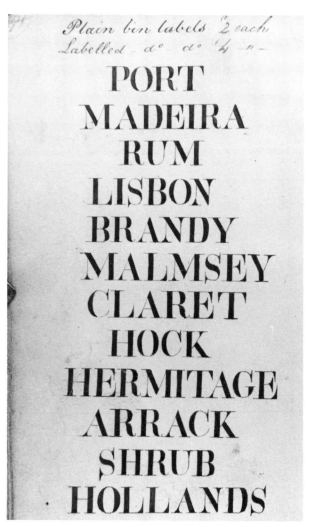

Plate 54. A small collection of square-cornered coathanger bin labels. The top three rows are of delftware (i.e. tin-glazed earthenware) and the lower ones of creamware. Rare names and spelling mistakes make this an interesting group.

Plate 55. A page from an 1807 notebook which shows some of the names available at that date from the firm of Josiah Wedgwood. Note the prices at the top of the page.

lower case lettering was employed. In either case emphasis was on clarity, an essential requirement in an ill-lit cellar.

Most bin labels were pierced with a circular hole, although other shapes are to be found. They were normally nailed directly onto the masonry of the bin itself and on numerous occasions the rusting of the nails has caused the metal to expand and the earthenware to crack.

The majority of bin labels are to be found with a straightforward generic name so that one will find 'Port', 'Sherry', 'Claret' and so on. A feature found on many labels is glazing of the lower section only, leaving the upper part unglazed or 'in the biscuit'. This enabled greater detail to be put on each label at the bin to indicate the contents more accurately. Thus a label may say 'claret', but with the chateau and vintage possibly pencilled above

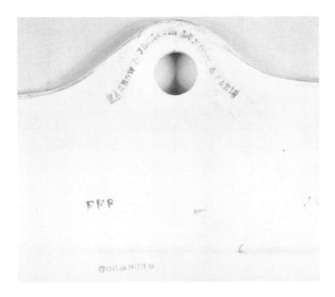

Plate 56. *The reverse of a bin label showing the maker (Wedgwood) and the retailer (Farrow & Jackson). This latter firm supplied an entire range of wine equipment for both the wholesale and retail trade until only recently.*

Plate 57. *A group of bin labels showing different shapes (rounded and square, coathanger and rectangular) and a variety of calligraphy.*

by the owner. Having said that bin labels typically have the generic name of the wine, on some examples a more specific nature is indicated; thus one may chance across the name 'Pale Sherry', 'Brown Sherry' or 'Amontillado'. Most coveted by collectors are single chateau labels and wines which are no longer consumed today. 'Paxaretta' and 'Vidonia' might qualify in the latter category. Mis-spelt labels are also sought after and not uncommon.

The reader may have noticed that all appurtenances associated with the wine cellar are of functional appearance. No more clearly is this demonstrated than in the total lack of decoration of the bin label. From this one may deduce that the cellar, while it might have been shown to a genuine wine enthusiast, was not a place of exhibition, regardless of the pride the owner might have in its contents.

So far we have concerned ourselves with the contents of private cellars, but quite clearly a substantial amount of wine was stored in the cellars of those whose business was its sale and distribution. The throughput of a commercial cellar would be quite enormous and it was completely impractical to label a bin by its generic name or even particular chateau. Thinking had to be amended and the solution found was to number each bin rather than to label it with a specific name. A ledger could then be kept by the cellarmaster with a cross-referencing number in the book to the bin numbers which appeared in the cellar. An accurate record could thus be kept of the contents of each bin.

Colour plates 17 and 18. A collection of wine bottle labels for Chateau Mouton Rothschild dating from 1945 to 1973. Each year Baron Philippe de Rothschild commissions an artist to design the upper section of the label and these have included many of the great artists of the 20th century.

76

Colour plate 19. An interesting miscellany of bin labels. The earliest is the delftware label for sherry (top left). The two slate examples are marked in paint and chalk. The wooden example is a rare one and the lead examples are both impressed and cast. The lower right-hand creamware one for sherry with blue lettering is unusually sophisticated, while the number 20 is either a house or hotel room number!

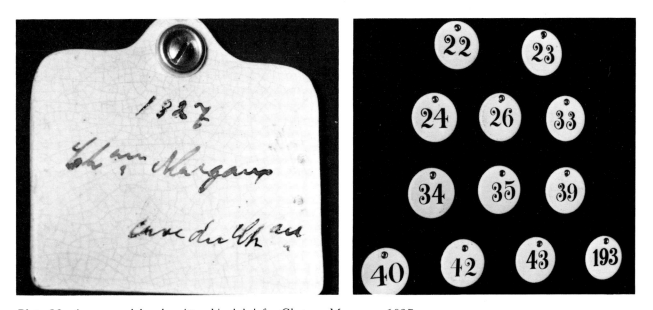

Plate 58. An unusual hand-written bin label for Chateau Margaux, 1827.

Plate 59. A small group of bin numbers. Numbers in excess of 100 are uncommon.

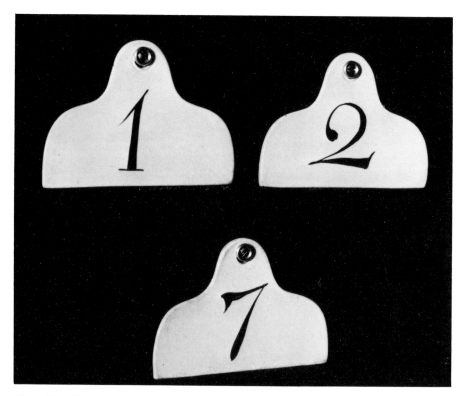

Plate 60. Three rare rounded coathanger bin numbers.

These small numbered labels are commonly found in sets running up to three or four dozen in number, but series of up to three to four hundred are indeed known. They tend to be of a standard size (between 3 and 4 inches in diameter) and as design has changed little since the system was first devised, it is difficult to determine their date unless marked by the pottery. Perhaps one word of advice to collectors is appropriate here. On more than one occasion, hotel room numbers have been offered for sale purporting to be bin numbers!

A list of the names of the various wines encountered on bin labels (and wine labels, which will be discussed in a later chapter), are to found in Appendix IV. It should be noted that, for reasons of economy of space, only the generic name of each wine has been listed and variations and misspellings have not been included.

CHAPTER 5
Corkscrews

So far this book has dealt with the making of wine, its commercial preparation for presentation to the retail trade, and its storage, both commercial and private. However, once the cork is drawn the final chapter in the wine's history has begun, for it must shortly be consumed.

Today, if one is to drink champagne, or a wine which seeks to emulate it, the cork will be firmly attached to the bottle with a wire cage. Before the middle of the nineteenth century vinification methods were far less reliable than they are today and a percentage of almost any wine was liable to a second fermentation with its attendant fizziness and the risk of popping corks. For this reason bottles were, and still are, made with parts of the neck wider than the rest in order that string or wire may be attached when necessary to hold the cork in place. The added thickness at this point also gives strength where it is most needed due to the pressure on the cork.

Although cork is now considered the most satisfactory way of keeping a bottle air tight, it was not the only method used in the past. (As this is being written, incidentally, plastic stoppers and screw tops are gaining currency.) The Greeks and Romans often protected their wine from the air by the addition of a tiny quantity of oil which spread over the surface. It would appear that amphorae were sometimes either additionally or alternatively sealed with pitch or plaster (or both) and on occasions with bungs of wadding tied on with string. Again these may have been further sealed with pitch or plaster. Elsewhere in Europe and in England tapered, wooden stoppers were inserted into the neck of the container and secured with string; alternatively, pieces of parchment, leather, hemp or linen were used. The effects of these various kinds of stoppering were enhanced by soaking the sealers with oil, wax or tallow and no doubt other unrecorded substances.

Early references to cork stoppers in Britain are not uncommon. In Shakespeare's *A Winter's Tale* the Clown refers to a ship in a storm as 'swallowed with yest and froth, as you'd thrust a cork into a hogshead' and Rosalind in *As You Like It* asks 'prithee, take the cork out of thy mouth, that I may drink thy tidings'. As cork was (and largely still is) a product of the Iberian Peninsula and in view of England's maritime trading links with that part of the world it would be surprising if corks had not been widely available. A wine bill at Woburn dated July 1653 mentions a quantity of 'claret wine' being delivered to the house accompanied by a gross of stone bottles and the same number of corks costing four shillings. They would however have been of conical form and used only loosely as short-term stoppers tied on with string. It was not until the later part of

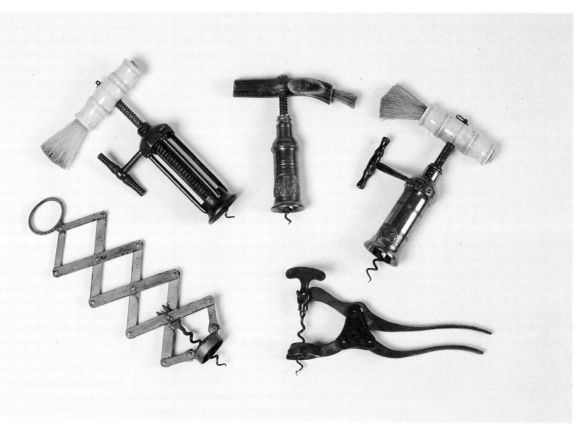

Colour plate 20. A selection of various corkscrews. Top row, left to right: a King's screw with a bone handle, skeletal cage and steel rack; a Thomason's screw with applied coat of arms on the bronze barrel and antler T-bar; a King's screw with bronze barrel and bone handle (a typical example). Bottom row: lazy tongs, Wiers patent of 1884 and a Lund's lever.

the century that it became the norm to drive the top of the cork home flush with the top of the bottle; it was this practice which prompted the invention of the device to remove it. While there are references to corkscrews in the seventeenth century, very few survive which can be dated with certainty and the history of corkscrews really begins after the year 1700.

The simple corkscrew has three parts. First, there is the spiral which is driven into the cork; this is called the worm or screw. At the other end is the second element, the handle and very seldom are the two joined immediately one to the other; usually there is a third element, the shaft. By reference to the form of each part of the corkscrew, collectors, or addicts as they prefer to call themselves, are able to identify the different models very precisely. Broadly, the worm or screw may be divided into two types, those with a central tapered spike around which threads a bladed spiral — these are known as Archimedean screws or augers, depending on the finer details and pitch — and those formed as a helix where the spiral does not have a central core. The worm may have a circular cross-section tapering to its point which is called a wire helix or it may have a flattened cross-section when it is called a bladed helix. Often a wire helix has a groove along its length; in this case the word 'reeded' is added to the description.

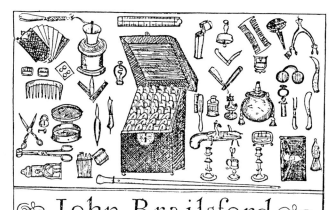

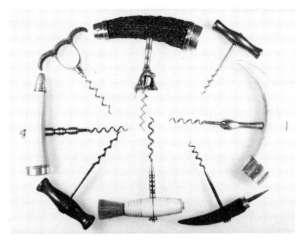

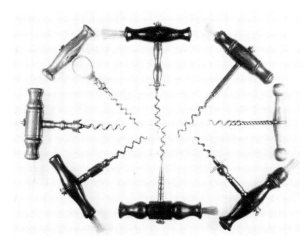

Plate 61. *The mid-18th century trade card of John Brailsford. It might amuse the reader to find two corkscrews amongst the implements shown at the head of the card.*

Plate 62. *Worms and handles. Clockwise from top. i. Stag's horn (antler) crossbar with engraved silver capped ends, 'bell' cap lifter on shank with bladed worm. ii. All steel 'T' bar corkscrew with Archimedean worm. iii. Boar's tusk grip with tapered helical worm. iv. Buffalo horn with steel spike to remove lead capsule with tapered helical worm. v. Turned bone 'pipe' shaped crossbar with reeded (or fluted) helical worm and brush. vi. Plain turned ashwood crossbar, flat steel shank with 'Speed' worm. vii. Ivory handle capped with silver ends, helical worm. viii. Leather covered steel 'three finger' pull with ciphered worm.*

Plate 63. *Shafts. Clockwise from top. i. Cast steel shaft in hour-glass shape with petal shaped button. ii. Square steel shaft. iii. Clough double twisted wire. iv. Turned steel shaft with knop and scalloped shaped button. v. 'Bobbin' turned steel shaft. vi. Blued steel turned baluster stem. vii. Turned steel shaft with four 'teeth' to grip the cork. viii. Steel shaft with large hole for centre finger, 'The Holborn Signet'.*

There are other screw types, but these are the province of only the most specialist collector.

The shaft may be plain or decorated. The amount and quality of the decoration often give a clue to the quality of the piece as a whole and most frequently provides as good a clue as any to its date. The shaft and the

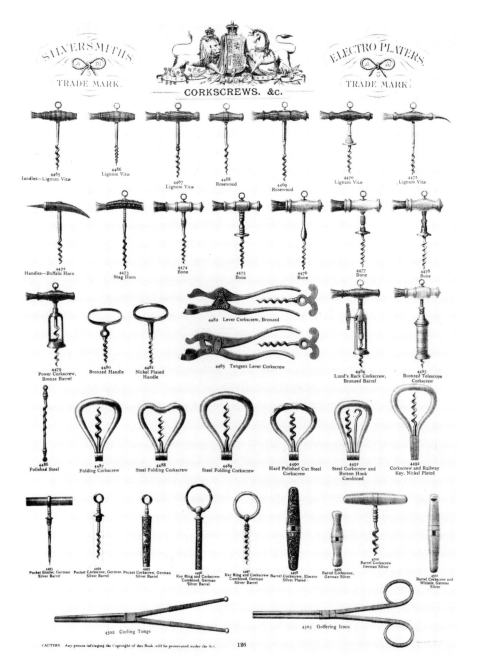

Plate 64. A selection of corkscrews from the catalogue of 'A.M. Silber, Silversmiths, Electroplaters and Cutlery Manufacturers, 1898'. Comparison of some of these corkscrews with some of those in the following plate, which date from exactly a century earlier, shows how difficult it can be to date corkscrews accurately.

worm are almost always made in one piece of high quality steel.

The handles of corkscrews are most frequently made of wood and turned on a lathe. It is often thought that many are also made of ivory, but this is not so. Ivory is actually a very rare medium for a corkscrew handle, although a great many are made of bone which of course can bear a close resemblance. Precious metals and stones are also occasionally used as

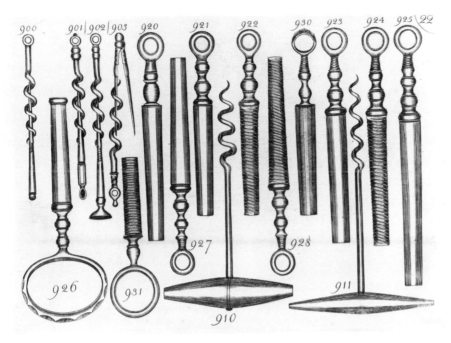

Plate 65. A page of corkscrew designs from an anonymous metalworker's catalogue of approximately 1800.

indeed are tusks and teeth, antlers and horns. A great many handles have one end fitted with a brush. This is to clean the top of the bottle after the wax or capsule has been removed.

Before delving into the evolution of the corkscrew, it should be made clear that corkscrews were often made to old designs, sometimes long after improvements had been introduced. It is frequently tempting to ascribe an eighteenth century date to a simple 'T' corkscrew made perhaps in the middle of the nineteenth century. Certainly a corkscrew for which a patent was taken out in 1802 has decoration clearly indicating a design of the 1840s and it may easily have been made a decade later than that. If one is tempted to date every corkscrew by the year of its first introduction, it is a sobering reminder to look at the catalogue of Silber & Fleming published in 1898 and then to remember that corkscrews are utility objects used frequently, and consequently age far more quickly than an art object stored on a shelf.

It would appear that almost all eighteenth century corkscrews were intended to be portable. Many fold in half, the handle forming a loop which protects the worm in the folded position. This variety was preceded at the very beginning of the century by a corkscrew with a very short worm (often little more than one and a half revolutions) protected by a sheath, a plain cylinder which screws onto the upper section of the shaft. The handle on such a piece was in the form of a signet ring — just a plain loop with a seal on it. Some of these seals are engraved with coats of arms, crests or initials and were presumably used to impress the hard wax with which the bottles were sealed after corkage. Later versions did not have the seal and by the end of the eighteenth century a separate seal was used for the

Plate 66. A good and rare folding bow corkscrew of unusually early date. It is silver, though unmarked, and has a steel worm. The silver bow bears the legend 'Francis Twisden, April 24th 1710'.

Plate 67. A simple corkscrew of about 1700-1710, with a handle formed as a signet ring and a sheath which unscrews to reveal a worm of only one to one and a half turns. Sometimes these seals are engraved with initials or a crest. Although silver ones exist this example is brass.

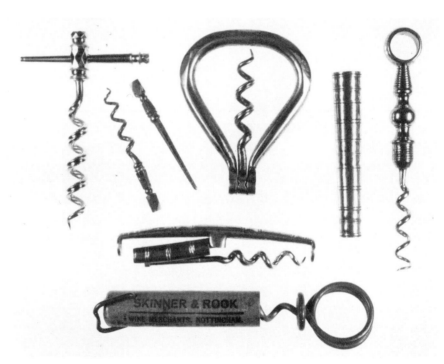

Plate 68. Pocket and folding bow. Top row, left: two examples of peg and worm pocket corkscrews, circa 1830, the cross bar 'peg' inserts into centre of worm; centre: faceted steel folding bow corkscrew; right: pocket turned steel ring, the protecting sheath forms a handle when inserted through ring, circa 1800. Below: double hinged folding pocket corkscrew, circa 1820. Bottom: pocket wood sheath wire corkscrew by Clough advertising 'Skinner & Rook, Wine Merchants of Nottingham', marked 'Pat. March 1910'.

purpose. Today most bottles are sealed with lead or plastic capsules and modern corkscrews are well equipped for their efficient removal.

A popular, though now rare, type of mid-eighteenth century corkscrew had a nutmeg grater incorporated in its design, but the most popular, particularly in Ireland where examples exist in silver, was the 'folding bow'

*Plate 69. Henshall type buttons. Left: lignum vitae pipe-shaped turned handle, brass baluster stem with brass Henshall type button, wording '*Parker * Potts & Denton*', circa 1840. Centre: rosewood handle stamped 'W.S.', steel heavy baluster stem with rare detachable threaded steel button, stem stamped 'Regd.', circa 1850. Right: turned bone handle, steel baluster shank with steel Henshall type button, circa 1830.*

as illustrated in plate 66, page 83. Another favourite eighteenth century corkscrew was that on which the handle had a very small ring. When the sheath was unscrewed from the shaft it was put through the ring to form a simple T-handled screw. This type has continued to be made into the twentieth century and is a particular favourite for canteens and travelling necessaires because of its extreme economy of space.

The most difficult variety of corkscrew to date is the simple T screw. Although the majority of these were no doubt made in the nineteenth century it is reasonable to suppose that some were made in the eighteenth. Typically they have a steel worm with a plain or decorated shaft, above which is a turned handle, often of bone. Steel examples dating from the present century abound and guides to dating lie principally in their turning and decoration. Many T corkscrews are equipped with brushes.

The closing years of the century saw the most dramatic changes in design. In 1795 Samuel Henshall applied for a patent to protect his first corkscrew design. It was a simple T screw, but with the addition of a button or flange at the head of the screw. When the worm had penetrated the cork and was fully driven home, the cork came into contact with the button which was gouged on its underside. This had the effect of making the cork rotate in the bottle which considerably eased the extraction.

By the same date (when incidentally it was quite common to call these objects 'bottle screws') examples were also being made which extracted the

Plate 70. Detail of a Henshall type button by Parker Potts and Denton dating from about 1840.

cork mechanically. The principle behind the mechanical corkscrew is that, having driven the worm through the cork, the worm and shaft, together with the impaled cork, can be prised from the bottle by having some part of the corkscrew impinge on its neck. Technically the most attractive designs are those which incorporate the principle of the rack and pinion, the lever or the counter-threaded screw. Some corkscrews have devices which firmly grip the bottle, while others use a scissors framework to gain mechanical advantage. Perhaps the least attractive are those with springs which only marginally ease the extraction of the cork during its first short movement.

The first major patent to be granted for a corkscrew in the nineteenth century was that given in 1802 to a successful Birmingham industrialist, Edward Thomason. Within ten years he was manufacturing approximately ten thousand corkscrews per annum at four shillings a piece. Although the duration of his patent was short, his invention was still being marketed at the end of the century and contributed substantially to his wealth and fame. Thomason's screws have a barrel, usually made of brass, which will locate on top of the bottle and into which the cork is drawn. Once the screw is driven fully into the cork a continuing turn of the handle engages a larger, concentric, reverse-direction thread which extracts the cork from the bottle. It is perhaps confusing for collectors that Thomason's patent is often found with a plaque on the barrel engraved with the names 'Dowler', 'Rogers' or 'Heeley', and others too. Presumably these were made after 1816 when Edward Thomason's own patent had expired. The plaques sometimes have Thomason's own motto 'Ne Plus Ultra'. Many different versions of Thomason's screw are to be found; some have plain barrels

Plate 72. Thomason type corkscrews by various makers with turned bone handles. From left to right. i. Oval plaque with lion and unicorn supporters reading 'Thomasons Patent. Ne Plus Ultra', royal motto around garter and on banner underneath. ii. Oblong plaque reads 'Josh. Rodgers & Sons. Sheffield.'. iii. Oblong plaque with lion and unicorn emerging from slanted oval with word 'Patent', maker's name 'Dowler' above. iv. Semi-circular plaque depicting the royal coat of arms lion and unicorn supporters and mottoes, below words 'Heeley & Sons'.

Plate 73. Thomason types with decorative brass barrels. Left to right: raised 'church screen' decoration; grape vine and bunch of pears; Gothic window decoration. All three handles of turned bone with dusting brushes, circa 1840.

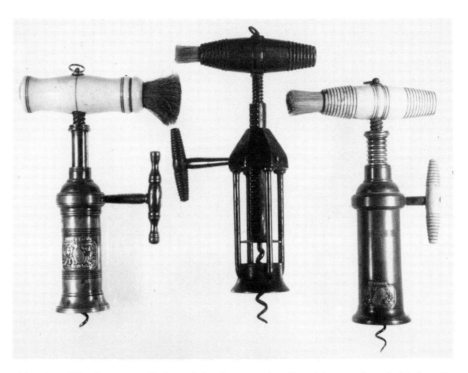

Plate 74. King's screws. Left to right: bone top handle with turned steel side handle, oblong brass plaque of lion and unicorn, motto 'Ne Plus Ultra' and maker's name 'Barlow' above; all steel cage with walnut 'pipe' top handle, ribbed steel side handle; bone 'pipe' handle, one end unscrews to replace dusting brush, wide rack with bone 'pipe' side handle, oblong plaque 'Dowler Patent' with lion and unicorn.

while others are decorated with Gothic motifs. A few rarities have decorated handles, but though the majority are made of bone, some are made of wood.

With much the same feel as Thomason's screw is the so-called 'King's screw'. The principal difference between them is that whereas the Thomason's screw has just one handle, the King's screw has a second handle (somewhat smaller) at right angles to the main shaft. This second handle is itself on a shaft which incorporates within its length a pinion which meshes with a rack on a sleeve encasing the main screw shaft like the Thomason's patent. Countless thousands of these were manufactured. Also unlike Thomason's patent, the cork is extracted without being rotated, but the price to pay for this is a separate operation with the second handle. Like the Thomason screws, King's screws are variously ornamented, but by machine rather than by hand. The barrels are usually bronze and the larger handles wood, mostly lignum vitae though sometimes mahogany or walnut, and occasionally bone. The subsidiary handles are often steel. More often than not one end of the principal handle is equipped with a brush for cleaning the neck of the bottle. A slightly earlier mechanical corkscrew was made, now called the 'Farrow & Jackson' type. A silver example exists marked 1796. These have a threaded shaft; the worm and the shaft are surrounded by a cage, on top of which

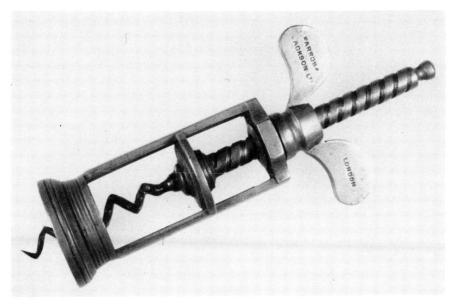

Plate 75. A brass corkscrew stamped on the fly nut 'Farrow & Jackson Ltd., London', with steel ciphered worm, circa 1880.

is a butterfly nut. This engages with the shaft and lifts it when rotated.

Although there were very few other patents taken out prior to 1850, and those that were appear to contribute very little original thought to the concept of cork extraction, around the middle of the century there was a plethora of patents for minor modifications to existing models. There then followed a positive rash of patents which employed lever actions of one sort or another. There were two halves to these corkscrews; the first part was a simple T handle screw with a hole in the shaft. When driven home into the cork the second half of the apparatus came into use. This consisted of a pair of plier-like levers, one half of which fitted round the neck of the bottle while the other had a hook which engaged in the hole of the first part. By closing the levers together the cork was extracted. Lever screws of a later date have folding levers which work on a rack system, not unlike the action of the King's screw.

A name to be found on many corkscrews which employ mechanical devices is that of Lund. Lunds were responsible for a large number of levers, but perhaps their most satisfactory design was the 'London rack', an inexpensive variant of the King's screw.

During the second half of the nineteenth century, and indeed into the twentieth it became common practice to give mechanical corkscrews names, hence the 'Perfect', the 'Royal Club', the 'Irresistable', the 'Victor' and the 'Challenge', and even today there is made a de luxe version of the Thomason's patent called the 'Vulcan'.

When dating corkscrews there are one or two points which should be borne in mind. First, one has to remember the maxim which applies to any object whether it be a corkscrew or not, which is that every item is the product of two things. One is the call for that thing to be made and the second is the technology with which to make it. It is the second of these

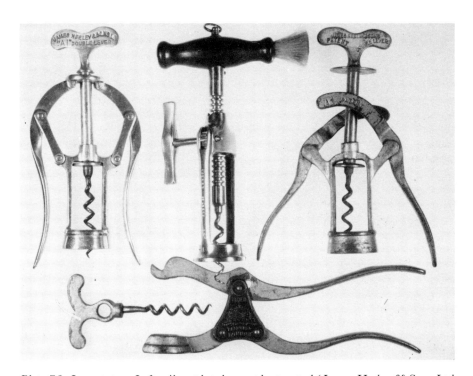

Plate 76. Lever types. Left: silver plated example stamped 'James Heeley & Sons Ltd. "A 1" Double Lever', polished steel rack stamped 'Lunds Patent London Rack', open steel frame stamped 'Lund Maker Cornhill and Fleet Street'. Centre: rosewood handle with brush. Right: unusual variation of a double lever, top stamped 'James Heeley & Sons. Patent Double Lever'. Below: frosted copper cast-iron two part lever corkscrew, bronzed iron triangle cast with royal coat of arms and words 'Lund Patentee London', reverse with words 'Sold by The Patentee 56 & 57 Cornhill. London' with a milestone 'London. Estabd. 1796. Trade Mark'.

two points which can often be the guide in the dating of the piece. Perhaps the latest in the long line of corkscrew designs demonstrates this last point better than any other namely the American designed 'Screwpull'. The plastic body has a springiness which earlier technology did not permit, and which is very strong. However it is the screw itself which demonstrates modern technology in its most advanced state. It is made from very high tensile stainless steel and is coated with polytetraflorethylene, an anti-friction substance of remarkable properties, mostly used in the manufacture of non-stick saucepans. The result is a corkscrew of unequalled efficiency, but the technology which has produced it has only been available during the second half of the twentieth century. Many corkscrews made during the last hundred years have been nickel or chrome plated, while others have been painted with metallic paint. These techniques were not available when now-antique corkscrews were made.

The greatest difficulty with dating is encountered when looking at a corkscrew made perhaps a hundred years ago, but to a design of a hundred years earlier. Machines were used in the eighteenth century to produce wire helices, but the hydraulic. presses and steam driven tools of the Industrial Revolution were responsible for producing artefacts quite unlike their eighteenth century predecessors. These considerations must therefore

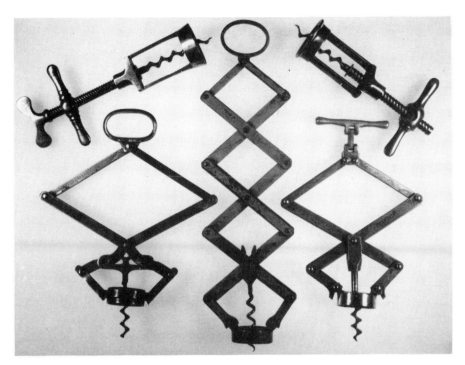

Plate 77. Mechanical corkscrews. Top left: 'The Victor', fly nut rotates on threaded shaft, circa 1910. Top right: 'Challenge', cross bar twists over tip of shaft, circa 1890. Below left: H.D. Armstrongs patent 'Irresistable', circa 1902. Centre: lazy tongs, Wiers patent of 1884, concertina type. Below right: cross bar handle stamped 'Perfect', French, circa 1910.

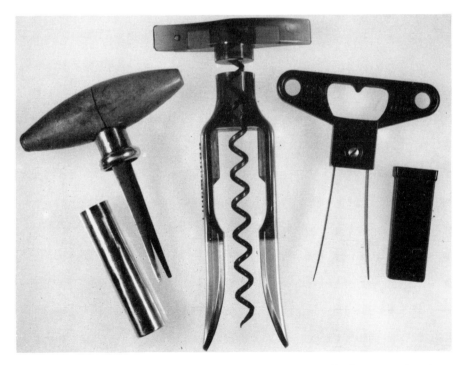

Plate 78. Cork extractors and the screwpull. Left: beechwood grip stamped on brass collar 'Patented May 9th. 98' (1898), brass sheath enclosing pair of steel prongs. Centre: the modern American corkscrew 'The Screwpull' with plastic bottle grips. Right: modern example in cast black metal raised words 'SAN BRI Made in France'.

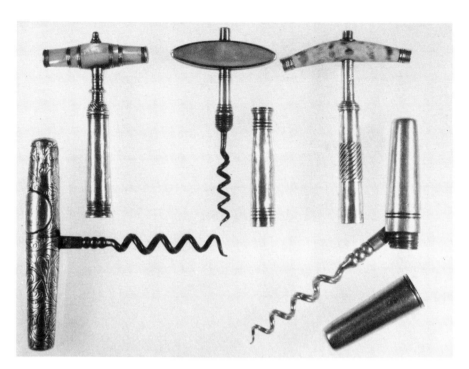

Plate 79. Silver corkscrews. Top row: three Birmingham examples of silver pocket corkscrews stamped with maker's initials on base of sheath, circa 1800 to 1820, left and centre with mother of pearl handles, right with ivory handle, by Joseph Taylor. Bottom left: Victorian London silver 1872 folding pocket roundlet, engraved honeysuckle design with owner's initial on applied disc. Bottom right: London silver 1912 pocket roundlet with gilded steel worm.

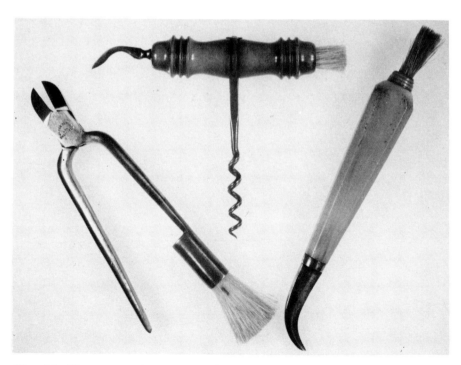

Plate 80. Champagne wire cutters. Left to right: steel champagne wire clippers with dusting brush stamped 'James Blyde & Co. Sheffield'; applewood handle with curved knife to trim lead seals and dusting brush, circa 1890; rare cow horn champagne wire cutter stamped 'Rodgers. Cutlers to His Majesty', G.R. with crown, circa 1820.

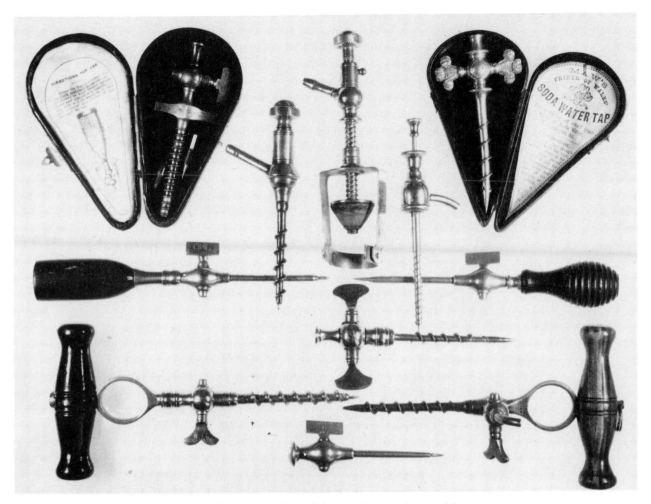

Plate 81. *English champagne taps. Top row, left to right: leather cased tap with instructions for use; brass patent 11030 (1884); silver plate by Buss & Sons, Manchester; silver plate with trocar through Archimedean worm; another leather cased tap. Centre, left to right: two detachable ebony handled trocar types. Underneath: brass Archimedean screw by G. Nazer, 31, Royal Exchange. Bottom left: ebonized handle silver plate with ring grip. Bottom right: rosewood handle, brass ring stamped 'Holborn Champagne Screw'. Bottom centre: silver plated 'Abyssinian' tap stamped 'Farrow & Jackson. London' and 'Patent 4N H*R'.*

be carefully borne in mind when assessing a corkscrew which does not bear some sign that makes for a confident assessment, such as a maker's name and model.

Although unsuitable for drawing corks from wine bottles mention should be made of a number of silver screws, sometimes with mother-of-pearl or ivory handles and invariably with a silver sheath to cover the worm, which were made in Birmingham from the late eighteenth century onwards. Birmingham incidentally, rapidly rose to prominence as a centre of manufacturing industry (particularly for the metal trades) at this time and a great many corkscrews were manufactured there. These silver corkscrews were made in large numbers by both Joseph Willmore and Samuel

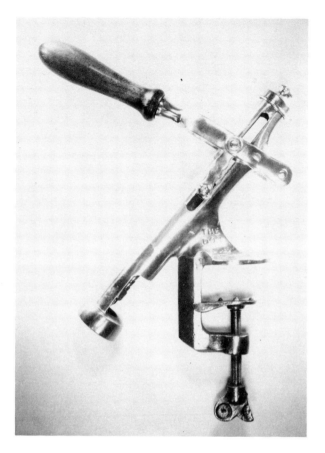

Plate 82. Brass bar corkscrew named 'The Don'. Chambers patent 1806/03. W.G. Edmonds & Co., Dublin. Ebony handle activates steep pitched worm.

Plate 83. 'The Rotary Eclipse' bar corkscrew which screws directly onto the top of a bar and dates from about 1880.

Pemberton and although interesting because they provide with their silver mark an accurate dating for a particular style, they none the less should not concern the readers of this book, for most of them were made for the withdrawing of corks from scent bottles and are of a size commensurate with that task.

When considering corkscrews one must include two devices which are specifically connected with champagne. First are champagne pliers. Usually the product of the late nineteenth and early twentieth century, these appear at first sight to be little more than an ordinary pair of wire cutters. They are, however, commonly fitted with a corkscrew which folds besides one of the handles and usually they have a brush at the end of the other. The second handle also often has a serrated edge which makes the removal of the capsule somewhat easier. The wire cutters are of course for removing the wire which anchors the cork on the average champagne bottle.

The other device is the champagne tap. Before the introduction of the modern half bottle of champagne there were presumably those who did not

Plate 84. Cast-iron bar corkscrew named 'The Safety. Patent 16777', R.G. Gilchrist's English patent of October 20th 1894, no. 16,777, manufactured by Gaskell and Chambers.

wish to consume an entire bottle. The champagne tap allowed this to be done without the wine losing its effervescence. Although made in France at the beginning of the nineteenth century, English examples date from the second half and were mostly made after 1880. Typically the champagne tap looks rather like an auger-type corkscrew. It is driven into the cork and when in position the central shaft is withdrawn, leaving a hole through the cork. The outside casing is fitted with a tap which can be used to allow a limited quantity of wine to be removed. The advent of quarter and half bottles, not to mention the full pint size, together with the modern invention of the bottle stopper, has rendered champagne taps obsolete.

The last type of antique corkscrew which deserves detailed description

Plate 85. Combination corkscrews. Top left to right: cow horn handled champagne tap, the brass shank incorporating a whistle; 'scissor' type with wire cutter; pocket folding combination tool set, faceted bow; penknife with button hook and corkscrew 'Spratt Patent' by Brookes & Crookes. Sheffield.' Middle: pocket carriage key, hoof pick and corkscrew; brass roundlet containing tweezers, gimlet, screwdriver, spike and corkscrew, advertising 'Cowbrough & Co Ltd Leeds. Nourishing Ale for Invalids'. Below: cow horn sided pocket tool kit, containing fifteen different steel tools and a corkscrew.

is the so-called 'bar' screw. If the worm of a corkscrew has a very coarse pitch — in other words it will look as if it has been pulled and stretched — it can be driven into a cork without rotating a handle; it can be pushed in directly. To have this facility the worm has to be finely machined and free from flaws. It means also that the worm has to be free to rotate and, having once penetrated the cork, the rotation has to be arrested so that when the screw is pulled, the screw does not rotate backwards the way it went in. The man originally responsible for this invention was Charles Hull who produced a manual version in the 1860s. However it was the large bar corkscrew which put this principle to best effect. A bar corkscrew is, as its name implies, a device of substantial robustness and is screwed or clamped to the bar of a tavern. In most examples the direction of the mechanism is tilted at an angle of between thirty and sixty degrees. The bottle to be opened is brought into contact with the lower end of the corkscrew, which has a flange approximately corresponding in size to the neck of the bottle. A large lever is then drawn towards the operator. This pushes the worm into the cork and automatically engages a device to prevent it from continuing to rotate. At this point it is impossible to pull the lever any further towards the operator. Pushing the lever back to its original position first extracts the cork, and in the final travel extracts the worm from the cork, allowing the cork to drop out of the bottom of the machine. The whole action is very speedy and a well maintained bar screw in the hands of an efficient operator can extract a cork in less than a second. These machines are many times the size and weight of our domestic hand-held model.

As show pieces in commercial premises bar screws were frequently made of brass which could be polished to match the beer pumps and other bar equipment. Some fine examples were made in cast iron and many had decorative wooden knobs or handles. As with other corkscrews their inventors and makers gave them names, the 'Don' and the 'Acme' being the most popular.

Anyone interested in buying a bar corkscrew today should remember that a good example may have drawn hundreds of corks a day for a very long while. Although no doubt they were made of the finest available materials at the time, such a work load means that many of them have mechanisms which are almost worn out. Despite this though they are increasingly collected and are now commanding high prices. Perhaps some of the original moulds used in making cast iron examples (many of which come from America) are still in existence because on occasion one sees unused examples whose authenticity is very much in doubt and which one suspects are modern reproductions made in old moulds.

In this chapter only the principal developments in corkscrew design have been described, but it has to be understood that many hundreds of patents were taken out for an enormous variety of patterns and it would be impossible to mention them all. A bewildering array of corkscrews was made combined with other items such as folding pocket and pen knives, button hooks, whistles, screw drivers, saws, carriage keys, walking sticks, umbrellas, whips and even the folding guards of carving forks. Some corkscrews did not have a worm, but instead, a pair of straight or angled steel pins or blades which forced the cork to rotate and move in an upwards direction. Indeed, the cork extractor, as opposed to the screw, has gained much currency in recent times, the idea being that the cork can be withdrawn intact and reused. In the 1960s attempts were made to extract corks by pumping air into the bottle via a hollow, thin spike inserted through the cork. There were two varieties, one which required the user to pump a piston to build up the necessary pressure and one which relied on compressed air cylinders. The idea failed because some bottles, particularly the flagon-shaped bottles used for a popular Portuguese Rosé, tended to explode!

Note: Due to the number of corkscrews in some plates the captions to the illustrations in this chapter are written in an abbreviated style.

CHAPTER 6
Wine Tasters

While watching the progress of wine from the vineyard to a gentleman's cellar we have seen that it has been almost exclusively handled by artisans and tradesmen. For this reason lavish materials have not yet been encountered; rather, unrefined glass, wood, steel and pottery have so far been used.

But there comes a time when the wine has to be consumed. In the first instance this is done in minute quantities for the purposes of professional assessment of its quality. Anyone who has had the privilege of attending a vintner's tasting of new clarets when the wines are only a few months or even weeks old, will be struck immediately by the totally undrinkable nature of the raw product. It is not merely for sobriety's sake that vintners at a tasting spit out the wine after tasting it. An experienced wine merchant is able to assess the potential of a wine from a very early stage and the job becomes progressively easier as the wine matures and develops. The professional is looking for a balance of fruit, tannin, acidity and alcohol in order to make his decision as to whether to purchase the wine. To do this a small vessel is required, hence the wine 'taster'.

By definition a taster or 'tastevin' only accommodates a very small amount of wine. It must be made of a material robust enough to withstand the rigours of daily use in a commercial environment and that material must be one which will not taint the wine in any way; it must either reflect light well or it must be of a light colour in order that the colour of the wine can be truly judged.

While porcelain tasters (see plate 93, page 103) are known to exist, it is not surprising that by far the majority of surviving examples encountered are of silver. Indeed the history of silver wine tasters reaches back over six centuries and there are several recorded references to them in fourteenth and fifteenth century manuscripts. A will dated 1426 mentions 'A tastour of selver with my owne merke ymade in the bottom'. Later in the fifteenth century during the Wars of the Roses an Act of 1477-78 placed an embargo on the export of gold and silver from England to the Continent. Wine tasters were specifically exempt from this order when used professionally. 'Any Merchant going over the Sea to buy any Wine to be brought into the realm, as far to carry with him only a little Cup called a Taster (un taster ou shewer) for wine.'

The earliest extant British taster dates from the sixteenth century (see plate 87). The standard English model is circular and between 3 ½ and 5 inches in diameter. The sides are plain and taper outwards at varying angles, although usually 45 degrees. The entire base is taken with a dome.

Plate 86. Two wine experts at a tasting, one taking the nose (or bouquet) while the other is assessing the colour. Shortly after this was taken the wine would have been tasted and spat out in the copper spittoon (or cuspidor) on the right.

Plate 87. Until recently the earliest silver wine taster was thought to date from 1631. However, a new contender has emerged while this book was being written. With canted sides and beaded decoration and a domed base, it is typical of English wine taster shapes. The base is decorated with a bunch of grapes inside a circle of scallop shells and unusually the piece rests on a foot. It is of heavy gauge silver and is hallmarked for 1603. Since the previous edition an even earlier wine taster of about 1580 made by Lawrence Gilbert of Colchester has been recorded. 99

Plate 88. *A wine taster made by William Townsend of Bath but assayed in London in 1775 (because Bath had no assay office). It is engraved 'James Moore, Bristol 1810'. James Moore was a wine merchant and a failed politician.*

Plate 89. *A very rare English wine taster approximately following the French models with a gadrooned lower section. It has a scrolled handle in the form of a caryatid and it rests on a moulded plinth. Made in London in 1701 by Samuel Wastell.*

They do not have a handle and are often engraved with the name of the vintner or owner around their outside edge. There is a well documented example made in London in 1646 and inscribed 'Michael Robinson, his taster, Nouem 2th 1670'. This design altered not a bit from the seventeenth century through into the eighteenth. Very few wine tasters were made after 1750 in England and fewer still seem to survive from the nineteenth century but absolutely the reverse is true in France where there was a constant and thriving business in the making of tastevins and indeed

Plate 90. A very rare glass wine taster similar to plate 89. The heavily moulded base would throw interesting reflections in the wine to aid assessment of its colour and the thumbpiece adds stability. A glass expert would date this to about 1720, but the resemblance to that in plate 89 makes it tempting to attribute an earlier date.

Plate 91. A shallow two-handled wine dish of about 1660 with punched and embossed decoration.

there still is. Plate 89 illustrates an English example made in 1701, but this is far more akin to French examples than those normally found in England. Also illustrated, in plate 90, is a very rare, if not unique, wine taster made of glass. The similarity of its design and date to the silver example in plate 89 is obvious.

For many years silver enthusiasts have conducted a heated debate on the subject of shallow two-handled bowls such as that illustrated in plate 91. They have flat bottoms and were fitted with two handles. The bowls vary in size from 2 inches to 4½ inches or more and the handles are of flat section or of wire construction, usually in simple C or S scroll form.

Plate 92. A miscellany of wine tasters or tastevins. i. French, about 1780. ii. French, about 1770. iii. Paris, about 1730, by Jean Platel. iv. London, 1788, by Thomas Daniel. Britannia Standard. v. Paris 1677. vi. Paris, about 1735. vii. Orleans, 1768, by Pierre Hanappier. viii. London, 1690. The last item is atypical and may be a 'cup of assay'. See text.

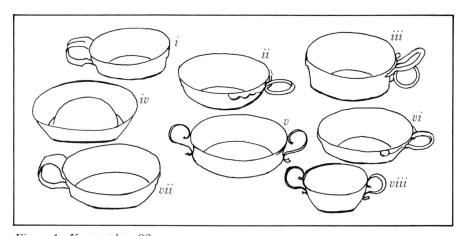

Figure 1. Key to plate 92.

Occasionally they are to be found plain, but usually they are decorated. This decoration can take the form of simple lobes or, more commonly, the sides and bases are embossed with floral and geometrical motifs. Often they are engraved with initials, sometimes accompanied by a date. These features may also be pricked. On later examples the sides and base may have gadrooned decoration and it is not unknown for the base to be embossed with bunches of grapes which makes the allusion to wine quite clear. Early books on silver referred to them as wine tasters but since the middle of the twentieth century many have argued that they are far too

Plate 93. *A polychrome Worcester porcelain wine taster, a considerable rarity, it was made in about 1755 and is 3¾ ins. wide.*

numerous to be tasters and that they were more likely to be sweetmeat or bon-bon dishes. Handled bowls which are unquestionably wine tasters have never been plentiful; some would even say that they were rare. But two-handled bowls that were made from about 1630 for some sixty years are among the most plentiful objects of silver during that period.

Credence must surely be attached to an entry in the records of the Court of Wardens at Goldsmiths' Hall dated 1st January 1639 which states '24 small wine dishes, 1 dwt worse than standard, are broken' (that is the silver was found to be sub-standard and the dishes destroyed). That so many should be made at one time makes it highly probable that the wardens were referring to the same shallow two-handled bowls. It would be gratifying to feel that the debate has been concluded and that henceforth they will be known as wine dishes. Wine dishes have parallels elsewhere with the long-popular Scottish quaichs and Dutch brandywine dishes.

Because of the nature of their use it is not surprising that there is a relative paucity of wine tasters of, say, the eighteenth century, when compared with decanters, wine glasses, or wine labels, as these latter objects were used by the public rather than a limited number of professionals.

In the wine-producing countries of Europe vastly more were made and correspondingly have survived. There are of course many regional variations, not only between one country and another, but between provinces and regions. Usually, in Continental Europe, it was customary for the wine taster to be suspended around the user's neck. This was done via a single handle. This was either a simple loop of silver with a sufficiently broad horizontal cross-section to allow a firm grip, or a similar

Plate 94. A very rare pair of English silver wine tasters of 1800 modelled on French examples. Late 18th and 19th century tasters are seldom found and the need for a pair is not immediately apparent.

loop of wire with a flat thumb piece. Solid thumb pieces or loops in the form of intertwined snakes are also known. The bowls on such pieces are shallow and circular and if the base is not flat, it is only very slightly domed. The most characteristic Continental element is the decoration itself. Variations of gadrooned decoration may be found, but a large number of examples display two quite distinct forms of decoration, one on either half of the bowl. This effect is quite clearly illustrated in plate 92, page 102.

An alternative form of taster is the mediaeval 'cup of assay', the vessel from which a small quantity of any liquid was tested (usually for poison) by a servant or assistant before it was consumed by the lord or master of the household. In the Middle Ages these tasting cups were apparently important pieces of plate although very little appears to be known about them today. A small two-handled cup in Harveys Wine Museum in Bristol may possibly be a later example of such an object.

CHAPTER 7
Wine Coolers

Early paintings and tapestries showing scenes of feasting frequently include in the foreground an oval tub containing bottles of wine. Close examination of these pictures leads one to the conclusion that the bottles were being cooled in these vessels and we can be sure that by the end of the seventeenth century this practice was indeed well established. In early pictures these wine coolers tend to stand on the floor in no particular position, sometimes near the dining table, sometimes near the edge of the room. Many of them were made in brass, copper or pewter, but lacquered or otherwise-decorated tin was perhaps most popular. They were universally oval in shape, standing on a rim foot. As utilitarian objects designed to be placed on the floor there is no doubt that they were frequently kicked and rapidly became worn. Brass and copper in particular are metals which abrade quickly so it is not surprising that very few of these survive. Lacquered tin equally betrays the passage of time, although a few examples do still survive in museums and private collections. They were also made in silver, the earliest surviving English example dating from 1667. Early silver coolers tend to have shallow basins raised on four claw feet in preference to the earlier rim foot and several well known examples can be seen in the Victoria and Albert Museum, the Bank of England and

Plate 95. A maiolica (Italian faience) wine cistern, painted in polychrome colours by Francesco Durantino in Urbino with subjects from the story of Diana and Callisto. This type of bulbous sided and footed cooler appears to have originated in Italy and this is an early example dating from 1540-50.

Plate 96. A silver wine cooler or cistern of 1677. It demonstrates very well the English silversmiths' preference for embossing silver rather than casting it into heavy shapes.

Plate 97. A large black marble wine cooler that will accommodate between two and four dozen bottles. The lower half of the body is carved with a vigorous calyx of gadrooning and the trumpet base conforms in outline with the top. It was made during the first half of the 18th century, but exactly when is difficult to determine.

other famous collections. However it should be pointed out that silver basins raised on feet are today called cisterns, while examples in other materials are called wine coolers. Another medium in which wine coolers were executed at this date was marble. In Britain this was a practice copied from the Continent where they were made in several countries in large numbers. They were of the same form as the base and precious metal models and were of a modest size, but crafted very robustly and of a great thickness commensurate with the brittleness of the material. Surprisingly earthen-

Plate 98. A walnut close stool or commode of about 1710. Such pieces have long been obsolete and commerce has dictated that if called wine coolers they are much more saleable. Wooden wine coolers appear not to have been made in England much before about 1730.

ware, a material in which many splendid wine coolers were made elsewhere in Europe, does not seem to have been used in England for the purpose.

The opening years of the eighteenth century saw very few wine coolers made. This is in line with a paucity of decanters. Whether or not this fact can be put down to the conflict and subsequent lack of trade between Britain and the continent of Europe can only be a matter of conjecture. At this time walnut was the fashionable timber for the finest furniture, although walnut wine coolers appear not to have been made at all during the entire first quarter of the eighteenth century. There are two items of furniture, however, which date from this period and which at first sight may be thought to be wine coolers. The first is an open-topped receptacle with a lining, usually of brass. Mostly square, although occasionally oval, they measure approximately twelve inches across. The brass liners were for holding hot coals which were used to keep kettles warm. This was a very common practice in Holland at the time and it is not unreasonable to suppose that the large number of Dutchmen immigrating to England with William III brought this practice with them. As a British habit, though, it died out fairly soon and confusion is more likely to occur when encountering converted 'close stools' or commodes (see plate 98). Before the advance of sophisticated plumbing these basic articles of convenience frequently masqueraded as elegant pieces of furniture of a totally different nature. Some appeared to be chests of drawers, others cupboards. Chairs of the most elegant and generous proportions were made with exceptionally deep seat rails to conceal the pot within. Such pieces will not concern us in this study, but their predecessors, which were simple pieces of furniture of similar proportions and size to wine coolers should be described. Most close stools were roughly cube-shaped, of about 18-22 inches in each direction and either raised on a plinth or supported on bracket feet and furnished with a lid. Supreme examples were covered in rich velvet and decorated with brass nailing; others were covered in leather and similarly decorated. Lesser examples were made in plain oak, but by the beginning of the eighteenth century they were being made in walnut, often cross-banded with typical feather-banding decoration. As long ago as the nineteenth century these objects were losing their appeal and those which were not broken up were frequently converted into wine coolers by substitution of the chamber pot and its supporting frame with a metal lining. Some, similarly lined, were used as coal or log boxes.

It would appear that wine coolers made their reappearance during the 1730s. As we have already said, during the first quarter of the eighteenth century much furniture was made in walnut. However, excessively cold winters in 1709 and 1711 had devastated the walnut tree population in much the same way as Dutch elm disease ravaged England in the 1970s. Owing to the practice of cabinet makers and carpenters laying down stocks of timber sufficient to last them for a generation or more there was no immediate problem, but by the early 1720s the crisis was a very real one. Following extensive lobbying of Parliament a law was enacted in 1724 to repeal the heavy duty on imported timbers and this allowed commercial importation of mahogany from the colonial islands of the West Indies. Its characteristic rich, red-brown colour and close texture was found to be an ideal medium for carving and cabinet making alike.

The earliest mahogany wine coolers (see colour plate 22, page 119) were very much like their silver counterparts of a quarter of a century earlier, being shallow, oval bowls with gadrooned decoration around the side and sometimes mask-head handles. However, rather than being set on a plinth, they were raised on four legs to complement other furniture of the period. These legs were of cabriole outline and usually had claw-and-ball feet and decorated knees. Initially made only for very wealthy families, their use had become more widespread by the 1750s and by that time the bowl had become deeper and the carving less sculptural. They were fitted with a zinc or lead liner. Whereas coolers of the 1730s had been fashioned from a single piece of timber, later examples tended to be coopered or staved and

Plate 99. An oval mahogany wine cooler with a lead lining glued to its inner surface. Sometimes removable zinc liners were fitted as an alternative. This variety remained fashionable throughout the middle of the 18th century, but this one may be later on account of the boxwood and ebony stringing, probably about 1780. Although in good condition and quite original, it bears little comparison with the far finer one in colour plate 23, page 121.

held together by bands of brass. Their capacity was also greater and they could hold a very substantial weight in the form of chilled water or ice, making the whole piece too heavy to lift safely. Consequently they were fitted with bungs or taps to allow removal of the water after use. Many were made with a detachable lower section comprised of the legs and a simple framework, and this continued to be common practice until the end of the eighteenth century.

While these developments in the shape of wooden examples were taking place, more and more grandiose coolers were being executed in silver. In the late seventeenth century these had been fashioned, as was the custom among English craftsmen, from sheet silver, but the introduction of the Huguenot silversmiths' casting techniques enabled wine coolers, or 'cisterns', to be made in very grand styles. These cisterns were little more than outrageous displays of ostentation. For centuries silver had been

Colour plate 21. A charming and rare example of an English wine cooler of about 1700. The metal body is japanned to simulate tortoiseshell and has gilt panels of floral bouquets alternating with trellis work. The stand is from another wine cooler some half a century later. It is customary to call wine coolers made of metal, 'cisterns' and those of timber, 'coolers'. This state of affairs should be rationalised.

Plate 100. An engraving by Gerard Jean-Baptiste Scotin II (1698-1745) of the wine cooler or cistern made by Charles Kandler for Henry Jernegan in 1734. The cooler (now in the Hermitage Museum, Leningrad) is certainly among the contenders for the grandest piece of silver ever made. Its construction was based on a combination of a sketch from George Vertue and a wax model by the sculptor Michael Rysbrack.

displayed in the eating room or chamber as an indication of a householder's wealth, and although by the eighteenth century this custom had diminished, it nevertheless still obtained amongst the richest families. Without question the grandest pieces of domestic plate ever produced were the wine cisterns of the early eighteenth century. Some silversmiths excelled in their endeavours to produce a lavishly sculptured basin. Many were three, four or even five feet across, but the grandest of all was that made by Charles Kandler, now in the Hermitage Museum in Leningrad, which weighs about 8,000 ounces (or about 250 kilos).

In addition to cooling wine these large cisterns were used for rinsing glasses and it seems appropriate to mention here that before lids were introduced in about 1760 wine coolers probably also served as jardinières. Usually the interiors were flat-bottomed and the cooler as a whole was an ideal height for raising plants to window level. It is therefore reasonable to suppose that plants cultivated in conservatories and brought into the house to flower could be put into these oval tubs to decorate a room.

It has been seen that until the middle of the eighteenth century almost all timber wine coolers were of oval outline and those made at the end of the period were furnished with brass bands. At this time they tended to be called cellarets, but today a clear distinction is drawn between the terms

Plate 101. An hexagonal mahogany wine cooler with segmentally veneered and crossbanded top on a fluted stand with moulded legs. This was made in about 1770. Note the introduction of the lid.

Plate 102. An item of furniture looking for all the world like a wine cooler, but which is in fact a cupboard for a chamber pot. Originally it was probably paired with a wine cooler. Note its similarities to the previous plate, despite its different shape, and that both the top and base taper inwards towards the central fluting moulding.

'cellaret' and 'wine cooler'. The former was simply a receptacle to keep wine at room temperature within the room, whereas a wine cooler was quite clearly designed to chill the wine and thus had to have a lined interior.

By the 1760s a variety of alternative shapes had begun to appear. Occasionally a square cooler is found, but far more frequently encountered are hexagonal and octagonal examples. (Rectangular coolers with canted corners are sometimes referred to as octagonal). Like their oval predecessors these typically had slightly tapering sides, being wider at the top. They were fitted with two, three or possibly even four, brass bands,

Plate 103. A mahogany cellaret of square outline. The severity of form is relieved by much fluted decoration, paterae, astragal panels and well-figured mahogany. It was made in about 1770.

usually of approximately one inch width, and they were either lead-lined or not, depending on their use. The interiors of lead-lined examples tend to be fitted with divisions for individual bottles. The upper section had a lid of conforming outline, a novel feature at the time. Below the body of the piece was an octagonal or hexagonal frame into which were tenoned three or four legs. These tapered in the opposite direction to the body and were usually chamfered on their inside edge. Contemporary accounts refer to this as a 'Marlboro' leg. Such wine coolers were produced in large numbers and were the stock-in-trade of a good cabinet maker. The word 'good' is important here as it takes a very skilled man to make such a piece;

Plate 104. A plate form George Hepplewhite's Cabinet Maker and Upholsterer's Guide *of 1788. A great many wine coolers survive which conform approximately to these designs. It is interesting to note that the octagonal cooler has a moulded top, while the oval one is plain, and that while the oval cooler has a fluted stand, the octagonal one is plain. These embellishments were easily interchangeable.*

each side of the body has to connect with the next with the most difficult of all joints to make, the angled, mitred dovetail.

Such wine coolers could be ordered in many different qualities. The top could be plain, or it could be cross-banded or segmentally veneered; it could be decorated with inlay, while its edge could be moulded in a variety of forms of varying complexity and cost. The brass fittings, though normally plain, could on occasions be fancy. It was quite normal on brass-bound furniture to use a rather straight and coarse-grained mahogany, although just occasionally an octagonal or hexagonal wine cooler is to be found veneered in a fine, flame-figured wood, in which case the brass bands are usually omitted. An inexpensive example would be fitted merely with a bung, but one of higher quality would have a tap. As far as the base was concerned, it could have a variety of mouldings to edge the join between the base and the top. The legs on a simple example would be plain, and on a better one would be moulded, while a better quality one again would feature fretted brackets to support the legs. Finally, most wine coolers were fitted with casters. On earlier examples the rollers would be made of laminated leather, while the rest of the caster would be brass, gilded on the best, lacquered on the less good.

Perhaps the very best brass-bound wine coolers are the oval examples made just before the introduction of lids, which had parcel-gilt cabriole legs with profusely cast and chiselled brass bands. (Chiselling was used to brighten up dull castings.) The mask-head handles were treated in the same manner, while occasionally the body too had finely cast brass appliqués (see colour plate 23, page 121).

Plate 105. A high quality mahogany wine cooler of essentially oval outline, but with projecting corners. Each face presents a serpentine form and this is repeated in the panel inlay with finely matched veneers. This piece was made in about 1790.

By the 1780s the Neo-classical movement had favoured a return to the oval cooler, but this time the outline was of a lighter and more refined nature. Although he died in 1786, George Hepplewhite's patterns of both oval and octagonal wine coolers were first published posthumously in 1788, and they already must have seemed quite archaic to their contemporary readers. By this date the vogue for brass banding, a characteristic of much dining room furniture including plate buckets, table wine coolers (to be discussed later), cutlery boxes and plate chests, had lost popularity.

In the final years of the century wine coolers were generally far more decorative exhibiting an increasing use of inlaid panels and a fashion for outlining furniture with boxwood stringing. Ovals gave way to cube-shaped or rectangular wine coolers, principally on square legs which were tapered towards the foot. Immediately before the close of the century legs became circular in cross-section and lids were sometimes domed in the fashion of a trunk. The end of the century also marked the end of the fashion for wine coolers on legs. Elsewhere in the book we talk about sideboards in greater detail, but it may be appropriate to state here that early sideboards were simply side tables made to such a height that a legged wine cooler could easily be situated underneath, but by the 1790s were incorporating so many drawers and cupboards that the cooler had to become squat and sit low on the floor.

Plate 106. A Regency mahogany wine cooler. The lid is formed as a giant patera while the body is carved with sinuous curves framing the lion mask handles. This variety of cooler had either mahogany, ebonised or ormolu feet, this example being ebonised. Note the similarity of carving to that on the design by Robert Adam shown in plate 229, page 217. Could the popularly-ascribed Regency date be questioned?

Plate 107. A wine cooler which, although of relatively undecorated form, is of high quality. The shape derives form Egyptian models and is described as 'sarcophagus'. This was made in mahogany in about 1815.

Plate 108. A pair of pale oak wine coolers in the Gothic style, closely modelled on a design published by Michelangelo Nicholson in The Practical Cabinet Maker *in 1826.*

Plate 109. Design for the above.

The years surrounding the turn of the eighteenth century constitute a great period of English history in which the naval victories of Admiral Lord Nelson, and more particularly the Battle of the Nile in 1798, fired the imagination of the populace and created a demand for allusory art and furnishings. Amongst the most obvious examples of this trend are the sphinx-head capitals to be found on much furniture, but perhaps a more subtle adaptation of Egyptian forms was the making of wine coolers in the form of sarcophagi with their typically outward sloping sides and sharply canted lids. This form seems to have predominated for the following thirty years after which wine coolers appear seldom to have been made, probably due to a further increase in the size and complexity of sideboards. Oak was a timber much favoured for these late post-1830 coolers and a final flourish before their demise appeared in a fashion for elaborate carving, particularly on the lids, of fruit, flowers, hunting scenes and trophies.

Ornamentation in the form of brass inlay was common during the

Plate 110. A superb pair of early silver table wine coolers by Louis Mettayer dated 1713. They bear the arms of Methuen and are decorated with various Classical motifs.

Plate 111. A pair of mid-18th century table wine coolers, brilliantly japanned in bright colours with chinoiserie designs. Although these are French, similar pieces were made in Britain.

Regency period and the squat form of wine coolers also lent itself admirably to carving. Many coolers of this date are fitted with lids which have finials carved in the form of the crests of the owner. Another type of Regency cooler comprised a vertically ribbed oval basin standing on hairy claw feet with a similarly decorated lid. A notable characteristic of these later, squat coolers, is their increased capacity, a feature which reflects the trend for accommodating a larger number of dinner guests at one sitting. Many coolers were consequently designed to hold upward of a dozen bottles.

In addition to large wine coolers, smaller, table coolers were made. A vogue for these first emerged in about 1700, or possibly a little earlier, for occasions when only a small quantity of cooled wine was to be consumed. Ice was a valuable commodity and was not to be wasted in a large cooler if only one bottle was required. The table wine cooler is basically a decorative cylinder or bucket in which chilled water was placed for the

Colour plate 22. A mahogany wine cooler carved from a single piece of wood and supplied to Blair Castle in 1738 by John Hodson. The resemblance to the marble wine cooler in plate 97, page 106, is clear and the unusual carved legs with paw feet match tables in the same room by the same maker.

cooling of one, or occasionally two bottles. The earliest examples were made in silver (and in at least one known case, in gold). The design of these now very rare objects followed the prevailing fashions. It is commonly believed that all brass examples, although sometimes identical in form to those made in silver before the middle of the century, postdate the year 1750. Also after this date, possibly during the 1760s, a few table wine coolers were executed in japanned tin. These were decorated with exquisite chinoiserie motifs and panels and had gilt-brass handles. All metal table coolers were invariably made in pairs and mostly had solid handles, some of which were formed as supporters for coats of arms. Moveable handles were generally in the form of lion-masks and rings. Slightly more common

Plate 112. A double-aperture table wine cooler in brass-bound mahogany. This variety is usually made to accommodate a single bottle. It has a detachable lid for emptying the iced water.

than these are staved, coopered and brass-bound mahogany coolers with detachable, tinned or lead linings. An example with an unusual addition — a coopered lid conforming in profile to a bottle — came to light recently. These were also made in silver and engraved to simulate their mahogany prototypes. (See plate 113, overleaf.)

Another common medium for the making of table wine coolers during the later years of the eighteenth century was porcelain. Examples produced in a large number of factories have survived and, in common with the majority of examples made during the nineteenth century, are in a variety of vase shapes. Perhaps the most common is that known as the 'Campana' which is in the form of a large, inverted and waisted bell supported on a turned stem and a square foot. It is also noteworthy for having a widely everted lip and a pair of handles which attach horizontally rather than vertically to the widest part of the body. Wine coolers were optional extras offered by the principal manufacturers to those buying dessert services. Although they frequently resemble them, they should not be confused with ice pails, which were designed for the cooling of compote of fruit. Ice pails usually have covers with upturned sides to contain ice, and separate liners for the contents, which were supported above ice packed in the base. Wine coolers naturally did not have covers or liners, but often had a heavy ring set in the base of the vessel to protect the fragile material from the weight of the bottle.

However, the most numerous of all table wine coolers are those executed in Sheffield plate. To make a table wine cooler in silver requires upwards of a hundred ounces, and sometimes a great deal more. Even in houses where the principal table service is in solid silver, it was quite in order to have the larger pieces plated and wine coolers, being the most substantial

Colour plate 23. A very fine coopered or staved mahogany wine cooler on a stand, having cabriole legs. It is profusely mounted in brass, cast with a variety of mouldings including guilloche, beading and gadrooning. Several similar wine coolers are known and it seems reasonable to assume that they all emanate from the same workshop of Samuel Norman. He supplied a similar cooler to Aske Hall for the Marquess of Zetland.

Plate 113. A delightful wine cooler made of silver and engraved with a handsome coat of arms. It might seem strange to a modern observer that a grand piece like this should pretend to be a milking pail, or perhaps amore lowly brass-bound mahogany wine cooler. It was made by Thomas Hemming in 1766.

piece of plate to be found in wealthy households from about 1790 onwards, came first in this category. With very few exceptions, almost all models to be found in solid silver are liable to be encountered in Sheffield plate and in the nineteenth century in electroplated silver as well. (An explanation of the differences between electroplate and Sheffield plate appears in the Introduction.)

During the Regency period, as with porcelain coolers, silver and plated examples were of vase shape, their decoration conforming to prevailing styles. Around 1805 much silver was wrought in the Egyptian taste and the

Plate 114. A pair of cream-coloured pottery table wine coolers of unusually simple outline and with mask handles. They bear the impressed mark for Davenport and were made in about 1825.

Plate 115. An impressive and rare pair of glass table wine coolers, the bodies being of campana shape. The lower halves are decorated with diamond cutting below a wide band of step cutting. They bear a strong resemblance to silver models (though without the handles) and were made in about 1825.

urn shape of wine coolers was admirably suited to this style. By 1820 the rococo revival was well established and silversmiths indulged the fashion for exuberant florid ornamentation. An often found later design is a much reduced copy of the Warwick vase, (the classical marble vase from Warwick Castle now in the Burrell Collection), which was so favoured by the great nineteenth century silversmith Paul Storr. After about 1830 few original ideas for their design emerged and although their use outlived that of their larger counterparts, few table wine coolers were made after the middle of the century.

CHAPTER 8
Wine Funnels

When pouring a liquid from one vessel into another spillage can easily occur and with a valuable liquid like wine it is particularly desirable that this should be avoided. In addition wine responds to gentle handling and does not like being shaken, splashed and generally aerated. Such problems can be minimised by using a wine funnel, an object, incidentally, commonly referred to as a 'port strainer'.

Furthermore, certain wines contain a fine sediment or coarse encrustation and, occasionally, errant pieces of cork, dislodged when the cork is punctured by the corkscrew, and for this reason good wine funnels are equipped with both coarse and fine filters. Any sediment at the bottom of a bottle will begin to emerge when the bottle is between three-quarters and seven-eighths empty, depending on the care with which the wine is being decanted, and a strong reflected light or a candle held beneath the

Colour plate 24. Decanting using period accessories. Note the way that the cranked spout sends the wine smoothly down the wall of the decanter and the positioning of the candle beneath the bottle which enables the sediment to be seen and the operation stopped. Where this is not practical a white tablecloth will often suffice.

124

Colour plate 25. Two very rare Worcester porcelain wine funnels. Both blue and white and polychrome decoration were fashionable at this period (about 1755) but funnels are very rare. The decoration is the right way up only when the funnel is in use.

bottle will show the person decanting when to stop. Alternatively, the muddy sediment in a brightly polished funnel will have the same effect. Good funnels are therefore made of a reflective or completely transparent material.

In order to prevent tainting of the wine, the cup or bowl section should be made to separate from the spout to allow easy cleaning. Most wine funnels are equipped with a detachable rim or interior ring which accommodates a muslin or other fine cloth filter. Being principally utilitarian objects they generally have little decoration, it being confined, where it does exist, to the moulded edges. A moulded rim of course also acts as a strengthener and prevents a metal edge from buckling or splitting.

A true wine funnel has a cranked spout; that is, it is curved near its tip to deflect the wine down the side of the decanter. When a funnel is not curved at its tip the word wine should be dropped from the description, for while no doubt it *may* have been used for wine, there can be no evidence for its exclusive use.

The earliest extant silver wine funnel is dated 1661 and very few others pre-date 1700. Indeed, examples from the early eighteenth century are also most uncommon and most of those that do survive are Irish. Whether or not they were expressly made for wine is a matter of conjecture. They mostly have conical bowls and a straight spout and were made in one piece.

Plate 116. A silver strainer and funnel with a hinged handle. Part of Roman treasure discovered in 1883 in a field at Chaourse near Montcorvet in North East France. It is part of a table service of 39 pieces, six of them being silver-plated bronze and the rest silver. The service dates from the 3rd century A.D. and, to judge from the coins found with it, was probably buried for safety some time during the second half of that century.

They do not prevent splashing, are not well designed to reflect the light and do not incorporate a metal filter. Occasionally they are pierced with a series of holes around the rim to allow the attachment of a cloth filter.

In a later chapter we will observe that wine coasters suddenly made an appearance in abundance in the 1760s; so it was the case with wine funnels. Although, unlike coasters, earlier examples do exist, it was not until then that they appeared in sizeable numbers. A typical wine funnel of that date has a broad, hemispherical or ogee bowl with a gadrooned or beaded rim. The bottom is pierced with a geometrical arrangement of holes forming the coarse filter for broken pieces of cork and larger pieces of crust. On the underside of the bowl beneath the filter is a small, plain collar which forms one half of the attachment for the spout. The upper end of the slightly tapered spout swells and has a moulding encircling its rim, while the narrow end is curved and shaped as may be quite clearly seen in the accompanying illustrations. Inside the junction of the two halves of the funnel is a thin silver ring pierced with small holes. This can accommodate the fine filter and fits snugly inside the upper section. Sometimes a crest or a set of initials is found on the bowl or tab at the base of the bowl. This design of funnel was current until the turn of the century when the entire body of the funnel was made in one piece. The upper section tended to be ovoid while the integral spout remained almost unchanged. A separate filter occupied the bowl section at the top and could be removed and used

Plate 117. An exploded view of a silver wine funnel that clearly shows the facility for the attachment of a fine muslin filter and the way in which a silver funnel can be separated for cleaning. This particular funnel was made by Hester Bateman in 1776.

as a filter for other liquids. This variety of metal funnel tends to be of heavier gauge than the earlier model and is frequently fitted with three short, vertically applied ribs which enable air to escape from the decanter as the wine is poured in. (See plate 118, second from left.)

By the 1820s the earlier form of construction had reappeared, only by then the funnel had attained a more grand proportion and frequently the rims were cast with foliate or other decoration appropriate to the period. Bowl shapes became more complex and the entire piece larger. Subsequent funnel design has relied on reproduction of all earlier forms and decoration.

A curious feature which is common to all funnels made after 1770 is the attachment of a small tab to the side of the bowl incorporating the coarse filter. It can only be assumed that this enabled the bowl to be detached from the spout and used to filter punch, tea or other liquids.

There were naturally a few variations. For a short while around 1775 it

Colour plates 26 and 27. Two views of an exceptionally rare, or possibly even unique, Battersea enamel wine funnel. It has an ogee bowl and slightly cranked spout. The magenta floral decoration is offset by a beaded gilt mount. This piece was probably made in about 1755.

was fashionable to construct funnels with a detachable upper rim. This was pierced with a band of small holes for attachment of the fine filter and fitted snugly into the top of the bowl. In Scotland, around 1800, funnels (and correspondingly their stands) were often oval in section and can consequently be easily identified. Similarly, North Country examples, are characteristically of unusually generous proportions.

A charming and rare variety of wine funnel is that made in glass. Glass funnels usually have a straight spout of narrow proportions and a plain conical bowl. Most bowls have straight or spiral ribbed decoration moulded into the glass during manufacture. However examples are also known with a cranked spout and quite plain bowl. (An example is shown in colour plate 1, page 19.) Perhaps these funnels date from the 1740s to 1760s as they bear a strong resemblance to wine glasses of the period. A delightful example with a faceted bowl dating from about 1770 is illustrated in plate 120.

Plate 118. A group of silver wine funnels and a stand. From left to right: 1764 with rare 'bath plug' filter; a funnel of 1809 with one-piece body; an 1814 example with a gadrooned body; one from 1776 (see plate 117) and the last dating from about 1790. The funnel stand was made in 1809.

Plate 119. A good wine funnel and stand of oval outline which is a north country or Scottish feature. Funnels with their original stands are now seldom seen and this one, with its gadrooned mouldings and gilt interior, was made in about 1810 by John McKay in Edinburgh.

Plate 120. A very rare glass wine funnel; the bowl is faceted with lozenges and the spout gently curved rather than being cranked. Glass funnels with cranked spouts are, in any event, rare. This one dates from the mid-18th century.

Porcelain funnels were also made and two examples are illustrated in colour plate 25, page 125. The straight spout implies that they were multi-purpose funnels, although the Worcester factory has confirmed that they were intended specifically for wine. It is interesting to note that the polychrome or blue and white decoration on these extremely rare objects was designed to be seen correctly when the object was in use. In the 'stored' position the decoration is upside down.

An exceedingly rare medium for wine funnels is enamel. It is suggested that the one illustrated in colour plates 26 and 27, page 128, is unique, although such an assertion will surely bring more examples to light. They are also found in other media; base metal is quite common and many pewter examples exist executed on similar lines to those in silver with two to three sections and cranked spouts. Certainly pewter was regarded as the poor man's silver.

Silver plated funnels were popular in the nineteenth century, particularly during the 1830s. Surprisingly, few examples are known with a date prior to 1800. Examples in copper usually have straight spouts and although they have tinned interiors and tinned gauze filters, one must suppose that these were for the decanting of coarser liquids. The same argument must surely apply to examples in brass and treen.

Although becoming increasingly popular with aficionados of wine, funnels are not generally collected. Because silver wine funnels are utilitarian objects they do tend to suffer from regular use. The cranked ends of wine funnel spouts are made from thin sheet metal and do not have cast or moulded edges; consequently they have frequently been damaged, bruised or bent and are very prone to splitting. The spout should be carefully examined for signs of removal of dents and for soldering where splits have been repaired before making a purchase. Very often the bowl too has been dented or bruised. In common with all silver, care should be taken to see if crests or coats of arms have been removed leaving the characteristic thin spot in the silver. Possible re-soldering or replacement of the tab should also be noted and of course care should be taken to make sure that each half of the funnel belongs to the other and that a marriage has not been made for commercial expediency.

Early silver wine funnels were hallmarked somewhere on their bodies, whereas by the end of the eighteenth century they were marked on the bottom half of the bowl on the junction between one half and the other. The lower half should carry at least the lion passant and the maker's mark, if not a complete set of marks. It should be remembered that it was quite normal for a silversmith to remove the effects of heavy punching of the hallmarks, thereby removing their crispness and consequently it is quite in order for bowl-marked funnels to have poor hallmarks. A clearly marked example will naturally carry a premium.

Because the majority of wine funnels appear to have been made in silver

Plate 121. Two unusual funnels. The glass example has a folded rim and a bowl of thistle shape, while the pearwood one unscrews into two sections.

Plate 122. A late 19th century wine filter. Both halves of the glass are engraved with a running band of grapes, vine leaves and tendrils and the filtration is effected by passage through a core of sinter (silica).

it may be assumed that wine was generally decanted not in the cellar, but in the main body of the house and by a gentleman, not his servant. After all, who would work objects in silver for his servant's use? This being so, it was necessary to provide a stand for the funnel to prevent any residual drops from staining the furniture on which the operation was performed. In the Wakelin ledgers of 1773 mention is made of a funnel salver although few funnel stands have survived from the eighteenth century. A funnel stand is a small, circular dish without feet and with a slightly raised rim. On many stands the base is slightly domed and it has been suggested that this profile will enable it to double as a taster. For strength and for decorative purposes the rim has a moulding and that moulding will usually match the rim of the funnel for which it was made. Regrettably only a small percentage of funnels have survived with their original stands. It is something of a puzzle that a substantial proportion of extant funnel stands emanate from Ireland.

CHAPTER 9
Decanters, Flagons and Jugs

Wine has traditionally been made in a cask or barrel which, until the middle of the nineteenth century, would have been exported from its country of origin still intact. The owner of a substantial house would have bought an entire cask from his vintner, while lesser clients would probably have purchased their wine already bottled on the vintner's premises. Château bottling is only a very recent development.

Until the 1670s wine was served at the table in jugs or dark green glass bottles. Contemporary paintings show that at the smartest tables these bottles were completely encased, but for the upper section of the neck, in wanding or osier- or basketwork, in a manner not unlike the modern Chianti bottle. The bottles themselves were frequently blown with rounded bottoms, balloon-shaped one might call them, with the foot rim, which

Plate 123. Proof for a trade card of about 1700. Note the top left-hand item.

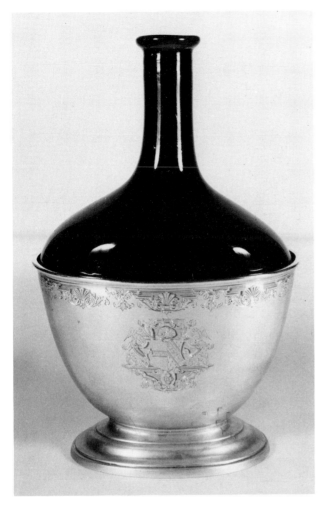 

Plate 124. A bottle of oval cross section sitting in its original silver stand. The latter is of simple outline, but highly crafted and is engraved with a band of shells and scrolls and a magnificent cartouche surrounding the coat of arms. It was made by Augustin Courtauld in 1723 and the arms are those of Veale impaling Young.

Plate 125. A Ravenscroft-type decanter jug made in about 1675. Note the pan top and chain-like trails around the shoulder. The lower half of the jug was blown into a mould to achieve the ribbed effect. Such decanter jugs were normally fitted with large hollow pear-shaped stoppers.

enabled the bottle to stand on a flat surface, being formed by the osierwork casing. Used concurrently with these were the pottery jugs described in the chapter on bottles.

Around the turn of the seventeenth century free-blown, round-bottomed glass bottles of oval cross section were made which sat in specially constructed silver coasters or bowls, but survivals of this form are extreme rarities.

The earliest decanters (that is, vessels designed specifically for pouring as opposed to storing wine) date from the 1670s and should more appropriately be called 'decanter jugs'. The term 'decanter', deriving from the necessity for one vessel to tilt or 'cant' when pouring liquid into

Plate 126. A rare and early decanter jug showing the influence of the Ravenscroft shape, but now with a narrow cylindrical neck. The trailed and moulded decoration has gone, but for the shaping at the base. This is perhaps a precursor of the cruciform shape.

Plate 127. A fine shaft and globe decanter with a faceted spire stopper. The late baroque armorials are in a floral and scrolled cartouche and are wheel engraved and of high quality. This decanter was made in about 1750.

Plate 128. A cruciform decanter of about 1720, the tall neck having a reeded collar or string rim. These decanters are said to be made for the more efficient cooling of wine.

another, did not appear until the eighteenth century. Some early decanter jugs are attributed to the glass maker George Ravenscroft and typically have a high-shouldered body, slightly tapering inwards to a simple foot. Above the body is a short, cylindrical neck, opening to a wider, cylindrical pan top. The pan top is connected to the body by a handle and has a nipped, or pincered, pouring spout. The decoration on the body can consist of moulded or applied, and reeded or fluted decoration in vertical panels, while the shoulder is usually ornamented with trailed glass chains or that favourite of the Ravenscroft factory, 'nipt diamond waies' decoration, elements which ultimately derive from Venice. It is likely that most of these jugs were originally equipped with a loose-fitting, inverted pear-shaped stopper of hollow construction, though very few are known to survive. It is perhaps interesting to note that the wide pan top of these jugs served to form as the bowl of a funnel, a sensible feature which it seems was never repeated, although it was certainly advocated much later by

134

Christopher Dresser in his book *Principles of Decorative Design*, published in 1873. (More will be said of this later.)

The next development by Ravenscroft and his contemporaries was the removal of the pan top and an elongation of the narrow neck while the body became shorter and more squat. This finally developed into the shaft and globe form in the same manner as bottles. Also like bottles of the period, decanter jugs were fitted with a sharp and angular ring of glass below the rim of the neck. This enabled the cork to be tied in place and at the same time provided the pourer with something secure to grip and strengthened the glass at the point where pressure from the cork rendered it vulnerable to breakage. Early examples of such decanters were also decorated all over with a variety of gadrooned, 'nipt diamond waies', raspberry prunt and other moulded and applied ornament.

By 1700 the vogue for baroque ornamentation in all fields of the decorative arts was waning and glass correspondingly became less decorated. By the second decade of the eighteenth century most decanters were completely plain. The general shape was still shaft and globe, but the handle disappeared. By the 1730s a new form had been introduced which had straight sides and a long, straight neck, but in section presented a variety of cruciform plan. Most authorities agree that the cruciform group corresponded with a fashion for drinking all wine, whether white or red, chilled and that the elaborate shapes presented a greater surface area for the quicker cooling of wine. However, wine coolers of this date, which have already been discussed, are distinctly scarce, a fact which casts doubt on this theory. It has been suggested that these decanters were made stable by being placed in a frame with four upright spikes, although none of the latter are known to have survived. Cruciform decanters seldom, if ever, have stoppers and therefore, like their predecessors, are fitted with string rings around the neck, sometimes narrow, sometimes broad and annular-moulded. A neck ring incidentally was formed by applying a moulded sausage of glass around the neck. Quite frequently the diagonal join can be seen and indeed may easily be mistaken for a crack.

Occasionally one encounters decanters of this date with an elevation similar to those of cruciform plan, but without the indentations, being either square, which is very rare, or octagonal or hexagonal. Rarest of all are cut examples. Cutting was yet in its infancy and very few cut decanters are seen. When they do appear they (not surprisingly) resemble contemporary cruet bottles which were fitted with silver mounts and stands, and they are therefore usefully dated. Although faceting is usually attributed only to the 1770s and '80s, surviving cruet bottles of this type in their original stands date from the 1740s and '50s showing that the technique has commonly been late-dated by some thirty years.

While the cruciform shape enjoyed a finite period of popularity, the shaft and globe was still being produced, and the 1740s and '50s saw the

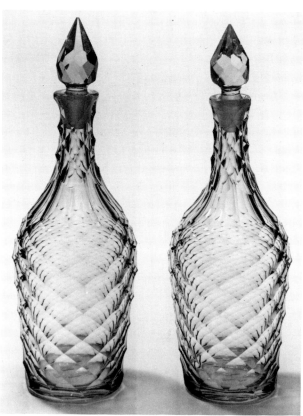

Plate 129. Two decanters with polygonal bodies of a period which corresponds to the cruciform decanter. They are however much less common.

Plate 130. A fine pair of magnum shouldered decanters. Apart from the vertical panels on the upper shoulders the entire surface of the decanters and stoppers are cut with lozenge-facets. This pair was made in about 1765.

Plate 131. Two shouldered decanters flanking a tapered one, each wheel engraved with labels simulating silver wine labels. These are all high quality decanters of about 1770.

Colour plate 28. A meeting of the Hell Fire Club in Dublin painted by a member, James Worsdale, in about 1735. The Hell Fire Club movement, which originated in England and was later banned, was a society of religious free thinkers and political radicals. Note a wanded bottle in a very fine silver table wine cooler.

development of this form of decanter at its most refined. They were by now frequently stoppered, although the stoppers were seldom ground to fit, the pegs being left with a 'fire' finish, and each being selected to drop in to the correct depth. They were normally of spherical form set with single or multiple tears of air for decoration, though by the middle of the century steeple or spire stoppers were fashionable. Shouldered decanters have a tapering body, widest at the shoulder and these, together with mallets (similar but widest at the *base*) were fashionable for the whole of the 1760s and '70s. (The mallet derives its name from its similarity to the stone-mason's or carpenter's tool.) Although spire stoppers were usual in the first of the shouldered decanters, stoppers in the form of a vertical disc faceted on the rim were introduced during the late part of their popularity and were used exclusively and in increasingly rich patterns in mallets.

With regard to decoration, many shaft and globe decanters were left plain, while others were engraved in the vernacular manner with generous sprays of fruiting vine with polished grapes, or floral wreaths, again with polished details. Some commemorative examples survive, notably with engraving of Jacobite significance. Cut examples are very rare. With

Plate 132. One of a pair of taper decanters, the neck having a broad band of hexagonal facets above panel cutting to aid the grip, while the stopper is star cut. The central band of cut and matted decoration is unusual, but the narrow fluted base decoration is often found and dates the decanter to about 1790.

Plate 133. One of a pair of so-called 'Classic' decanters with panel-cut shoulders, fluted base, three neck rings, everted lips and star-cut mushroom stopper. The pair was made in about 1810.

Plate 134. *A pair of square shouldered decanters with reeded or pillar-cut bodies and step-cut necks. They are of heavy quality and were made in about 1820.*

shoulder and mallet decanters the largest decorative group is that with descriptive labels and these are often collected specifically for this feature. Engraved or gilded labels for the contents of all, though principally wine, decanters were popular until about 1770. At the end of the century gilt labels were again fashionable, but on coloured decanters and almost exclusively on those for spirits (of which more later). Cut examples of shoulders and mallets are also seen, some with geometric flat cutting, others cut all over with hollow diamonds.

Following the mallet shape, the body, shoulders and neck of decanters gradually merged into one almost continuous tapering form and this type is now logically known as the 'taper' decanter. A parallel development produced the so-called Indian club. In this instance the taper finished approximately three-quarters of the way down the piece and the remaining one quarter curved gently inward. Its resemblance to the early twentieth century exercise club has given the form its modern name. Tapers are common, Indian clubs less so. Contemporary stoppers are vertical and of pear shape, sometimes with a cut and polished 'printie' or hollow in the centre of each side. These decanters coincided with a cool and restrained period in decoration and were frequently left quite plain. Where it occurred, decoration was shallow and followed current taste for the Neo-classical with festoons, stars, paterae and other pretty, symmetrical motifs,

Colour plate 29. Three decanters demonstrating the most popular colours. In the centre is an amethyst, triple ring-necked, square-shouldered decanter of about 1825. It is flanked by two taper decanters, each of about 1790.

either cut or engraved. Taper and Indian club decanters are the easiest type from which to pour, there being very little shoulder to catch the air bubbles which tend to make wine gurgle as it is poured into the glass. They are, incidentally, also the shapes most like the modern wine bottle which is probably no coincidence.

Neither the taper, nor the Indian club, originally had string rings around the neck, though a band of faceting was generally introduced on cut examples to give some grip. By the late 1790s, applied rings had been introduced to provide a better grip and keep the hand away from any tail-back of wine from the lip after pouring. At the same time, the lip itself, formerly barely everted, was flattened and extended in an attempt to prevent dripping. Rings varied in number between four and one but settled eventually to a normal three, although the Belfast factories favoured two. Occasional examples occur with a continuous applied spiral of glass, the top of which might be cut to resemble a serpent's head. At the same time decoration became more formal and it was common practice to cut

Colour plate 30. Coloured decanters were normally reserved for spirits and sold in sets of three. Because of the strength of the liquor they were often only half-bottle in size. Here is a group of three in a metallic painted frame; they have gilt decoration simulating wine labels and it will be noticed that the pear-shaped stoppers are initialled to correspond with the right decanter. Although very similar, the 'Hollands' decanter outside the frame comes from a different set which can be seen from the difference in the calligraphy of the capital letter.

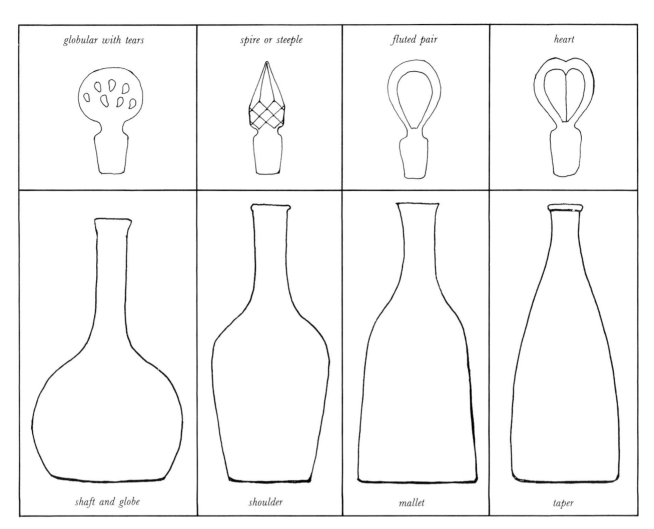

| globular with tears | spire or steeple | fluted pair | heart |
| shaft and globe | shoulder | mallet | taper |

Figure 2. This diagram shows outlines of decanter and stopper shapes.

the shoulders of the decanter with flat, vertical panels, and the base, for an inch or an inch and a half, with shallow, vertical flutes (see plate 133, page 138). These would complement the pierced coasters in which the decanters were placed on the table.

During the early part of the nineteenth century the widest part of the body of the decanter was gradually raised until a shape not unlike the shoulder had evolved with the largest diameter approximately halfway up. The decanter as a whole though was clearly different from the shoulder as the neck was broader and had applied, moulded neck rings which totally altered the visual proportions. A vast number of these decanters survive. Circular disc stoppers, again with central printies, known as targets or bullseyes, were normal at the beginning of the century but were soon superceded by flat, radially-fluted mushrooms.

By about 1820 the fluent designs of the Georgian period had given way to a square-shouldered formality (see plate 134, page 139). Cutting became almost de rigueur and continued to be so until about 1850. This form of decoration had become popular as a result of advanced technology in the form of steam-driven cutting machines. One of the advantageous properties of English lead-glass was its ability to take cutting well and full

target or bull's-eye

cut mushroom

star-cut mushroom

Indian club

classic

pillar-cut

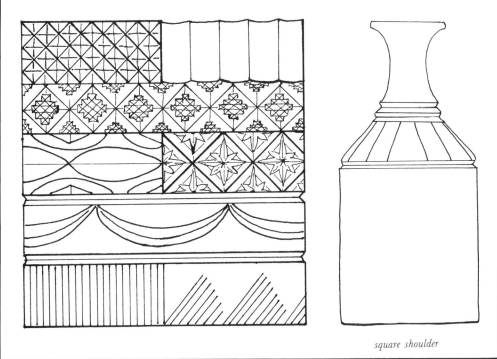

square shoulder

Figure 3. Diagram showing the different styles of glass cutting such as, strawberry, hobnail, etc.

Colour plate 31. A simple glass decanter blown with four interior divisions, each one separately stoppered. Although made from the beginning of the 19th century onwards, this one dates from the second half. Such decanters were intended for different coloured liqueurs, a type of beverage which gained popularity at this date.

Plate 135. A square shouldered decanter with panel-cut shoulders, the body divided in panels with 'V' cutting. It has two neck rings and shows a late form of the mushroom stopper.

use of the new technology was made by blowing decanters of thick metal and then cutting patterns on large areas. Glass collectors have many words to describe precisely the different cut designs — strawberry, hobnail, diamond and so on (see figure 3, page 143).

Following the arrival of the square-shouldered decanter a profusion of designs emerged. There were barrel decanters, cylindrical fluted ones, examples with waisted bodies and revived forms of the shaft and globe, the

Plate 136. *A pair of Victorian decanters of plain shaft and globe outline, but with an opaque white flashed coating which has been cut to reveal clear glass beneath. They were made in about 1845.*

Plate 137. *A very fine Victorian magnum decanter which has a body of ovoid shape divided into panels and cut profusely with star cutting. The long neck is panel cut and the ovoid stopper matches the shape of the body. The star-cut foot dates this decanter to the beginning of the second half of the 19th century.*

Plate 138. *A Victorian decanter. The body is of pear-shaped outline, profusely cut with a plethora of neo-baroque ornamentation. The elaborate shape and the foot date it to the second half of the 19th century, about 1855.*

flagon and the taper. During the Victorian period the majority of designs were characterised by fancy decoration, and/or outline. If the shape itself was not ornamental, then it could be relied upon to have coloured, cut or applied decoration in some form. Much of the latter was in one of the many historical revival styles found in every other form of decorative art. Fresh ground was not broken until the 1870s when Christopher Dresser introduced his highly innovative and starkly simple designs. He particularly disapproved of cutting. In his opinion the '...somewhat elaborate effects...rendered in glass by very laborious engraving, whereby different depths of cutting are attained...rarely produces an effect

Plate 139. A claret jug deriving from the designs of Christopher Dresser who advocated a return to simplicity. The silver marks and engraved registration mark enable this jug to be dated to 1887.

Plate 140. Three icing or champagne decanters; the left-hand two are mallet-shaped and are each blown with a pouch or sack which will accommodate ice. The plain left-hand example has a pear-shaped stopper with a printie, while the centre one is festoon cut and has a base cut with flutes. It has a heart-shaped stopper. The right-hand decanter is of Indian club form and is divided into vertical panels on the body and has a horizontally ribbed neck. The cavity for the ice may be reached from the underside of the decanter which unscrews. It dates from the 1830s.

proportionate to the toil expended upon it; and if a bottle so engraved is filled with a coloured wine, the entire beauty of its engraving is destroyed.' The pendulum of fashion did not swing again until the turn of the century with the decorative swirling ornamentation of art nouveau only to swing back again more recently to the plain and simple designs of Scandinavia.

Not all decanters followed the general trends outlined above. A charming rarity is the icing decanter which is usually of taper or Indian club form and has a cavity blown in a bubble in its outside to contain ice. This may or may not be stoppered with a cork. These decanters usually date from about 1790 and are said to have been used principally for Champagne. Ice decanters appeared again in the 1830s, but by then the ice pocket was generally underneath and closed by a metal mount which screwed into place and was sealed with a cork washer.

Britain has been known throughout the world for its addiction to port and a notable venue for its consumption is the regimental dinner in the officers' mess. Some regiments have developed their own individual procedure for passing the port, but in all cases it is passed clockwise around the table. Etiquette demands that one never asks for the port, one always waits for the decanter to be passed and in regiments where one officer was

Plate 141. A fine set of four so-called ship's decanters. Their utter simplicity makes them much favoured with serious drinkers and the survival of a pair of bottle size, together with the matching half-bottle size pair, is most unusual. This set was made in about 1810.

particularly loquacious it became the rule that the decanter did not touch the table until it had completed its round. Decanters with rounded bottoms and frames to hold them are said to exist to cope with this contingency.

Far more common, but still outside the mainstream of design, are 'ship's decanters', so-called because the suggestion was once made that their broad base and low centre of gravity gives them stability at sea. One cannot imagine any sea captain who was not already inebriated being so foolhardy as to produce such a valuable object in anything but the calmest of seas. Nevertheless, the logic behind the name persists and early examples have frequently been copied by later glass makers. Ship's decanters are formed of a single large cone, or a cone with a neck on top. Just occasionally the outward curve is trumpet-shaped. Some decanters appear to be halfway between a ship's decanter and the normal design of the period in which they were made and these are loosely referred to as 'semi-ships' or 'Rodney' decanters, after Admiral Rodney (see plate 142, overleaf). All decanters of 'ship' type may be decorated in a similar manner to their more ordinary contemporaries.

Although not strictly speaking within the terms of reference of this book mention should be made of spirit decanters. During the late eighteenth century, sets of decanters were made in coloured glass, principally blue, but sometimes green or amethyst, with gilt labels saying, 'Rum', 'Brandy', 'Gin', 'Hollands' (Dutch gin), and occasionally 'Shrub', a cordial made usually from citrus fruit and rum. Similar colourless sets were also made. Such sets were often sold in a skeletal frame of silver or plate or one of iron, either painted or covered in red leather (see colour plate 30, page 141). Sometimes these decanters were square (with or without canted corners) or oval and these shapes were generally presented in mahogany

Plate 142. A magnificent set of four so-called semi-ship's decanters or Rodneys. Like the previous plate, a rare survival of four decanters in sizes. The cutting includes diamond, fan and panel varieties and the stoppers are an unusual form. The set was made in about 1810.

Plate 143. Two tantaluses. The left-hand example is a typical, if inexpensive, model dating from about the turn of the 19th century. The square bottles are cut all over and have globe stoppers. Many tantaluses have swivelling tops, but this example has a front that lets down which is operated by a key. The right-hand tantalus is of the Art Deco period of the 1930s and was perhaps inspired by Dresser's designs of some fifty years earlier. The decanters are signed 'Orefors, Sweden'.

cases with lids which could be closed and locked. They were known as case bottles and represent part of a wide series of decanters enclosed in purpose-made boxes which are sometimes of considerable quality. Many of them, gilded with classical ornament, were imported from Bohemia and the Low Countries and subsequently fitted up in Britain.

After 1850 the lockable tantalus (so called because it 'tantalised' the would-be drinker) largely replaced the earlier open frames. De luxe

Plate 144. An early silver claret jug. The ovoid body is decorated with a band of bright cutting and wrigglework and has an oval cartouche similarly executed, enclosing an engraving of a woman attended by a dog and pruning a vine inscribed underneath 'Amicitiae sacrum'. It was made in 1787.

Plate 145. A quite exceptional early cut glass claret jug. The tapering body is engraved with a profusion of trailing vines, while opposite the handle are the coat of arms of George, Prince of Wales, later George IV, as used between 1801 and 1820. The underside is lightly engraved with the name 'Lee' who was presumably the engraver. It was made in about 1805.

versions often had containers for glasses and cigars. Around the turn of the century these were sometimes referred to as 'liquor frames'. An attractive variation was a single decanter divided vertically into three or four sections. These were for colourful liqueurs such as curaçao, chartreuse, crême de menthe and kummel. (See colour plate 31, page 144.)

There are two other types of 'decanter' which must be included here, although not of the same form, the first is the claret jug, the other the pilgrim bottle. Quite why claret, as opposed to any other wine, should require an individual form of decanter remains a complete mystery. The first jugs which appear to have been used for serving claret (although not exclusively) were those made in silver during the 1770s. Unlike hot water jugs, which they resemble, these early claret jugs do not have insulated handles. True claret jugs, in glass rather than silver, were first made in

Plate 146. *A typical 19th century claret jug with silver gilt mounts, owing much of their design to the mounts of tigerware jugs of the 16th century. Its decoration is embossed and chased and the thumbpiece is cast as an heraldic crest. It was made in 1861.*

Plate 147. *A fine 19th century claret jug of good simple form. However, its importance and charm lie in the wheel engraved decoration which takes the form of Roman warriors and horsemen, appropriately set off with formal motifs in various bands. It dates from the 1860s.*

earnest during the early years of the nineteenth century when complete services of glass were introduced, comprising vessels for every possible purpose. The first glass jugs, therefore, were lipped and handled versions of decanters and followed precisely the pattern of whatever suite of glass was being purchased. The vogue for decanter-type claret jugs was short lived and soon an individual type emerged in which most had a body of glass mounted in silver, silver plate or silver-gilt, depending on their quality. As a result of the 'Jacobethan' revival, a great many claret jugs were made between 1850 and 1880 with silver or silver gilt mounts emulating those found on Elizabethan tigerware jugs. (These do not resemble decanters in shape.) Like decanters, claret jug design then fell under the influence of Christopher Dresser and, much later of the art nouveau and art deco movements. Perhaps the most interesting are those which depart totally from standard designs such as jugs in the form of animals and birds. These were possibly derivatives of the prototypes in rock crystal made in Augsberg and Nuremberg in the sixteenth and seventeenth centuries but, whatever their origins, it cannot be denied that they are one of the most charming of wine antiques.

If the claret jug in the form of a squatting duck is the epitome of a charming wine item, then a pilgrim bottle may be described as one of the grandest and rarest (see plate 149, overleaf). It is perhaps difficult for us to appreciate today that prior to the seventeenth century the aristocracy were very mobile, entire households moving from one estate to another in different parts of the country. Much of their wealth was accordingly invested in small, portable valuables, in particular in plate. The pilgrim bottle, basically a flask with chains, was inevitably included in such a collection of valuables. Contemporarily they were called 'flagons', what we call a flagon now being described as a 'livery pot'. Most early pilgrim bottles were of flattened pear shape and were executed in silver or silver-gilt. The majority of surviving examples are in the collection of English Silver in the Kremlin. The grandest, some standing almost three feet high and undoubtedly made for display rather than actual use, were made in the closing years of the seventeenth and early years of the eighteenth centuries. A few were made in the nineteenth century, mainly as presentation objects, and were straightforward reproductions of earlier forms.

Occasionally unusual stoppers may be encountered. A known phenomenon, though very rare, is the tasting stopper. These may be in the

Plate 148. An amusing claret jug in the form of a cockatoo, the crest forming the thumbpiece. The handle, being drawn from bottom to top, is a late feature in glass making, but no later than the design would suggest. It was made around 1870-80. These animal and bird claret jugs are among the most sought after.

151

Plate 149. One of a pair of pilgrim bottles in the Duke of Devonshire's Collection at Chatsworth, made by Anthony Nelme. These magnificent objects were made for ostentation and this particular pair, which display a wealth of Baroque ornament, were made in 1715 and are some of the latest originals. In the 19th century a number of reproductions of earlier examples were made, sometimes as presentation pieces; amongst those on public display are the Duke of Wellington's pilgrim bottles at Apsley House, London.

Plate 150. A travelling decanter set. Inside the plain mahogany box (on bracket feet with castors beneath) are sixteen, magnum-sized, square decanters accommodated in baize lined partitions. As a piece of furniture it would be tempting to date this to the late 18th century, but the presence of star-cut mushroom stoppers, each numbered to accord with the appropriate decanter, clearly puts this piece at around 1810. Such sets were presumably used by travellers and soldiers. It is not clear whether they were for wines or spirits.

form of a pear-shaped stopper, but hollow, and date from around 1800. Their function is quite obvious. Another variety recently encountered is a stopper in the form of a cup, the stem forming the peg.

In the eighteenth century and for the first couple of decades of the nineteenth, decanter stoppers were ground into the necks of the decanters with an abrasive paste which left a coarse matt finish. After about 1810, at first in the best workshops and later universally, it became the practice to fit and polish the pegs of stoppers on a stoppering lathe. Therefore if a decanter is encountered of an eighteenth century or very early nineteenth century design, but with a polished stopper one of three situations obtains; first, the whole piece may be a reproduction; second, the stopper might be a later replacement, in which case the stopper peg will be polished but the interior of the neck not, and third, the decanter might have started life as a carafe and had an alien stopper added to it. In the latter event, the stopper will be a poor fit since only the peg will have been on the lathe. In any case it can usually be determined by the feel if a decanter has held a polished stopper. The term 'carafe' incidentally may be loosely applied when reference is made to early decanters without stoppers. A true carafe can usually be identified by having a slightly wider neck than that of its corresponding decanter.

As already mentioned, Christopher Dresser advocated that decanters should have necks of funnel shape. In his own words, decanters are '...objects which are meant to be filled many times and therefore should have a funnel-shaped mouth. It must also be convenient to use and hold and the upper funnel should be of such a character that it will guide the liquid in a proper direction when poured from the decanter.' He also stated that the decanter should have a foot so that it would raise the body of the vessel above the white tablecloth so that the light may readily render apparent the brilliancy of the colour of the wine. This latter feature was actually already established practice and can be seen on decanters dating from about 1850 onwards.

Decanters of course were made in all sizes and were not always for wine or spirits. Small decanters, which held up to three-quarters of an imperial pint, but often very much less, were made for sauces as is proved by their engraved labels. Wine decanters start from a similar size, the smallest sometimes being called 'one go's'. The majority though, were made with pint and quart capacities in line with bottles (although this no longer accords with our modern twenty-six fluid ounce bottles). Magnums (two bottles) and larger sizes are known, the largest of all being a twenty-one bottle decanter once owned by André Simon. Some decanters were no doubt used for a variety of purposes such as a large decanter of six to eight

Plate 151. A very late 18th century Indian club decanter. It is quite plain but for the cartouche and monogram which bear a strong resemblance to the punch bowl in plate 254. However, the interesting feature is the stopper, the peg of which is hollow. This enabled it to be used as a taster and this variety is much sought after by collectors.

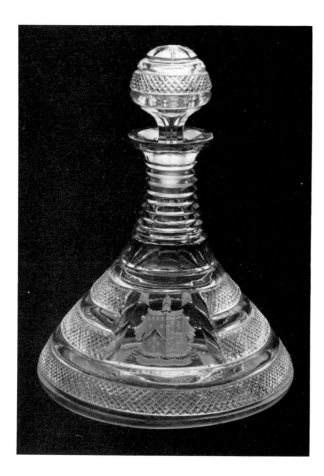

Plates 152 and 153. A really magnificent so-called ship's decanter. This important piece would merit the attention of a serious collector for several reasons; first, it is of a desirable shape; second it is of magnum capacity; third, the decoration, which comprises bands of diamond cutting interspersed with flat sections and a step-cut neck and panel-cut shoulder, is very good, fourth, it is of high quality and fine condition and has its original stopper. Finally it is beautifully cut with the coat of arms wheel-engraved (detail). The coat of arms is that of Admiral Sir George Cranfield Berkeley who married Emily, daughter of Lord George Lennox, in 1784, whose arms his are impaling.

bottle capacity dating from about 1810 which was wheel-engraved with bunches of grapes, barley-hops and a cow. Details of decanter and bottle sizes can be seen in Appendix II.

When discussing decanters one cannot fail to mention those enamelled in the workshops of William and Mary Beilby of Newcastle. This brother and sister team started working with enamels on glass in about 1762. Many of their designs are armorial and therefore were clearly made for a specific client. Another supreme craftsman famous for his decoration on both porcelain and glass is James Giles. A contemporary of the Beilbys, his speciality was gilding. His work appears on both blue and green decanters and indeed, on rare, opaque white ones. Much of his work is alleged to have been done on Bristol-made glass notwithstanding the fact that he was working in London. Giles employed in his workshop a number of painters and they worked on wares from the Worcester, Bow and Longton Hall porcelain factories and also imported Chinese porcelain. He was principally a decorator of porcelain bought in the white, mostly from Worcester, but also from many Continental factories. His repertoire on glass included, predictably, much of the style of contemporary porcelain decoration such as exotic birds and bouquets of flowers. An extensive series of scent bottles survives with hollow diamond cutting, gilded with stars at the intersections, and decanters were sometimes handled in this way. In the 1760s, he was working in the rococo manner on shouldered decanters. Coinciding with the introduction of mallets the workshop's style shifted

Plate 154. An exceptionally large decanter or carafe dating from the early years of the 19th century. It is wheel-engraved with a cow, an apple tree, bunches of grapes and barley, clearly indicating that it was intended for a number of different beverages.

Plate 155. A shouldered decanter with a faceted spire stopper. it is beautifully enamelled with the word 'Claret' surrounded by a rococo cartouche and with pendant vine leaves and a bunch of grapes. Holding this photograph to a mirror might indicate that on the reverse are painted the words 'faith and loyalty'. It was made in the workshops of William and Mary Beilby in about 1765.

Plate 156. A fine cut mallet decanter, beautifully decorated in the neo-classical taste. It bears a strong resemblance to opaque white decanters with gilt decoration known to have been decorated in the workshops of James Giles.

towards Neo-classicism resulting in a dramatic series of decanters in 'enamel' or opaque white glass, decorated with rams' heads, garrya husks, paterae and Greek key ornament, and some with vases taken from classical sources. Work by both the Beilbys and Giles are highly prized collectors' items and are most uncommon. A later well known Bristol artist was Isaac Jacobs, who worked on 'Bristol' blue and amethyst glass. He is chiefly

Plate 157. A mallet-shaped opaque white decanter, the entire body cut with lozenge facets. The centre and corner of each facet is decorated in gilt and like the last decanter this was made in the workshop of James Giles in the early 1770s.

Plate 158. The base of a decanter which has been blown into a mould. The fluting round the base is an inexpensive way to emulate the cutting of more costly decanters, but the interest here lies in the impression of the maker, 'Penrose, Waterford'.

known for his use of a simple, bold Greek key pattern, but he also decorated decanters with gilt labels, mostly for spiritous liquors and usually in sets of three. Jacobs' work is sometimes signed on the underside and is naturally highly collectable. It is the presence of the mark 'I. Jacobs, Bristol' on the reverse of a few pieces of gilt blue glass that has given the term Bristol to all blue glass, notwithstanding the fact that most contemporary houses made it.

Until now, little or nothing has been said of Irish glass. Specialist glass books, some of which are listed in the bibliography, outline the history of glass in Ireland as well as England with more detail than can be attempted here. The glass-making industry in Ireland was founded at about the same time as that in England. It met at first with a mixed amount of success, but by the middle of the eighteenth century was well established, notwithstanding the English Excise Act of 1745 which placed a ten shilling per pound weight duty on all glass exported from the country. Furthermore all glass imported into Ireland had to come from Britain. In 1777 the duty on glass in England was doubled, but in 1780 Irish glass was exempted and restrictions in respect of the export of glass from Ireland was removed. Not surprisingly this had the most dramatic effect; glass makers from England rushed to Ireland to set up glass houses in Waterford, Cork, Dublin and Belfast. (Almost every book, incidentally, written on glass this century has pointed out, quite correctly, that more glass has been ascribed to the Waterford factory than was ever produced in the whole of Ireland!) With the exemption from duty the Irish were able to take full advantage of the properties of lead glass by blowing it thick and then cutting it thinner. Much Irish glass therefore has cut decoration, although the popularly held notion that all cut glass of the eighteenth and nineteenth centuries is Irish is absolute nonsense. Glass making industries continued to thrive in Bristol, London, Stourbridge and Newcastle and many products from these centres were also cut. Nor is it true that Irish glass has a particularly blue or grey colour. Every melt of glass varies from the next and because of the interchange of ideas and ingredients between England and Ireland, technology, and thus the colour, was much the same in the two countries. Certain forms of decoration, however, can be ascribed to

156

Plate 159. A silver-plate and wheel-engraved glass claret jug made by W. & G. Sissons in Sheffield in about 1870. Generally fine claret jugs had silver mounts and the best, silver-gilt. This is clearly an exception to this rule. The fern decoration is typical of its date.

Plate 160. A beautiful claret jug of coloured glass overlaid with silver in the Japanese style. it was made in Birmingham in 1897 by Elkington & Co.

particular factories with varying degrees of certainty. The most obvious are those which are blown into moulds with the name of the manufacturing company in the mould (see plate 158, page 156). Examples of these factories are the Waterloo Company of Cork, Francis Collins of Dublin, Penrose of Waterford and Edwards of Belfast. Another group which can be fairly certainly identified are those which were blown into moulds so that the fluting around the base of the decanter is moulded rather than cut. Certain varieties of moulded neck ring and moulded target stopper are also associated with particular Irish factories, and all these groups can be placed in the category of 'probably Irish', but not certainly. A few Irish factories are associated with particular designs of cutting. Finally, there is a group of decanters which are particularly heavy in relation to their size and which display a particularly un-English appearance, but nevertheless retain a substantial degree of technical competence. Many of these pieces are decorated with a form of cutting known as 'lunar slices' and such pieces are often also described as 'probably Irish'.

Finally a word must be said about the rarity of individual types of decanters today. Decorative (rather than purely utilitarian) seventeenth century decanter jugs are in very scant supply, most extant examples being either in museums or other public collections or in the hands of a very few specialist glass collectors. Very occasionally early shaft and globe decanters may be found in specialist shops and here also, though rather more frequently, cruciform decanters can be seen. Decorated shoulder and mallet decanters are most avidly collected and are accordingly also difficult to obtain, although taper and Indian club decanters are, on the other hand, fairly numerous. By the end of the eighteenth century decanters were being made in very substantial numbers and singles are even now relatively easy to obtain. In general, with the exception of decanters which incorporated the most sophisticated decoration, the price decreases the more recently the piece was made.

As the stopper is constantly removed and replaced, it is quite common for the neck of a decanter to become chipped or cracked and once this happens, either the whole object must be discarded or where the damage is only slight, the neck can be ground and re-polished. In any event the result of this occurrence has meant that a great many decanters which started life as one of a pair, now survive only as singles and both collectors and drinkers are prepared to pay a premium to acquire a pair. Very occasionally a set of four may be found though there can be little doubt that sets of substantial numbers were made, sometimes in a variety of sizes, sometimes all the same. While on the subject of size, it should be said that half bottle or pint decanters find little favour with the buying public, and are correspondingly inexpensive. By contrast, magnums and larger decanters are very sought after and because they were only made in small numbers command a substantial premium. It is perhaps fortunate that the

Plate 161. This claret jug, in contrast to the previous plate, has a completely plain body mounted in silver with a flower bud, the stem of which forms a handle. It was made by E.H. Stockwell in London in 1880. These last two examples show the remarkable variety that claret jugs can take.

serious wine drinker on the whole prefers his glass to be completely plain so that the clarity and colour of his wine may be easily judged while it is still in the decanter, while the glass collector by contrast is looking for rarities of design and decoration. This means that the collector and drinker can usually go their own separate ways without encroaching upon each other's interests. If this were no longer to obtain, it would be a sad day and another upward spiral of prices would occur which would put many practical objects beyond the means of many people who can best appreciate them.

CHAPTER 10
Wine Labels

Many wine antiques sport alternative names. In a previous chapter we mentioned that in the eighteenth century the object known as a corkscrew was then a bottle screw, while in another chapter readers will see that what we have called a wine funnel, they may know as a port strainer. By the same token the term 'wine label', would mean nothing to a man hearing it two hundred years ago, for he would have called the same object a 'bottle ticket'.

The introduction of the wine label was a logical development. The first vessels to indicate their contents have already been described in the chapter on bottles when reference was made to pottery flasks with handles, but for the seventy or so years following 1670 it appears that little further was made with the name of the wine on it. (A recent article has noted a reference to a bottle ticket dated 1723, but no examples have survived prior to the 1730s, and it has not been possible to confirm this reference.) Sealed bottles gave the name of their owner, together with perhaps his home town and the date, but never indicated their contents. To date the only reference work on the subject is Dr. Norman Penzer's *Book of the Wine Label* and in it he expresses the view that prior to the introduction of the silver wine label, parchment labels, resting on the neck of the bottle, were used. Alternatively he suggests that parchment was gummed to the bottle's side. This theory, however, is not proven, for no parchment neck labels have come to light and in any case it is notoriously difficult to stick anything to glass. Whatever did fill the hiatus between about 1670 and 1735 is for the time being fanciful conjecture.

The very earliest silver wine labels are of a design known as 'escutcheon shape' because of their resemblance to the escutcheons or backplates of furniture handles. They have an outline composed of S and C scrolls about a symmetrical axis and are curved so that they rest easily on the shoulder of the bottle. (With one exception, which will be descibed later, all bottle tickets are held in place with small chains, the ends passing through holes drilled into either end of the label. In Scotland small loops were incorporated into the label design itself for the same purpose.) Many escutcheon labels may have a smooth surface with the name of the wine engraved on it, but the better quality ones are decorated with a variety of work known as flat-chasing; it normally takes the form of a fruiting vine covering the entire surface but for the central area where the name of the wine is engraved. (Early wine labels seldom have their names pierced; this is a feature dating from after about 1785.) A similar simplified version of the escutcheon-shaped label is a broad rectangular label with a wavy edge, which made its appearance after about 1740. Another design of early label

Plate 162. Five labels of escutcheon outline. As can be seen, these can either be plain like the top three, engraved like 'Old Hock' or flat-chased like 'Mountain'. It is perhaps interesting to note today that 'Old Hock' was considered a term of approbation. These labels date from the 1730s or early '40s.

Plate 163. Two wine labels of so-called 'broad rectangular' outline. They have gadroon edges typical of the mid-18th century. 'Mountain' is a wine that comes from Malaga.

relied on a cast technique (rather than cutting from sheet metal) and these are in the form of a pair of cherubs or putti holding suitably Bacchanalian vessels amid a profusion of fruiting vines (see plate 164, page 163). Between them is a banner bearing the engraved name of the wine. A number of Sheffield plated labels have also survived dating from the period immediately following the invention of the Sheffield plating process by Thomas Boulsover in 1742 (see plate 164, page 163).

As a result of research and study undertaken by members of the Wine Label Circle since its foundation in 1952, it can fairly safely be stated that wine labels were first available between 1730 and 1735. An entry in the accounts of Earl Fitzwalter records 'May 11th, 1738. Paid Edward, the silversmith in Lombard Street, for 14 tickets, silver, for wine bottles, at 5s. 6d. each £3-17-0d.' Because hallmarking laws excluded the need to

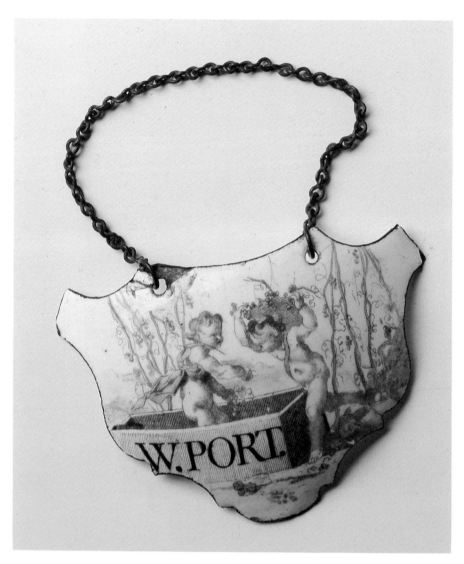

Colour plate 32. A 'Ravenet' wine label. These magnificent and large wine labels were made at the Battersea enamelling factory and the labels take their name from the engraver of the transfer prints which decorate them. Typically they have cupids, either treading the grapes, as in this case, or simply lolling around with bunches of grapes amongst the barrels.

hallmark anything weighing less than 10 pennyweights, in theory before 1784 but in effect before 1790, most early wine labels are marked only with the maker's mark (and sometimes with the lion passant also).

When a silversmith uses a punch to stamp his wares, notwithstanding that the punch is made of steel and is tougher than the silver it is punching, it nevertheless wears out over a period of time. Consequently a replacement punch has to made which will in its turn have to be registered with the Goldsmith's Company. Records have been kept of all these punches at Goldsmith's Hall together with the date of their introduction, and it is therefore possible by closely studying each mark to identify its date to within a short period of time. Several early makers of wine labels have been identified in this way, amongst them John Harvey and the

162

inappropriately named Sandilands Drinkwater. Although the former was working as a silversmith prior to 1735 no wine labels appear to exist with his stamp before that date, a fact which reinforces the theory that the wine label was not yet in common usage.

Despite their proven existence during the 1740s, the popularity of silver wine labels seems to have waned rapidly for there is a relative dearth of surviving examples dating from about the late 1740s to the early 1760s, a period which happens to coincide with the full flowering of the Rococo style in England. Where furniture was concerned escutcheons developed into the heavy cast rococo handles as advocated for example by Thomas Chippendale in his *Gentleman and Cabinet Maker's Director* first published in 1754. However, with wine labels, which would seem to be the perfect vehicle for similar treatment, this development did not take place. This is more surprising when one considers that the silver trade was in the vanguard of decorative design and characteristically rococo asymmetric acanthus leaves, icicles and rockwork abounded on silver generally and on furniture and other decorative wood and metalwork. There are a few, though very few, surviving wine labels which incorporate decoration of a

Plate 164. Two so-called 'Bacchus and banner' wine labels. These can vary considerably in quality — some are thin and some are heavily cast.

Plate 165. Four Sheffield plated wine labels. The one for 'Port' at the top is a very early example dating from soon after the invention of the process by Thomas Boulsover in 1742. 'Mountain' and 'W. Wine' date from the 1760s or '70s whereas the 'Sercial' is from the end of the century.

Plate 166. Three examples of neo-classical wine labels. The 'Claret' is prettily pierced with repetitive motifs while the 'Port' is surmounted by an urn draped with garrya husks — a typical neo-classical theme.

rococo kind, but in a very mild form. Armorial cartouche designs, which are found on any worthwhile piece of silver of the period, similarly do not appear. Why then was there this gap? It can possibly be accounted for by the introduction of another medium, namely that of enamel, and certainly escutcheon-shaped labels were made at the Battersea enamel factory and at Bilston and other Staffordshire factories.

The enamel labels from Battersea must represent the pinnacle of achievement for a wine label collector (see colour plate 32, page 162). This factory was only working between 1753 and 1756, but during that time it produced some exquisite examples of the enameller's art. The process involved the fusing of a layer of white opaque glass to a sheet of copper and to this was applied a transfer print, a technique newly discovered for the decoration of pottery and porcelain. The print would then be hand coloured and fired to produce the final result. Battersea wine labels, often known as Ravenet labels after the engraver of the transfer print, are large by comparison with other wine labels of the period. Most usually they depict bacchanalian putti or cupids, either treading grapes in a trough, drawing wine from casks, or generally lolling about amongst the barrels. The names of the wines are in black Roman lettering. The general use of the term 'Battersea' to describe all enamel wine labels is seldom

Plate 167. Three examples of wine labels decorated with bright cutting. It can be seen how tiny slivers of silver are removed, very often in a chevron pattern to leave a glistening surface. Another popular edging was beading, though the two forms of edging are seldom found together.

encountered nowadays as it is commonly realised that a large number of labels were made in the Staffordshire area during the third quarter of the eighteenth century. These Staffordshire enamel labels differ from the Ravenet examples by being painted rather than transfer-printed. They outnumber them by many times and are generally smaller. The lettering also tends to be black, and the decoration is usually floral, mostly incorporating representations of roses.

However, notwithstanding their reluctance to adopt the Rococo, wine label makers were not slow to utilise neo-classical motifs and by the 1760s were producing rather simple labels in a variety of shapes — the crescent, the scroll, the wide vase (sometimes known as the goblet), the kidney, the simple narrow rectangle and the oval (both pointed and rounded). These shapes coincided with the introduction of 'bright cutting', a form of decoration much favoured by neo-classical silversmiths. Very small slivers of silver were removed from the surface and each slice left a facet which reflected a bright light — hence its name. On its own this form of decoration is not entirely pleasing and it was sometimes enhanced by the additional technique of wrigglework, a repetitive zig-zag line. Some labels were also decorated with swags of husks or with a simple form of stylised drapery. Some indeed were actually shaped to simulate drapery and are often mistakenly described as 'festooned'. Festooning is a particular method of hanging curtains and it is quite inappropriate to use the term here. Most of these labels tend to be small and are characterised by prettiness and elegance rather than magnificence.

Also encountered at this date are wine labels which incorporate a small oval or shield shape forming a cresting, on which can be engraved the crest or indeed the full coat of arms, of the owner, although the latter is extremely rare. One of the most sought after today is the heraldic wine

Plate 168. A desirable form of wine label for collectors are those incorporating crests, in particular naval or military ones. The above plate has four such examples. The label for 'white wine' has a vacant cartouche which might have been engraved with such a device.

label which normally took the form of the family crest with the name of the wine on either a scroll, a crescent or a rectangle beneath the crest or upon the wreath on which the crest stands. Some regimental wine labels were made in the form of a gorget. (Later examples from the nineteenth century would take the form of the regimental crest.)

Towards the end of the eighteenth century wine label design seemed to be losing much of its novelty and many labels are merely repetitions of earlier forms. In about 1800 though, a totally new approach is felt, for in place of the thin, light-calibre tickets, pierced and shaped from sheet metal, we suddenly find bold cast shapes of substantial size and weight, brilliantly chased and often gilded, either totally or in part. These cast labels take the form of garlands of fruiting vines, leopards' pelts with fruiting vines, shells or bacchanalian figures with grapes (see colour plate 33, page 171). After about 1820 a single vine leaf became a popular design, though the majority of these were die-stamped from thin sheet metal rather than cast. Their making was occasioned by the manufacture of presses capable of delivering sufficient force to stamp out the metal shapes.

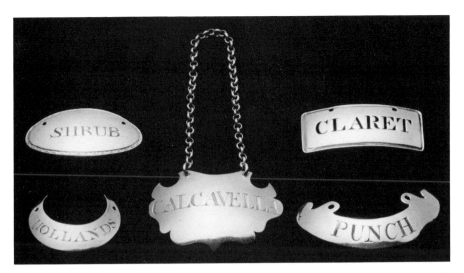

Plate 169. *Five examples of plain wine labels. These represent the types most readily available to those starting a collection, though an early example like 'Calcavella' or an unusual name like 'Punch' are perhaps rather more difficult to find. Pierced labels, like the 'Claret' example above, are a relatively late form.*

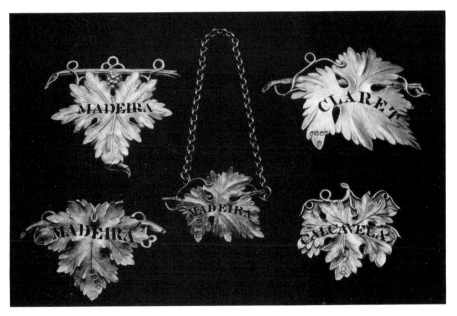

Plate 170. *A very popular type of wine label after 1820 was the vine leaf. These came in a variety of sizes, qualities and weights and this is a typical selection which also demonstrates the fact that the most common of all wine labels is 'Madeira'.*

In about 1830 the initial label became extremely popular (see plate 171, overleaf) though the form had been known previously, very late in the eighteenth century. Early examples are to be found with initials pierced with Roman letters. With the exception of the Scottish ones, which can be plain, later examples usually reflect the florid taste of the times and are commonly cast with decorative edgings or engraved scrolls. As Queen Victoria's reign began another variety, frequently known as 'architectural'

Plate 171. An increasingly popular area for collection are those labels in the form of initials. A few were made at the end of the 18th century and the beginning of the 19th, but most were made from the 1830s to the 1870s. They can vary enormously in size and are popularly acquired in accordance with the initials of the collector.

Plate 172. Wine labels were made well into the Victorian period, notwithstanding the fact that paper labels were introduced on wine bottles after 1860. Mid-19th century labels are often referred to as 'architectural', but this is a misnomer and these four examples are clearly far more cartouche-shaped than architectural.

was introduced. The word 'architectural' should be avoided in this context as it conjures up notions of columns and classical porticos and these labels are in fact cartouche-shaped. They have raised, cast or pressed borders, often incorporating scrolls, but sometimes straight lines also.

Occasionally it was inappropriate to hang a label around the neck of a decanter and instead a mounted cork was inserted in the top. These are usually composed of two silver discs which are attached to either end of a cork with a simple pin. Above the larger end is a ring, or sometimes a flat disc, joined at right angles and upon which may be engraved some initials or a crest. Sometimes one encounters a crossing piece, heavily cast and engraved, and such an example is to be seen in plate 173. Some are fitted with a threaded shank so that a fresh cork can be fitted from time to time.

After 1860, when it became legal to sell wine by the bottle from various retail premises and the use of the gummed paper label became widespread, the 'bottle ticket' trade was drastically reduced and few, if any, labels for unfortified wines were made after that date. During the late Victorian period, spirits as well as Port, Madeira and Marsala were decanted and labels in the form of cut-out words were made. The turn of the century seems to have marked the demise of label design until recently.

Having considered the evolution of their design, let us now describe the decoration in a little more detail. We mentioned that on silver escutcheon-shaped labels, flat chasing is found, while during the Neo-classical period bright cutting and wrigglework were employed. Some wine labels have pierced decoration which can be described as 'fretted' and this is a sought after and relatively unusual variety (see plates 166, 167 and 168). Much bright-cut silver has feather-edged decoration which was an inexpensive way of producing a form of gadrooned edge. The feather edge was popular

Plate 173. Some wine labels take the form of a silver mounted cork and were clearly used in place of a stopper. Most examples of this type were light in weight and were obviously made as economy models. The illustrated example however is heavily cast with a shell and has a gadrooned border.

Plate 174. Two pairs of neck ring labels. The left-hand pair, for 'Sherry' and 'Port', are made of ivory while the right-hand pair for 'Madeira' are silver. Although silver ones usually date from around the beginning of the 19th century, these were made in 1854.

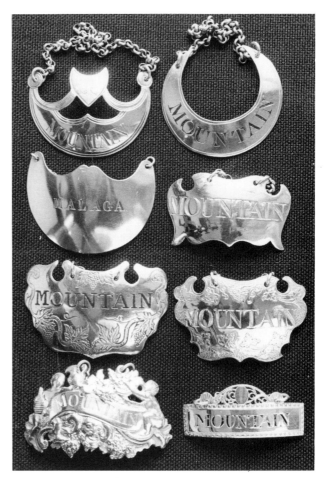

Plate 175. A typical product of India made of a pair of tiger's claws mounted with silver filigree. Many of these still survive.

Plate 176. A collection of wine labels for 'Mountain'. Already this small group is beginning to show interesting variations. Mountain was a wine that was very popular at the time when wine labels were first made and these are all 18th century examples.

during the 1770s and 1780s, while the bolder gadrooned edge was fashionable both before and after that time. On the heavier quality, nineteenth century examples, when not pressed, the gadrooned edge will be formed by an applied cast moulding. Also popular was the reeded edge which was either single, double or triple, see plates 169, 174 and 176 (top left). Occasionally a wine label will have a beaded edge, though this is rare and rarer still is a beaded and reeded edge. Many borders incorporate small shells while others have satyrs or other forms of mask head. A popular allusive type was the border which comprised cast or pressed flowering vines.

The substantial majority of eighteenth century wine labels were made in silver, but during the nineteenth century other media were employed, mostly copying silver prototypes. A number of ivory labels were made in rectangular form with cut corners and reeded edges and one would expect these to date from about 1800. More common though in ivory are splayed

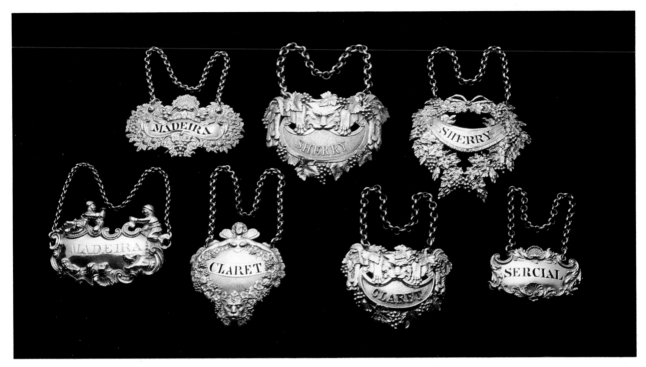

Colour plate 33. Without doubt the grandest wine labels were made at the beginning of the 19th century, mostly by Benjamin Scott, Digby Smith and Paul Storr and a little later by Edward Farrell. Whereas earlier labels were delicate, light and often pretty, this variety have much substance and were cast and often gilded. For some reason 1806 seems to have been a very prolific year for good labels.

neck rings (see plate 174, page 169). Neck rings were also made in silver from about 1790 onwards, but ivory examples tend to be flatter and were clearly intended for use at the base of the neck of a shaft-and-globe type decanter of about 1840. Silver examples are approximately three eighths of an inch wide. There was of course a substantial English presence in the Indian sub-continent where emigré silversmiths had been established since the eighteenth century. They too turned their hand to the making of silver wine labels which they marked with their own devices. Mounted trophies, particularly tigers' claws and boars' teeth, for use as wine labels, were not normally marked and may have been made by native craftsmen.

Another apparently popular, though now uncommon, material for wine labels is mother-of-pearl. These again tend to be nineteenth century, notwithstanding the fact that many copy the earlier escutcheon form. Wine labels exist in other media also; a charming Victorian label executed in

Plate 177. A collection of wine labels of South African origin. The 'Constantia' is a fine example, while the 'Van de Purll' is probably unique. However, when a group of others suddenly appeared on the market comparison enabled the central 'Rustenberg' label to be identified as a fake, while 'Cape-Vin' and 'Havepoot' are probably re-engraved. The faker gave himself away when one day he engraved a label 'Pinopage', presumably as a mis-spelling of Pinotage, but he didn't realise that the pinotage grape was not cultivated until the 1920s.

beadwork is known to the authors, but such an item must surely be regarded as an unusual collector's piece.

During the nineteenth century a large number were made in porcelain of cartouche shape with polychrome decoration composed of floral borders. They usually had tinned chains.

One of the most interesting aspects of the wine label is of course the name that it carries. Silver wine labels at any rate, are datable as we have already discussed, so they give us a clear indication of the type of wine being consumed at any one time. Furthermore, wine labels were very frequently made in sets — a dozen or more labels being not uncommon. Again, this can clearly indicate the preferences of the family to whom they belonged. There was a notable trend during the eighteenth century for Portuguese wines, a fact occasioned by the Methuen Treaty of 1703 which

Plate 178. A very grand set of silver-gilt wine labels made by Benjamin Smith in 1807. These heavy, cast labels are among the grandest made and it is particularly pleasing to see a set intact which clearly shows the drinking preferences of the original owner. They would complement the decanter wagon in colour plate 36, page 181 or other rich silver-gilt plate of the Regency period.

has already been discussed in Chapter 2. On Scottish labels, because of the 'Auld Alliance', a higher percentage of French wines are named. In Appendix IV a list of all the different types of wines can be found which the reader may find interesting. For an explanation of some of the names Dr. Penzer's book is recommended. It will be noted that the names found on tickets for sauces, flavourings, cordials and spirits have been omitted.

Wine labels are collected for their names as well as their various shapes and forms. Spelling mistakes were quite often made and can add interest and value to a label. Abbreviations too are not uncommon, 'R. and W. Port' for example (red and white port) being fairly often encountered. A sad and reprehensible trait among twentieth century collectors and dealers has been to buy sets of labels to split among their friends so that each will have an example of a particular type and at the same time reduce the burden of the high costs that a good set demands. The inferences that may be drawn from an intact set are lost and set-splitting is a habit for which certain collectors should have their knuckles rapped!

CHAPTER 11
Wine Coasters
and Decanter Wagons

Whereas many of the articles concerned with wine drinking evolved only gradually over a number of years, coasters seem to have mushroomed in popularity rather suddenly during the 1760s. Their purpose is quite straightforward; a decanter can easily accumulate dribbles of wine down its side and these will stain the surface upon which the decanter is placed. By resting the decanter in a coaster this problem is obviously avoided. Furthermore, if two or more decanters are on the table together, the coasters prevent them from touching one another and chipping in the process.

The term coaster is derived from its ability to 'coast' along the polished surface of the dining table and according to the *Oxford English Dictionary* was first used in an 1898 catalogue of the antique dealers Mallet & Son of Bath (and more recently of London). Coasters had previously been known variously as 'wine', 'bottle' or 'decanter slides' or 'decanter' or 'bottle stands'.

It has been said in the past that early coasters were meant for bottles whereas later ones were for decanters. There seems nothing to substantiate this view as decanters pre-date coasters by many years. However, as

Plate 179. A fine piece of silver made by Paul Crespin in 1723, one of Britain's finest silversmiths. Being about 5ins. across it could be a coaster — but then for that matter it could be a stand for anything else. The engraving of the Royal arms indicates that it was probably part of an ambassadorial service.

Plate 180. One of a pair of late rococo silver coasters. The scalloped rim adds a lightness to the design enhanced by the detail of the piercing. They were made by Thomas Lamborn in 1770.

Plate 181. One of a wonderful pair of silver coasters by Edward Aldridge which would be absolutely plain but for the fact that the sides are pierced to simulate Chinese trellis work. That the base is similarly covered in trellis pattern is exceptionally unusual. This pair of coasters are very crisp and in almost new condition despite being made in 1770.

already mentioned in the chapter on bottles, silver receptacles of bowl shape seem to have been made prior to 1760 to hold the glass serving bottles which preceded decanters, although few of these seem to have survived or can at any rate be positively identified. The illustration in plate 179 is decidedly coaster-size, but could be a dish or stand for almost any circular bowl or vessel. The question of where decanters were placed during the first half of the eighteenth century must for the moment remained unanswered. We can however be sure that all early coasters had baize-lined bottoms which indicate that they must have been used at the end of the meal after the tablecloth had been removed and the servants dismissed.

In style silver coasters followed prevailing fashions. Rococo was still fashionable in the 1760s and many rococo coasters are characterised by hand-pierced decoration of asymmetric patterns of scrolling foliage or Chinese birds, or a mixture of both. Many had gadrooned or moulded wire rims (see glossary), either straight or wavy in outline. The majority of coasters of this date and those made in the early 1770s had high sides, perhaps as much as one and a half to one and three quarter inches. By about 1800 their height had gradually diminished to about one inch although some were as little as three-quarters of an inch.

Changes had naturally taken place in design too. During the 1770s rococo frivolity was replaced by more ordered neo-classical patterns in the form of repetitive geometric piercings. A favourite was a continuous band of vertical lines simulating fluting, a pattern found on a great deal of domestic silver of this date. Many of these decorative piercings were produced on machine driven hand presses. Much use was also made of

Plate 182. Two coasters, the left-hand example being Sheffield plated, while the right-hand one is silver. The quality of piercing and engraving of the silver one is higher, commensurate with the more highly regarded material. Coasters of higher quality have bases of silver, whereas both these are of turned mahogany. The silver coaster is hallmarked for 1795 and the Sheffield plated one is of a similar date.

Plate 183. The central coaster is the height of simplicity and made of pewter. The left-hand example is also made of pewter, but the wavy rim, bright-cut decoration and piercing are clearly emulating silver models. It dates from about 1780-90. The right-hand one is made of paktong, a silver-coloured alloy invented for Imperial Chinese use and used in Britain during the 18th century. This one was made in about 1775.

'bright cutting', sometimes enhanced by wrigglework. This remained popular thoughout the 1770s and 1780s and after a short lull re-emerged in the 1790s. (It is occasionally seen on coasters dating from about 1820.)

By about 1800 a now-classic type of coaster had evolved with a plain unpierced rim of ogee or double-ogee outline (see plate 184). Countless hundreds of these were made, not only in silver, but also in Sheffield plate. Sheffield plated coasters incidentally, rapidly began to outnumber silver examples at this date and indeed, by about 1850, silver examples were quite rare.

Early in the nineteenth century however one finds the only coasters ever made which were truly grand examples of the goldsmith's art. These magnificent coasters were made by Digby Scott and Benjamin Smith and the celebrated silversmith Paul Storr for the retailers to the Royal Household, Rundell, Bridge and Rundell (see plate 185, page 178). This particular type, many of which exist in long sets, are of silver gilt and are

Colour plate 34. A very pretty pair of lacquered papier mâché coasters. The polychrome flowers stand out boldly against the black background and are offset by the gilt mouldings above and below. This pair retain much of their original brilliance and gloss and may be dated to about 1810-20.

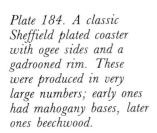

Plate 184. A classic Sheffield plated coaster with ogee sides and a gadrooned rim. These were produced in very large numbers; early ones had mahogany bases, later ones beechwood.

very large, being six inches in diameter. They are high-sided, about three and a half inches, and are cast with a profusion of fruiting vines, cherubs and leopards between a top border of ribbon-tied reeding and a lower border cast with a running band of stylised leaves. They were made en suite with large sets of baskets, salvers and trays.

For a while, after about 1805, there was no prescribed shape or design and it is difficult to be quite so precise about their evolution until the 1830s and 1840s when the Gothic Revival style was popular. While its most famous manifestation is the great Palace of Westminster, it was equally applied to such humble items as the coaster, and rims were made in the form of Gothic traceries. A rococo revival, which had slightly preceded the former, is also evident in some coasters, but can be distinguished easily from its earlier counterparts by the reproduction of decorative detail only, not overall design. Further historic revivals were represented in a similar way until about 1880 when the making of coasters seems to have ceased until modern reproductions were made in the twentieth century.

Generally speaking, nineteenth century coasters were made with bulbous or everted sides as opposed to the strictly vertical sides applied to

Plate 185. A fair number of these magnificent silver-gilt coasters have survived. They are unusually large, being 6ins. in diameter. The name of the firm who produced them usually appears on the base rim together with the Latin inscription as follows: 'RUNDELL BRIDGE ET RUNDELL. AURIFICES REGIS ET PRINCIPIS WALLIAE'. They were usually executed by either Digby Scott and Benjamin Smith or by Paul Storr, and the majority are dated 1806 (though a few are later).

those of the eighteenth century. Concurrently, turned beechwood replaced the mahogany, lignum vitae or rosewood (the latter unusual though), which was used prior to 1800. One might observe that these beechwood bases illustrate one of the earliest uses of varnish as opposed to polish, to seal wood and enhance its colour. Being circular, coaster bases of all dates were easily produced on a lathe and with the exception of some Sheffield plated examples had ribbed or otherwise moulded patterns. Coasters are sometimes found with a silver button in the middle of the base on which the initials, or the crest, of the owner are engraved. The majority are baize-lined underneath, a thin groove having been made approximately a quarter to three-eighths of an inch (six to nine milimetres) from the edge into which the baize lining was pressed to form a 'finished' edge (see plate 187).

During the eighteenth century the finest quality coasters had a base of sheet silver overlaying the wood and a few were made with solid silver bases. Such pieces were often engraved with the full heraldic achievement of the owner in contrast to the crest found on less expensive examples.

The earliest examples were hallmarked somewhere on their vertical sides and sometimes an unpierced section was left specifically to hold the marks. This was a straightforward operation as the coaster would be sent to the assay office before it had been pierced, all the decoration being added after

Plate 186. An imposing Regency coaster, the thin, pressed metal, silver-plated body being composed of a running band of vine leaves and grapes. This encases a blue glass liner, the survival of which is fortunate. This is to hold a magnum decanter and dates from about 1825.

Plate 187. The underside of a coaster. Notice how the turned wood is bevelled and grooved to accommodate the baize bottom. Wirework coasters of this nature are almost invariably Sheffield plated. The everted sides are typical of the post-1820 period.

Colour plate 35. A group of four treen coasters. The large coaster at the rear has a baize-lined base (not shown) which a contemporary tray would lack. It must have been made for an exceptionally large decanter of six-bottle capacity or more, or alternatively a ship's decanter. The small coaster in the foreground is finely turned in pollard oak while the other two are of mahogany. These items are difficult to date, but are thought to be late 18th century.

its return. Silver based coasters are usually marked somewhere on that surface. By 1780 the hallmarks had been moved from the side to the moulded rim of the base. Again, the marks were stamped before the piece had been finished and in particular before the wooden base was added. In order to fit the base and complete the process of finishing the silver itself, it was necessary to rework the base rim and in doing so the silversmith quite frequently defaced or otherwise damaged the hallmarks. This, together with the fact that marks in this position are further abraded by frequent cleaning, has meant that many late eighteenth century coasters have very poor hallmarks. One occasionally chances upon a freak set on which the hallmarks are good and clear and these must be regarded as a bonus for those to whom hallmarks assume some degree of importance. This is a regrettable trend fostered by commercial interests and while agreeing that it is a pleasant bonus to know the date, maker and city of origin, these surely must take second place to design, quality and condition of the object overall. Silver coasters are now very desirable and command high prices far in excess of their melt value.

An inspection of the base of a coaster may give an indication of deception. Many 'false' coasters have been made from cruet strands (objects never favoured amongst silver collectors) by removal of the vertical

Colour plate 36. A splendid pair of silver-gilt decanter wagons which have the facility for being hooked together. They are of exceptional quality and are cast in the form of continuous fruiting vines. They were made by Benjamin Smith in 1828 as part of a service for the first Earl of Hastings whose armorials they bear.

Plate 188. A common find in a house is an incomplete cruet. Note the lack of one bottle and the stopper of another.

handle and the three supporting feet. These can be recognised as cruet stands by their flat, rather than turned, bases and by the hole where the handle was fixed which will be filled underneath. Marks will normally betray the removal of the feet.

The nineteenth century also saw a variation in coaster sizes, in line with that of bottles and decanters. Magnums, as with decanters, are rare, but more are to be seen dating from after the turn of the century than before it. It has always been a mystery why half-size coasters should also be so rare, as half-size decanters are by contrast quite common. It may be that half-bottle decanters were deemed to be for liqueurs or other drinks not coasted around the table. Even rarer is the square section coaster, presumably also for a decanter holding a liqueur, rather than wine. Especially rare are coasters large enough to accommodate a ship's decanter and while on the subject it is interesting to note that a pair of silver coasters

Plate 189. *This second plate shows how easy it is to dismantle the cruet to make a coaster. The counterfeit item can be distinguished by the lack of turning of the wood base or its complete replacement with a new one. This cruet was made in 1782.*

made in 1800 by Robert and David Hennell for Admiral Lord Nelson and bearing his crest, are only five and a quarter inches in diameter. They must have been made for decanters of normal shape rather than those we today call ship's decanters.

During the 1790s other media had come into use for the manufacture of coasters; most common was papier mâché (see colour plate 34, page 179), a material which was formed by bonding together layers of paper with glue. Once the required shape had been moulded, it was coloured and lacquered. A great many shades were employed, but the most common was black, followed by rich hues of red, green and blue. The decoration of eighteenth century papier mâché coasters tended to be very stylised, consisting of gilded diaper patterns, wriggles and rather uninspired representations of oak leaves and grapes. Some had chinoiserie or freely painted floral patterns and a particularly attractive finish was simulated lustreware. After the decade 1800 to 1810 when the straight side fell into disuse, papier mâché coasters often relied on simple horizontal ribbed moulding for decoration and strength. These ribbed coasters tended to be high-sided, undecorated and quite often furnished with a Sheffield plated, reeded rim. They were usually a brilliant scarlet colour, although sometimes black, and occasionally had additional mounts in the form of diminutive rings and hooks with an oval back-plate which enabled a pair of coasters to be linked together. One of the earliest exponents of the art of papier mâché was Henry Clay of Birmingham who had first perfected and patented the process of pasting layers of paper under pressure in 1772,

Colour plate 37. A most unusual decanter wagon in the form of two Roman chariots back to back, a clear allusion to Classicism. This is reinforced by the ram's head handle and numerous running floral motifs. Perhaps the most unusual feature is its manufacture in gilt copper. It dates from about 1810.

Colour plate 38. A blue glass plate or stand. The central area is about the same size as a coaster and it is quite possible that this is a coaster. This has been photographed with a strong light behind it and the signature 'I. Jacobs Bristol' can be seen in reverse behind the Earl of Verulam's crest. The 'Greek key' edge is typical. It is this and a few other signed pieces which have given rise to the silly fallacy that all blue glass was made in Bristol.

Plate 190. A rare glass coaster. The wavy notched sides and diamond, step-cut body and star-cut base portray a sophisticated provenance, but one cannot help wondering about the efficacy of such a piece. It is not surprising that very few survive.

although the earliest recorded reference to papier mâché coasters is dated 1792. Clay frequently stamped his work and although he died in 1812 the firm remained in business for a further fifty years. Another firm which signed much papier mâché work was Jennens & Bettridge who had taken over Clay's workshop in Birmingham after the latter had moved to London.

Occasionally coasters are found in media other than silver, Sheffield plate and papier mâché. Throughout the period they were made in treen. Very rare early examples have rococo carving and one example exists in the Pinto Collection in Birmingham of ply construction with a fretted, pierced side. Any wooden, fretted, pierced or shaped gallery was incidentally constructed in this way with cross-grain laminations. Particularly delightful are treen coasters (see colour plate 35, page 180) with very shallow sides and an ogee outline. These were often topped with an astragal moulding and the rim was occasionally inlaid with chequer stringing. A rarer type is that which has a line of inlaid brass and a shaped outline reminiscent of a silver salver.

Other metals used included japanned tin, pewter, brass and paktong, the latter being a silverish alloy originally perfected for Imperial Chinese use. In his monograph *Old Pewter* H.H. Cotterill illustrates a pair of pewter

Plate 191. A rolled paperwork coaster. Popular belief has it that rolled paperwork was an amateur pastime, but the turned wood to accommodate the paperwork is certainly professionally made and inlaid with chequered stringing. Rolled paperwork coasters are seldom encountered and this one dates from about 1800.

coasters which apparently have painted decoration of fleur-de-lys. They have tall, straight sides, are unmarked and date from the late 1790s. Pewter coasters may have similar decoration to those in silver of the same period, that is, bright cutting. It might be appropriate to add here that one type of Sheffield plated coaster which does not have a solid silver prototype, is that made of wire work resembling a modified form of garden railing (see plate 187, page 179).

Very rarely coasters were made in glass and pottery. Glass coasters seem a ridiculous and senseless notion, but nevertheless they exist and one is illustrated in plate 190, page 185. Potteries were producing creamware coasters with pierced, fluted sides in line with silver examples during the 1790s (see colour plate 5, page 25).

Throughout the eighteenth century it was fashionable for ladies to employ themselves in the decorative arts by crafting objects. A very popular pastime in the closing years of the century was the making of items in rolled paperwork. These pieces were mostly purchased in 'kit' form from professional makers. Tea caddies abound in this medium and even whole pieces of furniture are decorated in this way. Two magnificent cabinets are displayed in the Lady Lever Art Gallery at Port Sunlight. It is therefore not surprising that one occasionally encounters a rolled paperwork coaster, or indeed a pair. The technique involved the curling of coloured, gilt-edged paper into tight coils and sticking them to a plain ground with the gilt edge outermost. Although very distinctive in its pristine state, as witnessed on the insides of cupboards and boxes which have been protected from the light, the colour of this form of decoration soon deteriorates. Because coasters are not stored in an airtight and light-free box, surviving examples are only a shadow of their former brilliance.

Plate 192. A silver double coaster with elegantly scrolled and reeded ends which was made by John Schofield in 1793. It has a nicely reeded and ribbon-tied border and there are little circles to accommodate the stoppers when they are not in their decanters. It runs on four silver and laminated leather rollers. The decanters have wheel-engraved vine decoration, triple neck rings and bull's-eye stoppers and are slightly later in date than the coaster.

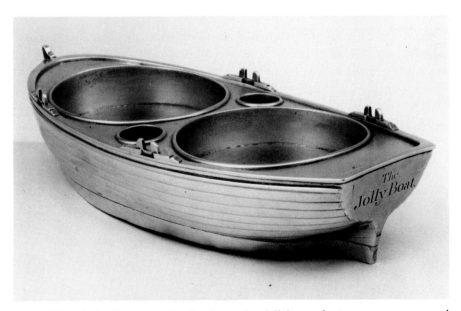

Plate 193. A double coaster in the form of a jollyboat, the transome so engraved. Clinker-built construction is clearly simulated and the apertures for the stoppers are quite obvious. Similar examples in papier mâché with silver or Sheffield plated mounts are known and these items are very collectable.

Plate 194. In contrast to grand pieces in silver gilt, this decanter wagon is Sheffield plated. Note the simple gadrooned rim and spoked wheels which also contrast sharply with colour plate 38, page 181. These wheeled wagons were a feature of the 19th century (earlier ones having concealed wheels) and this one was made in about 1815.

Not all coasters conform exactly to the standard pattern. Some were equipped on one side with a tall shield, about nine inches high as a rule, and constructed of plied mahogany. These rarities were designed to protect the decanter and its contents from the heat of the fire when being used away from the dining table. More common and for use while still at the table were double coasters either in the form of small jollyboats or mounted on a wheeled framework in the form of a wagon. As the end of the eighteenth century approached, the numbers of people sitting down to dine together increased, and dining tables and chair sets correspondingly increased in length and size. Jollyboats and decanter wagons were a logical development in line with this trend. The prevailing predilection for neo-classical ovals conveniently suited this requirement and many of these double coasters closely followed the designs of the cruet sets which they accompanied. Jollyboats were made in silver, Sheffield plate, mahogany and lacquered papier mâché, the latter being either with or without silver or Sheffield plated mounts. During the nineteenth century the crisp symmetry of the earlier examples evaporated. Early jollyboats and wagons had concealed castors beneath and receptacles for the decanter stoppers visible from above. Nineteenth century decanter wagons on the other hand, by their very nature had wheels, and a handle at one or both ends

Plate 195. An amusing (if utilitarian) decanter wagon. The horizontal members are made of black lacquered papier mâché, while the vertical ones are lacquered brass, as are the handles and wheels. Originally the wheels would have been shod with leather tyres (as indeed might those on colour plate 36, page 181). Slightly better versions would be gilded rather than lacquered brass. When first made the decanters were raised above the surface of the papier mâché on raffia mats, but those seldom survive. Decanter wagons enjoyed very short popularity at the beginning of the 19th century.

to facilitate movement from one diner to the next. Again examples can be found in silver, Sheffield plate and papier mâché and also in gilded copper. Just occasionally, during the Sheffield plating process gold was substituted for silver although this technique is rare and the authors have only seen one example of such a decanter wagon. Ivory embellishments are sometimes found, particularly on the handles and wheels. As miniature examples of carriages of the period they are often to be found with leather tyres although these have frequently long since perished. On better examples of papier mâché, the brass enrichments were gilded, while on lesser examples they were only lacquered. Originally, of course, they would have presented the same appearance.

Colour plate 39. A group of opaque colour twist wine glasses. These are much sought after by collectors, primrose yellow being a particularly rare colour. The glass on the left is a 19th century European copy, the bubbles in the bowl displaying the use of soda glass. The glass second from the right is a delightful rarity, being an air and colour mixed twist.

Colour plate 40. A commemorative goblet made in about 1725-30 and engraved with a medallion portrait of William, Duke of Cumberland. The highlight of his military career was the defeat of the Jacobites at Culloden in 1746 so this may be termed an 'anti-Jacobite' glass. Williamite glasses on the other hand were engraved to commemorate William III's victory at the Battle of the Boyne in 1690. The engraving post-dates the glass by 25-30 years.

190

CHAPTER 12
Drinking Glasses and other Drinking Vessels

Without question the wine antique given the most serious attention of collectors to date is the wine glass. There are many, many books written on this subject and in this chapter we can only hope to give a brief workable history by explaining the principal influences on design and methods of production.

The earliest known drinking glasses date from Roman times, but it was Renaissance Italy which really set the art of the glass maker in a prominent place in the field of decorative arts. The principal province famous for its manufacture was Venice and its products found a ready market throughout Europe and also in England. It is not possible to distinguish between window and vessel glass before, perhaps, the middle of the seventeenth century, but throughout the previous seven centuries at least, vessel glass was being both imported and made here, usually in the same glasshouses as window glass. There is little doubt that vessel glass was a mere fragment of the total output for most of the long period. Many of the glasshouses were ephemeral affairs, set up by families of nomadic makers who settled where ingredients and fuel existed together, and moved on when the fuel was spent. Their products could be very refined, generally in green glass, and strongly influenced, wherever made, by Venice. In England a monopoly was granted by Elizabeth I to John Le Carré, a native of France, in 1567. Monopolies were not granted merely to favour a particular craftsman, but were also a means by which the Crown could raise revenue by charging fees for the privileges granted. Due to internal squabbles amongst his associates, Le Carré was unable to meet all the terms and conditions imposed by the monopoly and in 1574 it fell to a Venetian glass maker who had settled in London, Giacomo Verzelini. A handful of pieces by Verzelini have survived and are in public collections and naturally show a marked Venetian style, albeit demonstrating some English influences. Some pieces are dated (the earliest known being 1577) and most are engraved.

There was considerable Government concern at the wholesale use of woodland as fuel, and by the beginning of the seventeenth century patents were being granted for the making of glass in furnaces fired by coal. Wood was finally banned by Royal Proclamation in 1615 and this date signals the emergence of Sir Robert Mansell who, with other speculators, took over virtual control of the glass industry. The establishment of the major glass centres of London, Bristol, Stourbridge, Newcastle, etc., dates from these times, and there soon followed the Glass Sellers' Company (1664) to

Plate 196. A 16th century Venetian wine goblet with a rounded funnel bowl resting on a stem interrupted by a large knop typically moulded with gadroons, swags and lion masks. It stands on a plain flat foot.

191

Plate 197. A magnificent goblet from the workshop of Giacomo Verzelini, engraved with diamond point and dated 1578. Note the soda glass, the narrowness of sections of the stem and the ribbed knop reminiscent of its Venetian predecessors and yet exhibiting a peculiarly English appearance.

Plate 198. A goblet of the period of George Ravenscroft. The lower section of the bowl has 'nipt diamond waies' decoration above a broadly inverted baluster stem with a ribbed central knop between various shallow annular knops. The almost flat foot is folded. Of particular note is the 'crizzing', a feature of early lead glass before the recipe was perfected. This glass was made in about 1680.

control first the importation and second the sale of glass vessels, as opposed to window glass, the preserve of the Glaziers' Company.

The next individual to have a profound effect on glass making was George Ravenscroft who was responsible for introducing lead glass to England. The addition of lead oxide to the melt was known to the

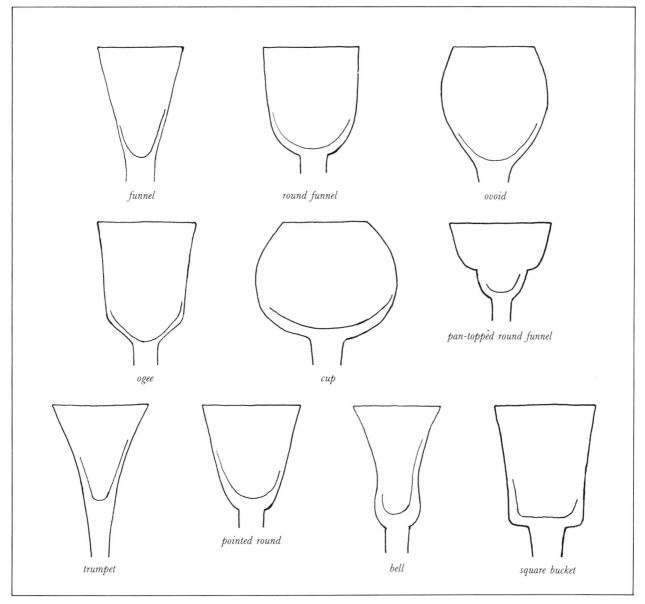

funnel   round funnel   ovoid

ogee   cup   pan-topped round funnel

trumpet   pointed round   bell   square bucket

Figure 4. The most common forms of bowl shapes.

Venetians and others, but it was the English who perfected the technique and who justifiably became famous for the rock crystal-like quality of their glass with its blue-grey or black colour and its weight and robustness. It was the solidity and good handling qualities of lead glass in sharp contrast to the lightweight glass of Venice and Bohemia which gave rise to the development of a distinctly English type of drinking glass which was to become the envy of all Europe for the succeeding one hundred years. It is this development which will be the focus of our attention in the following pages.

There can be little doubt that English drinking glasses are collected for two simple reasons, the first being that a substantial number survive and the second being that there is a wide variety of examples of each of the many types which evolved in the late seventeenth and entire eighteenth century. Because their development was fairly complex, this study becomes easier if it is subdivided on the basis of first, the shape and construction, and second, the decoration.

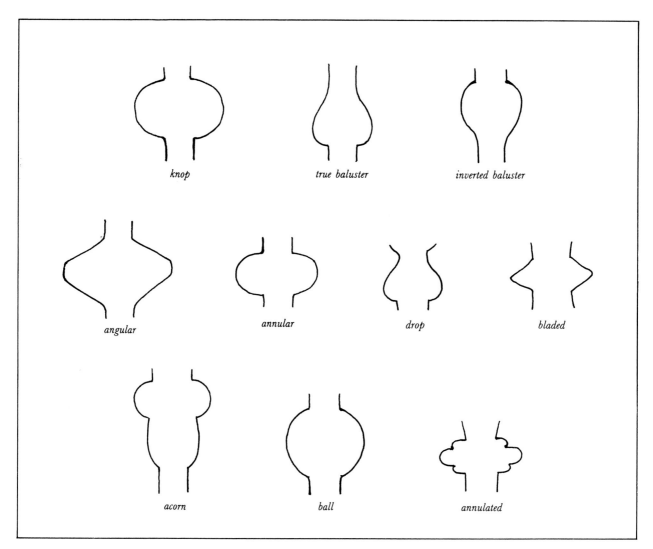

knop   *true baluster*   *inverted baluster*

angular   *annular*   *drop*   *bladed*

acorn   *ball*   *annulated*

Figure 5. Different shapes of the knops on glass stems.

The basic constituent parts of any glass are the bowl, the stem and the foot. Individual glasses are made in parts, the simplest being in two (the bowl and stem being one part, the foot the other), and others (most frequently) being in three, but sometimes in four, five or even six pieces. There are a wide variety of bowl shapes and glasshouses employed the range to maximum effect. It is very difficult to describe each bowl shape in words and for this reason a diagram showing some of the most common forms is included here (figure 4, page 193). Descriptions are also given in some of the captions.

The stem of a drinking glass can be plain or it can have swellings. In glass collecting terminology, these swellings are called 'knops' and the different shapes of knops are, like the bowls, given particular names. These too are illustrated in figure 5, above.

The development of the feet of drinking glasses can more easily be explained verbally. They are usually conical, some being of a sharper angle than others. Some are almost completely flat whereas others enable the stem to start a full three-quarters of an inch above the table level. Where feet are not conical they are usually of domed outline, again of varying heights. Long before English glass had become pre-eminent it had been realised that great strength was to be gained if, when the foot was made,

194

Plate 199. A group of baluster glasses which display some of the many knop forms, the angular, annulated, ball and acorn among them. It should be noted that there are several conical feet and one domed foot and all are folded. The bowls are rounded or straight funnels, but for one, which is bell shaped. They all date from between 1710 and 1730.

Plate 200. A particularly fine and well proportioned drinking glass with a well drawn acorn knop below a rounded funnel bowl and above a base ball knop.

the base rim of the glass was folded underneath, (or very occasionally on top of itself) thus forming a double layer of glass around the edge of the foot. When this technique is employed the glass is said to have a 'folded foot'. It is intended to give extra strength to the rim so that it will not chip when put down. Although this technique had evolved in Venice and was repeated in the Low Countries, it was also widely adopted in England and was used until approximately 1750 to 1760 when it dropped from fashion, only to re- emerge later in the nineteenth century when the revivalist movements made their presence felt.

Another variety of foot is the 'firing' foot. During the eighteenth century there were many drinking societies and during the course of an evening's meeting it was common for one of the members to enjoin the company to drink with him in a toast. In order to signify concurrence with the toast being proposed, the assembled company would bang their glasses repeatedly on the table thus producing a sound like an fusillade of rifle fire, hence the expression 'firing glasses'. To withstand this treatment it was necessary to make the foot of the glass of substantial thickness and indeed their survival bears testimony to their effectiveness.

As previously stated the lead glass produced in England enabled manufacturers in this country to produce wonderfully heavy and solid

Plate 201. A group of glasses showing two light balusters in the centre flanked on the left by two heavy balusters and on the right by two balustroids. They are arranged chronologically from left to right and date from about 1700-1740.

Plate 201. Three Silesian stem glasses of varying complexity.

glasses quite unlike the frail, light soda glass products of the Rhineland and Venice. Glasses made during the period beginning in the 1680s and ending approximately in the middle of the eighteenth century are often collectively referred to as 'balusters' and may be subdivided under the headings 'baluster' (or 'heavy baluster'), 'light baluster' and 'balustroid'. (These terms are used by glass cognoscenti amongst themselves and opinions

196

Plate 203. Two wine glasses of extreme simplicity, but each very well made. The left-hand flute has a single tear drop and the stem and bowl are drawn from a single piece of glass. The right-hand goblet bears a strong resemblance to a popular modern piece of glass. Glasses with cup bowls are often called mead glasses, but this is a very modern term without justification. Both these glasses were made in about 1740.

Plate 204. An unusual wine glass with an ovoid moulded bowl, and a stem with a tear drop large enough to accommodate a coin. The coin is dated 1706 and the glass is probably contemporary.

differ about their precise definitions. There may be some overlapping of the various types depending on personal opinion.) In the very early eighteenth century a typical English drinking glass displayed this new solidity and had a rounded funnel bowl, a heavy baluster stem and a conical folded foot. Just occasionally, the glass forming the foot would be made from a particularly heavy gauge metal and on these occasions the foot is not folded. Also only occasionally, the bowl may be conical or bell-shaped rather than funnel-shaped. The baluster shape of the stem may be the right way up or (more usually) inverted.

During the period 1720 to 1735 heavy balusters gave way to 'light balusters' although the transition from one to the other was not precise, but took place only gradually. As the name implies the baluster stem had become lighter in general feel, (though not necessarily in actual weight). The stems were elongated and the appearance of the knops became less heavy in the process. The rounded funnel or 'trumpet' bowl still predominated, but other shapes were introduced — the waisted funnel, the bell, and occasionally the bucket, the tulip and even the ogee bowl. Towards the end of the period the full range of bowl shapes were employed including the pan top and the double ogee. The folded foot remained the most common type, although it is generally not found on glasses of poor quality.

Most of the light balusters were elegant glasses of some quality, but a contemporary range of cheaper glasses, less well made, existed for a less discriminating market. These are the balustroids, glasses with multiple knopping, often elaborate, but often inept in design. They occur in some quantity and are dateable up to the middle of the century.

Outside the mainstream of design, but made during the same period, are a group of glasses with 'Silesian' stems. Silesia was a glass making area of what is now Czechoslovakia and glasses showing Silesian characteristics were made in England as a mark of respect following the accession of George I to the English throne in 1714. They have moulded stems, tapering inwards from the top, and may be four, six or eight-sided. On drinking glasses such stems were fashionable until about the 1740s.

Probably the most common of all English wine glasses are those with straight stems. These were first made during the second quarter of the eighteenth century and show almost the entire range of bowl shapes. They may be encountered in all different sizes ranging from cordial to giant goblet. Although the folded foot was the commonest form during the period when these straight-stemmed glasses were made, one encounters a higher proportion of plain conical feet than previously, as they were the cheapest kind of glass to produce. A plain stem was sometimes enlivened by the introduction of an air bubble within it. This may have been a small almost spherical bubble immediately beneath the bowl, or it may have been elongated slightly to form a tear drop. Sometimes, although only rarely, this elongation extended downwards so far that the entire stem was hollow. Bubbles are found in the knops of baluster glasses also.

The demise of the baluster stem is often attributed to the Excise Act of 1745 which taxed glass products according to their weight. As the stem contributed largely to overall weight, its reduction was a logical development. However, the trend towards straight-stemmed glasses had already begun and it is more likely that the Act merely accelerated an existing change of fashion. The Act may also have been responsible for the corresponding demise of commemorative coin glasses which seem to have been made during the first half of the eighteenth century (see plate 204, page 197). All examples have baluster stems with fairly pronounced hollow knops in which a small coin has been inserted. Obviously this type of stem is the only form capable of containing an object of this width. The practice was revived in the nineteenth century.

Colour plate 41. A group of five fine drinking glasses. The left-hand two on opaque twist stems are by William and Mary Beilby, the far left-hand example being decorated with a mythical Chinese ho-ho bird (a favourite chinoiserie motif). The other three glasses were all decorated in the workshop of James Giles and display three different stem types, proving that all three types were fashionable within the period that Giles was working (up to 1774).

Colour plate 42. A magnificent large goblet enamelled in polychrome by William and Mary Beilby. It has the royal coat of arms on one side and the Prince of Wales' feathers on the reverse. This is one of a series thought to have been commissioned in 1762 (when the Beilbys started) to commemorate the birth of the future George IV.

Plate 205. A group of air twist glasses. From left to right: a rounded funnel flute; a broad rounded funnel goblet; a bell bowled wine glass; two trumpet bowled wine glasses (the first Jacobite); and an engraved pan top wine glass. They all date from the 1740s. The diminished use of knops is typical and was largely occasioned by increased taxation on the weight of glass.

Plate 206. A group of opaque twist stem glasses. The third and fifth from the left are single series while the others are double. They display a wide range of tape, spiral, corkscrew and gauze forms and date from around the 1760s.

Perhaps the greatest area of interest for the wine glass collector lies within the category of straight-stemmed glasses which followed in about 1750, namely the 'twist' stem. When a gather of glass with several air bubbles in it is drawn out and twisted, the bubbles form a multiple spiral. This process produces the 'air-twist' stem with which collectors are so familiar. A high percentage of air twist glasses have plain, straight stems, though a few are known to have knops, occasionally in the middle of the

Plate 207. A facet stem wine glas of robust simplicity. It is worth noting that the bowl is blown thickly, the stem has shortened and the foot flattened in comparison with glasses of even ten years earlier. The proportions and general deterioration of workmanship signal the decline of English supremacy in wine glass making in the 1770s. Such a glass may be had quite cheaply.

Plate 208. A wine glass similar to the preceding example but of more elegant proportions with a longer stem and higher foot. However, the great feature of this glass is the diamond point stipple engraving which is probably by David Wolff. This very time-consuming technique leaves a light impression which can only be seen with the clarity shown here when placed in a strong light against a dark background.

stem, but more commonly, immediately below the bowl. Very rarely the knop is just above the base. A multiple knop, twist-stem glass is considered a prize possession by collectors.

Between 1755 and 1760 opaque twist stem glasses became popular in which opaque white glass was introduced into the stem and then twisted in the same way as an air bubble. The opaque rods were sometimes of solid form, but more usually were multi-stranded, producing a lace like effect.

Colour plate 43. A Lambeth delftware wine goblet decorated in blue on a white ground in an attempt to copy the products of the Orient and Holland. The initials 'TL' and the date 'August 30 1717' add greatly to its collector interest. Only one other similar goblet is known at the time of writing.

This emulated Venetian latticino glass which had been popular for some time. The first opaque twist stems had single series twists, that is to say there was only one group of threads in the stem whatever the pattern. Soon makers added a second gather of glass and further threads outside, producing a double series twist, a product of increased sophistication (see plate 206, page 200). Double series stems exist in airtwist wine glasses too, but these are as rare as are single series opaques. Further experiments produced stems with both air and opaque white spirals, and the addition of coloured threads was popular in the late 1760s and '70s (see colour plate 39, page 190). Blue, green and red and combinations of these are the most frequently encountered, but probably the acme of achievement is the acquisition of a yellow twist. It seems amazing that the sound practice of employing a folded foot should drop from favour at about the same time that opaque twist stems were being made. Consequently glasses of this type with folded feet are quite uncommon and do not appear at all after about 1760.

By about 1765 to 1770 twisted stem glasses were becoming unfashionable and the glass making industry was developing a new form of decoration. As early as the 1730s and 1740s British craftsmen had been exercising their ingenuity by experimenting with cutting techniques and had met with some success. There are two characteristics necessary to produce cut glass satisfactorily — weight and solidity. Soda glass was

Plate 209. Two glasses of the early 19th century showing the utter degeneration of form. The left-hand glass (perhaps a rummer) is well cut with diamonds, panels, steps and a star, while the right-hand one is amusingly engraved with a couplet and dated '13th January 1807'. It reads: 'Wine wets the wit, improves its nature's force and adds a pleasant flavour to discourse'.

blown particularly thin — indeed that was its attractive quality — but it was usually far too brittle to take a cutter's wheel. Lead glass by contrast enabled this particular technique to be practised to great effect. Cutting appears early on wine glasses but only came into wide popularity in the 1770s. The most solid element of a wine glass is its stem and it was this area which was decorated (see plate 208, page 201). On a typical facet stem drinking glass of the 1770s and later, the stem was cut into small diamond, hexagonal or scale-shaped facets. The decoration extended upwards slightly onto the lowest area of the usually funnel-shaped or ovoid bowl. On very rare specimens the treatment was also applied to the foot. After only a very short period of time the remainder of the bowl was being decorated, but with engraved motifs, initially bands of stars placed immediately below the rim, but towards the turn of the century neo-classical swags, shield-shaped cartouches and monograms within formal borders.

In various forms faceted glass saw the retail glass trade through to the end of the century, by which time the stems of drinking glasses were becoming progressively shorter and rummers and other large capacity

Plate 210. A light baluster wine glass of a type associated with Newcastle, with a finely wheel-engraved band of baroque decoration on the bowl and foot It dates from about 1740.

Plates 211 and 212. A very fine light baluster goblet with a complex knop stem and a conical foot. The wheel-engraved bowl is of exceptional quality and interest (see detail). It has long been held that such glasses were made in Newcastle and engraved in Holland. It seems perfectly reasonable however that they may have been made there as well. The detail shows a drinking party seated at table with a floor length tablecloth, contained in a scrolled baroque cartouche. In common with paintings of the period note that wine glasses are held by the foot. The glass dates from the 1740s.

vessels were being increasingly used. In 1835, when the glass excise tax, and consequently restrictions on weight, were finally lifted, cutting tended to become deeper and design more exuberant. During the nineteenth century machinery was introduced to the industry and steam-driven cutting tools enabled decorators to produce fine patterns on thinly blown glass.

The four major centres of the glass industry were London, Bristol, Stourbridge and Newcastle but it is very difficult to say exactly where most pieces were made. Recent research refutes the theory that early Newcastle glasses are mostly typified by an elongated light baluster or balustroid stem and, even in those instances where the stem is plain, are of unusually narrow proportions. Many were also said to be characterised by a narrow band of exquisite quality engraving around the rim of the bowl, varying from half an inch to one inch in depth (see plate 210, page 203).

A great many eighteenth century glasses were engraved. In the first instance it was common practice to engrave the bowl of the glass with a

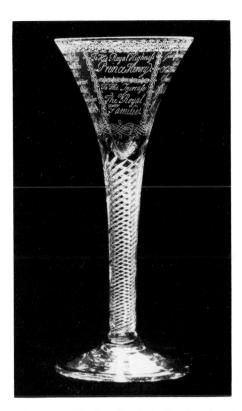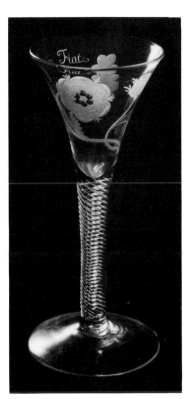

Plate 213. A flute glass decorated with ears of barley clearly indicating that this glass was for the consumption of ale. Similar glasses may be decorated with hops or vines which are equally clear allusions.

Plate 214. One of the few surviving wine glasses engraved in diamond point with the Stuart National Anthem. This anthem, which ran to several verses and supported the Jacobite pretenders to the throne in exile, always finished with the word 'Amen', hence the name of these glasses. They are among the most sought after glasses by collectors and are usually given names after the famous collections in which they have at one time been. This glass, now in Harveys Wine Museum, is known as the 'Russell Glass'.

Plate 215. A Jacobite glass very similar in form to the more highly prized Amen glass, but engraved with the rose, the pair of buds and the oak leaf associated with the Jacobite cause. It is also engraved with the word 'Fiat' making the association even more firmly attributable. Despite their defeat in 1745, Jacobite fervour remained strong in the 1750s which was when this glass was made. Normally of course the word 'Fiat' would be read from the outside of the glass, but here we have reversed the photograph to make it readable.

symbol to signify its contents. Thus one might encounter a tall, thin glass engraved with an apple moth, a twig with leaves and an apple or two. Quite clearly such a glass was intended for cider. Other glasses were engraved with hops or barley (for the consumption of ale) and yet more with grapes and vine leaves. Engraved decoration also reflected prevailing styles. The Rococo, for example, was represented by wheel- and occasionally diamond-point engraved chinoiserie decoration or fruit and flowers. On some pieces bunches of grapes and vine leaves and tendrils proliferated. Engraving was sometimes combined with oil-gilded decoration.

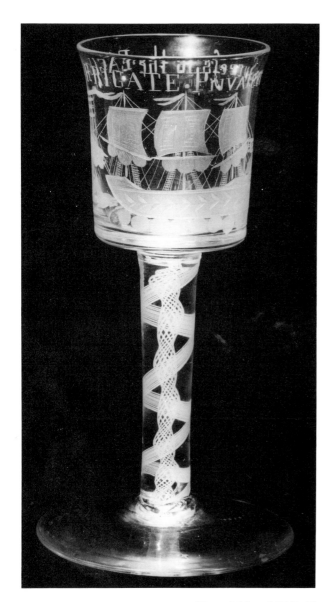

Plates 216 and 217. Two 'privateer' glasses. Privateers were privately owned frigates which, for monetary reward, harassed enemy shipping. Most of them sailed from Bristol. The most successful was the Eagle frigate which plate 216 shows. However this is a fake and compares very unfavourably for quality with the genuine glass in plate 217. Privateers are some of the most copied of all glasses. Both of these purport to date from the late 1750s — one does!

Very popular subjects for engraved decoration were flowers and leaves and many of them have obvious Jacobite associations. Some are extremely explicit, others less so, and some no doubt have been misconstrued as bearing Jacobite emblems when they do not. Among the former are a series known as 'Amen' glasses on which the entire Jacobite version of the National Anthem may be found, usually ending with the word 'Amen', hence the name (see plate 214, page 205). Equally forthright are those with portraits of Prince Charles Edward, usually in Highland costume. Less obvious are those with mottoes, the most common of which is the single

Plate 218. A group of glasses showing different types and capacities. On the left are three goblets of varying sizes, the third one being a so-called mead glass (see plate 203, page 197). Next to it is a wine glass of distinctly smaller capacity, a common size in the mid-18th century. Fifth from the left is a flute engraved with barley ears indicating its use for ale, though similar glasses were used for cider, perry or champagne. Next to it is a ratafia glass with its very narrow flute bowl, while the right-hand glass is a cordial.

word 'Fiat' (see plate 215, page 205). These are almost always accompanied by engravings of roses and rosebuds (emblems signifying the Old Pretender and his younger sons), oak leaves and stars and sometimes the thistle with its Scottish allusion. A vast number of surviving glasses display some of these symbols, but are without the word 'Fiat' and may or may not have alluded to the cause. They can vary considerably in quality. No doubt when drinking with people of similar persuasions a Jacobite supporter would have been prepared to use one of his more obvious glasses, whereas when he was in the company of people whose opinions he did not know, one suspects that his less explicit glasses were used and if comment were made, the symbols were passed off as mere decoration. We do know for sure that water was frequently found on the table and when drinking a toast to the King a Jacobite would swing his glass across the table before taking the wine to his lips so that he could be seen to be drinking to the King 'across the water'. True Jacobite glasses date to within a few years of the rebellion of 1745, but many others with only Jacobite-type decoration date from the 1750s and 1760s and their attribution is in doubt.

Glasses have also survived with decoration alluding to or commemorating many other causes, events and personalities, William III's victory in Ireland and Nelson's naval successes being examples. A number of eighteenth century glasses are known with engravings of ships and the words 'Success to the...' followed by the name of a privateer around the rim. It seems likely that these originated in Bristol, a major port from which privateers set sail. Occasionally glasses are found simply engraved with the crest or coat of arms of their owner.

Plate 219. Part of a 19th century drinking service including two different sizes of decanter and a variety of drinking glasses. In descending capacities these are: goblet, red wine, white wine, hock, sherry (or port) and two sizes of liqueur. In addition there are three sizes of beaker or tumbler and (not shown in the photograph) a water jug. Not included in this particular set, though common in some, are finger bowls, carafes, jelly and custard glasses and ice plates.

Some of the most delightful glasses are those, decorated in enamels, which came from the manufactory of William and Mary Beilby (see page 154). In order to achieve the desired effect the decoration was painted in enamel colours and then fired onto the glass. A high percentage of surviving examples have white decoration applied to the bowl. The most simple have merely trailing vines with bunches of grapes, but more elaborate examples have little vignettes or landscapes. A considerable series were enamelled with armorials of local families in rich colours. The grandest of these carried the Royal Arms on one side and the Prince of Wales feathers on the reverse. These glasses, of which at present only nine examples are known, are said to commemorate the birth of George III's firstborn son in 1762 (see colour plate 42, page 199). Apart from armorials, the workshop produced very little work in colour. Coloured landscapes are

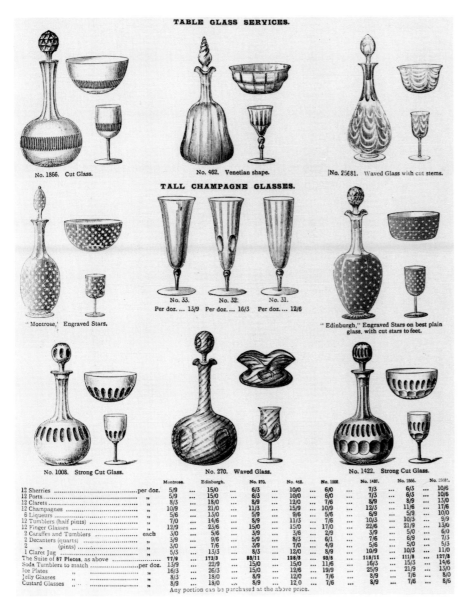

TABLE GLASS SERVICES.

No. 1866. Cut Glass. No. 462. Venetian shape. No. 25681. Waved Glass with cut stems.

TALL CHAMPAGNE GLASSES.

No. 33. Per doz. ... 13/9 No. 32. Per doz. ... 16/3 No. 31. Per doz. ... 12/6

"Montrose," Engraved Stars. "Edinburgh," Engraved Stars on best plain glass, with cut stars to feet.

No. 1008. Strong Cut Glass. No. 270. Waved Glass. No. 1422. Strong Cut Glass.

	Montrose.		Edinburgh.		No. 270.		No. 462.		No. 1008.		No. 1422.		No. 1866.		No. 25681.
12 Sherries ....per doz.	5/9	...	15/0	...	6/3	...	10/0	...	6/0	...	7/3	...	6/3	...	10/6
12 Ports........................ "	5/9	...	15/0	...	6/3	...	10/0	...	6/0	...	7/3	...	6/3	...	10/6
12 Clarets........................ "	8/3	...	18/0	...	8/9	...	12/0	...	7/6	...	8/9	...	8/9	...	13/0
12 Champagnes .... "	10/9	...	21/0	...	11/3	...	15/9	...	10/9	...	12/3	...	11/6	...	17/6
6 Liqueurs .... "	5/6	...	13/0	...	5/9	...	9/6	...	5/6	...	6/9	...	5/9	...	10/0
12 Tumblers (half pints) .... "	7/0	...	14/6	...	8/9	...	11/3	...	7/6	...	10/3	...	10/3	...	9/9
12 Finger Glasses .... "	12/9	...	23/6	...	15/0	...	15/0	...	17/0	...	22/6	...	21/9	...	13/0
2 Caraffes and Tumblers ....each	3/0	...	5/6	...	3/9	...	3/6	...	2/9	...	3/9	...	5/0	...	6/0
2 Decanters (quarts) .... "	3/9	...	9/6	...	5/9	...	8/3	...	6/1	...	7/6	...	6/9	...	7/3
2 (pints) .... "	3/0	...	7/6	...	3/9	...	7/0	...	4/9	...	5/6	...	5/0	...	5/3
1 Claret Jug .... "	5/3	...	13/3	...	8/3	...	12/0	...	8/9	...	10/9	...	10/3	...	11/0
The Suite of 87 Pieces, as above	77/9	...	173/3	...	93/11	...	128/3	...	93/6	...	115/11	...	111/8	...	127/3
Soda Tumblers to match ....per doz.	13/9	...	22/9	...	15/0	...	15/0	...	11/6	...	16/3	...	15/3	...	14/6
Ice Plates " .... "	16/3	...	26/3	...	15/0	...	12/6	...	19/9	...	25/9	...	21/9	...	13/0
Jelly Glasses " .... "	8/3	...	18/0	...	8/9	...	12/0	...	7/6	...	8/9	...	7/6	...	8/0
Custard Glasses " .... "	8/9	...	18/0	...	8/9	...	12,0	...	7/6	...	8/9	...	7/6	...	8/6

Any portion can be purchased at the above price.

Plate 220. A page from the 1902 catalogue of the Army & Navy Stores showing different glass patterns available at that time. The price list indicates that a full suite of 87 pieces (for a dozen people) could cost anything from 77/9d (i.e. just short of £4.00) to 173/3d (approximately £8.66).

extremely rare and, in general, the use of colour was restricted to minor detail on a very few glasses.

The use of gilding on glass is seldom seen. A series of decorated glasses is attributable to the atelier of James Giles, and these are gilded with fruiting vines, hops and barley, and neat bouquets of garden flowers with attendant insects. William Absolom of Great Yarmouth was another independent decorator of both china and glass, who embellished goblets in unfired (or cold) gilding with a series of naïve subjects, such as local buildings, coaches and various military toasts. Yarmouth Church and local

Plate 221. A typical toasting glass of the mid-18th century. Few of these glasses survive because traditionally, having consumed the contents, those toasting one another would snap the stem between their fingers.

ships are sometimes portrayed. (The same subjects are however more often engraved.)

Like decanters, drinking glasses were made in a wide range of sizes. The smallest are known normally as 'cordials', when eighteenth century, and 'liqueur' glasses, when nineteenth. The next size up are simply 'wine glasses' while larger glasses with a capacity say, of six fluid ounces or more, are known as 'goblets'. Outsize goblets, which may not necessarily have been used as drinking vessels, are referred to as 'large', 'giant' or 'mammoth'. Tall thin glasses are called flutes and exceedingly narrow flutes are known as 'ratafias', ratafia being a liqueur or cordial flavoured with fruits and or, more particularly, their kernels. Different members of the glass collecting fraternity try to classify the various capacities in a strict sequence, but, as different glasses within the same set may vary only marginally and there is no historical precedent for such classification, it can be rather confusing to those who do not share the same credo.

The last quarter of the eighteenth century saw the introduction of suites of glass with decanters and various sizes of drinking glasses all decorated to match. By the nineteenth century, the practice was considerably extended, in line with the fashion for service 'à la Russe' and a complete set may have comprised a dozen or more glasses for each place setting. The smallest were for liqueurs then, in ascending order, the remainder were for brandy, port, sherry, white wine, hock and red wine. In addition there may have been up to three different sizes of beaker for water or fruit juices, as well as champagne flutes and goblets (also for wine, but of larger capacities than ordinary glasses). Matching decanters, of more than one size, may also have been present and also water jugs, ice plates, and jelly and custard glasses. An interesting extra, also en suite, might have been a carafe and tumbler which a guest might have taken to his room for overnight use. These enormous sets could be purchased more or less plain, although most were engraved or etched and almost all were, to a greater or lesser extent, cut. De luxe sets would be additionally gilded. Some were moulded in a wavy form of decoration.

There are three types of glasses which do not fall within the accepted range of types, but which should be included here. The first (for true romantics) is the 'toasting' glass, a glass with a very tall, very slender stem and invariably with a trumpet bowl. Having 'touched bowls', producing the familiar clink, the drinkers would consume the wine and break the stems of glasses by simply snapping them in the hand. Also used for toasting, was the 'toastmaster's' or 'deceptive' glass, in which the (again) trumpet-shaped bowl is blown with very thick sides producing a capacity which appears normal for the size of the glass, but which is in fact even less than a cordial. Their origin is obvious and relies on the need for the toastmaster to keep a clear head while the rest of the party are free to indulge themselves (see plate 222, overleaf). Finally, there are trick glasses

Colour plate 44. A magnificent silver-gilt wine goblet and cover, most elegantly engraved with scallop shells and lozenges. The complex knopped stem and terraced foot are very similar to contemporary Venetian glasses. This was made in London in 1598 and stands 16½ ins. high.

Plate 223. A trick beaker which dates from the beginning of the 19th century. A careful look at the photograph will reveal that the sides of the glass are double skinned and that the liquid is only between the cavity formed by the two skins, the centre of the glass being empty. Such a light-hearted piece was probably part of a conjuror's equipment.

of various types. One is in the form of a tumbler (though stemmed examples are known), and has completely hollow sides. A red liquid simulating wine is introduced through a hole in the bottom which is then sealed with a cork and a liberal dressing of wax. These were possibly made as theatrical props or conjuror's accessories or even merely as a joke (see plate 223, above). One recently came to light with the date 1823 engraved on it with a diamond point. Another is engraved with a border of flowerheads all, except say four, of which are drilled through the centre. Those who know drink from the intact side; the uninitiated drink from where they please and are doused with wine accordingly, to the diversion of their friends.

Drinking vessels

Glass was of course not the only material used for drinking vessels. What of the period prior to Mansell and Ravenscroft? It has always been well known that silver and gold do not taint the flavour of wine and though there may be a few dedicated wine buffs who disagree with this theory, it cannot be denied that silver was, and still is, the medium mostly chosen by professional wine tasters for their tastevins. In any event, before the advent of glass as a commercially viable medium for domestic drinking vessels, wine cups or goblets were made in silver and or gold or silver gilt.

There are two basic categories of early silver or silver-gilt cups. The first comprises rather grand 'standing' cups (see colour plate 44, page 211) which invariably had lids, though these have not always survived. The huge variety of styles, together with the rule that they were always decorated, usually to a very high degree, indicates that they were objects of some considerable status and were principally intended for display. Although no doubt some were actually used for drinking wine, this use was probably ceremonial and because of this they are really outside the scope of this book. On close inspection many are shown to be of secondary quality in so far as the silver is of thin gauge and the repoussé or other decoration is not well executed. A number of seventeenth century examples of these cups have survived in turned wood, most of them skilfully decorated with armorial devices. Their exact purpose is unclear, but was probably ritual. Large silver standing cups, sometimes called

Plate 222. A deceptive glass of about 1820. The thick walls are quite apparent in this photograph, but when filled with wine, refraction makes it difficult to appreciate at a casual glance that the glass is not a normal one. When toastmasters were obliged to keep a clear head such a device was invaluable.

Plate 224. *A wine cup delightfully engraved in the interior with flowing scrolls and stylised flowers. The hallmarks are for 1592 and the maker's mark can clearly be seen on the rim. The wide bowl is typical of 16th century wine cups.*

Plate 225. *A wine cup of 1636. Were it made in glass it would be said to have a rounded funnel bowl and the stem is clearly an inverted baluster with knops above and below. Such utter simplicity was fashionable in the 1630s and '40s and there are some who would say that this design has never been improved.*

'loving cups', are of course still passed ceremonially at dinners, particularly at those held by the various livery companies and guilds.

The second category includes a smaller, simpler variey of cup known merely as the wine cup or goblet. Although dating back to the early Middle Ages, by the 1570s their form had been standardised and a typical example had a shallow saucer-shaped bowl, not dissimilar to a champagne saucer, and a stem formed as an inverted baluster of rather angular proportions below two elements of spool turning. Beneath the baluster was a further turned element above a spreading conical foot of low profile, usually with one or two stepped mouldings at the rim. Towards the close of the sixteenth century the baluster slimmed down and the turned elements above and below it diminished. Perhaps the most notable change was that the bowl became deeper and closer in shape to the rounded funnel bowls seen on later glasses. By about 1600 most wine cups were being decorated. Between about 1610 and 1620 they became quite tall with very elongated stems and the bowls were decorated with strapwork and foliage. However,

Plate 226. Fashionable during the middle of the 17th century were stemless wine cups, where the rather flat-bottomed bowl sat straight on a trumpet foot. This example has lobed decoration with panels of matting. It was made in 1650 during the Commonwealth and may be compared with the previous plate for having much thinner metal used in its construction. Soon after this was made glass superseded silver as the principal medium for wine vessels.

decoration soon became unfashionable again and during the 1630s, when a large number seem to have been made, the average wine cup was quite plain. The rounded funnel bowl became wider at the base and evolved into an ogee shape. Occasionally a bucket bowl may be found of this date. However, whatever the precise shape, the base of the bowl was no longer pointed and the sides were almost vertical. The bowl was raised from a single piece of metal and better quality examples were cleverly arranged so that in the finishing the rim was of fairly substantial thickness to prevent the bowl from tearing. The majority had stems composed of more or less baluster elements and display a lovely balance in their design.

During the years of the Commonwealth a new form of cup evolved with a bucket-shaped bowl. They were almost without exception stemless and had high, conical or trumpet-shaped feet joined directly to the base of the bowl. Most commonly they had repoussé or flat-chased decoration, usually arranged geometrically in panels, but occasionally they had acanthus leaf or other floral decoration. These straight-sided bowls with their flat bottoms sometimes appeared lobed when viewed from the top.

Examples of these various forms were made until the 1660s and 1670s after which their manufacture suddenly declined. It was not until the last quarter of the eighteenth century that a substantial number of silver and silver-gilt goblets were made again. Typically these later examples were of about half pint capacity and had ovoid bowls generally following the form of other silver of the period. A high percentage of surviving pieces bear presentation inscriptions and whereas those made at the beginning of the period were frequently decorated with bright-cutting and wrigglework, towards 1800 they tended by and large to be undecorated. For the most part they seem to have been made in pairs and this, together with the fact that surviving early seventeenth century examples are to be found with

Plate 227. A pair of parcel-gilt silver wine goblets typical of late 18th century silversmithing. Most goblets of this type were presentation pieces, but the inscriptions on these are far better than many. The wording, the sentiments and name of the recipient or donor may add much value to an otherwise ordinary pair of goblets. Typically they have ovoid bowls and trumpet bases and in this instance are resting on square plinths. These were made in 1795.

pricked initials, gives rise to the speculation that they may traditionally have been made as wedding gifts. During the nineteenth century many styles were revived and consequently a large number of silver, silver plate and electroplate cups are to be encountered which at a glance might appear to be seventeenth century, but which on close inspection turn out to be examples of revivalism.

It is perhaps difficult for us to appreciate in the twentieth century that some of the objects which we take for granted today were at one time of great rarity and correspondingly of great value. In this category come both the coconut and the ostrich egg. In the sixteenth and seventeenth centuries, both these items, having had their tops removed, were mounted in silver or gold. The foot or lid was often formed from the part of the object cut away to make the cup. Drinking cups were also made in the seventeenth

Plate 228. A cylindrical beaker with a slightly tapering body with a flared or everted lip. It is pricked with the initials 'RRS' and dated '1686', although it was made in 1680 and bears the appropriate hallmarks. The running band of acanthus leaf decoration around the base is typical of that period and the base is strengthened by a complex wire moulding.

century in treen, generally to contemporary silver patterns. Again, further examples were made during the nineteenth century. Some of the best pieces were mounted in silver. Beakers and wine cups and goblets of similar form were sometimes made in horn.

Also during the seventeenth century it became fashionable for persons of quality to carry with them when travelling a set (usually a pair) of silver tumblers in a leather case. Samuel Pepys recorded in his diary in 1664 'Thence home, taking two silver tumblers which I have bought'. Tumblers were raised from a single piece of silver, the rounded base being left proportionately thicker to provide stability. The outer surface was sometimes engraved with the crest, coat of arms or name of the owner and often with the date. During the latter part of the seventeenth and early part of the eighteenth century tumblers were included in more sophisticated travelling cases together with a set of cutlery, a nutmeg grater, spice box, corkscrew and other essentials for the table. At this time tumbler cups temporarily replaced the straight-sided beaker as the most common drinking vessel in the average domestic household. They are differentiated from beakers by having rounded, as opposed to flat, bases. (A set of four treen tumbler cups are clearly shown in the engraving on plate 248.) Beakers often have an applied moulding for added stability around the base but this is not always the case. Many people regard tumblers and beakers as being synonymous. Although always made in a wide variety of materials, in the twentieth century the beaker shape has been adopted for the average informal drinking glass.

CHAPTER 13
Wine Furniture

The earliest piece of furniture particularly associated with wine is the side table. Paintings of the late seventeenth and early eighteenth centuries often show at the edge of a dining room a marble-topped table of fairly small dimensions, upon which were kept the accoutrements of wine drinking. As already explained in the chapter on drinking habits, all the serving and drinking equipment was held away from the dining table until a diner required to drink. When summoned a servant would bring the ready-charged glass from the side and, as soon as it was empty, remove it. The prevailing fashion in furniture design when these tables were first made dictated that they had cabriole legs and these were joined by a framework composed of a complex moulding some four or five inches deep. Within this moulding there may or may not have been a drawer for storage of the napkins, corkscrews and other accessories necessary for the serving of the wine. Colour plate 8, page 33, shows just such a table. It is commonly thought that all marble-topped tables of this type were pier tables, that is, they were placed against the piers between the windows of a room. Without doubt some elegant and highly decorative examples did occupy this position, but the wine table fulfilled a different function and was by comparison relatively plain. A pier table was also taller than a serving table — needing to cover the dado rail which normally stood thirty-four to

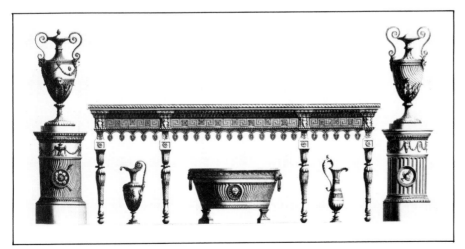

Plate 229. A design for a neo-classical side table flanked by two different designs of pedestals with urns and with a cellaret or wine cooler below. The ribbed decoration on the cellaret and the left-hand pedestal bear interesting comparison with the wine cooler in plate 106, page 116. This design, by Robert and James Adam, was for Osterley Park and, although executed during the 1770s, was not published until 1822.

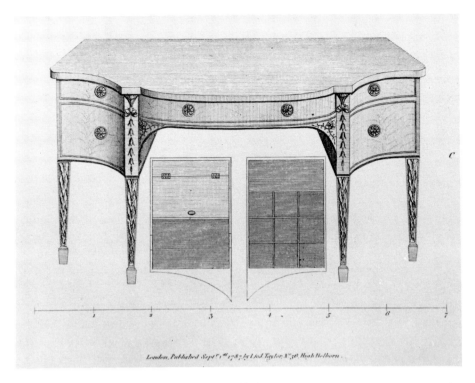

Plate 230. A plate from George Hepplewhite's Cabinet Maker and Upholsterer's Guide *published posthumously in 1788. This is perhaps everybody's idea of what an elegant sideboard should be; serpentine in shape and with a silver-drawer flanked by drawers and cupboards. Although only four legs are shown, six in reality would have been fitted. The centre of the plate is taken with two alternative fitments for the cellaret drawer and the text makes it quite plain what their purpose is.*

thirty-six inches above the floor. The average table height was approximately twenty-eight inches. A few wine tables were made with a raised, moulded lip which was designed to contain any spillage which may have occurred.

During the first half of the eighteenth century this small table was gradually enlarged until, by the 1760s, more often than not it too covered the dado and stood some thirty-six inches high. It had a wooden rather than a marble top, sometimes with a shallow drawer underneath. It was flanked by a pair of cupboards, on top of which stood two large wooden urns. The cupboards, which were approximately square and of bottle-sized dimensions, could have one of several functions. They usually contained on the one hand, racks for the warming of plates over a tray of hot coals, while on the other, they were fitted either as a wine cooler or cellaret, or more probably as a basin in which to rinse the glasses and silver plate. George Hepplewhite, in his *Cabinet Maker & Upholsterer's Guide*, referred to a pedestal included in one of his designs as 'used as a pot cupboard'. The urns above either supplied water for the basin, in which case they were lead-lined and fitted with a tap, or they were fitted with divisions for holding cutlery. By the 1780s the different components of this ensemble had been variously combined to form the 'sideboard' which soon became an important feature in the dining room and the principal piece of furniture from which food and drink were dispensed.

Plate 231. *A serpentine mahogany sideboard modelled approximately on the designs in the previous plate, though with embellishments quite in keeping with other patterns in the book. Unusual features in this board are the three pull-out slides beneath the top and the centre legs which are canted. Although appearing to have five drawers, it has in fact only three — the outer ones each simulate two drawers; each has been fitted with divisions to hold bottles.*

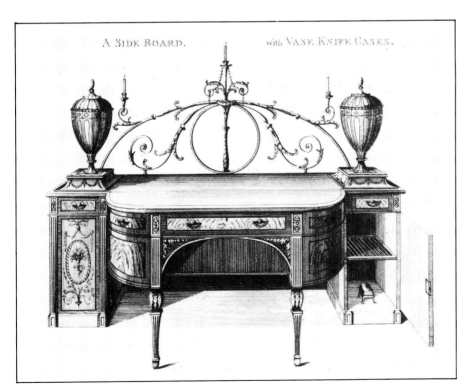

Plate 232. *A sideboard with vase knife cases from Thomas Sheraton's* The Cabinet Maker and Upholsterer's Drawing Book, *1802, showing a combination of Adam and Hepplewhite designs. The pedestal on the right shows provision for warming plates. The cooling and storing of wine and the rinsing of glass and plate could also be catered for within the pedestals.*

Plate 233. A large early 19th century mahogany pedestal sideboard. Notice the brass rail superstructure to take curtains to prevent the walls from being splashed during serving and the simple Greek key inlay and lion's mask handles. However, the interesting aspect of this piece is that one drawer bears the trade label of Blease and Seddon of 24 Dover Street, London. Thomas Seddon was a famous cabinet maker and this partnership survived from 1802 to 1809 from whence this piece dates.

Sideboards can be found in many qualities and a variety of shapes and forms. Commonly they have six legs, four at the front and two at the back, and they may be straight, bow or serpentine-fronted. They may be plain or decorated with inlay. Their dimensions vary greatly, the smallest being perhaps little more than three feet long and the largest in excess of twelve feet.

The standard late eighteenth century form of sideboard consisted of a shallow central drawer flanked by a pair of cupboards, a pair of drawers or one of each. Designs for these were included in the famous eighteenth century pattern books of George Hepplewhite, Thomas Sheraton and others. By about 1810, if not a little earlier, additional space was provided by the extension of the side sections down to the ground to form pedestals. The central drawer remained intact, thereby retaining their essentially 'kneehole' appearance.

The next development was an upwards projection of the pedestals and the provision of a wooden splashboard to join them together. This replaced the brass rail hung with curtains which had previously been fitted from the 1770s onwards to the back of the sideboard to prevent the wall from being splashed with food and wine. By the 1820s sideboards had attained quite grandiose proportions but there was sufficient space below the central

Colour plate 45 . A very grand suite of sideboard furniture comprising a side table, a pair of pedestals and urns and a wine cooler. This set was supplied to Harewood House in 1771 and was made to complement the Robert Adam interior. It was probably designed and certainly made by Thomas Chippendale. Overall the pieces are embellished with an almost complete vocabulary of neo-classical motifs and are among the most splendid examples of furniture made in 18th century England.

drawer to hold a free-standing wine cooler. This separation of a part of the sideboard specifically designated for wine from the main body of the piece soon became the norm and although sideboards were made throughout the nineteenth century those made after 1850 very seldom made any provision for wine at all.

Very frequently people who are not accustomed to the precise terminology used by furniture historians will mention, when discussing furniture, an object called a 'wine table'. This expression is modern and probably derives from the need of people at parties for a small table on which to stand their wine glass. These are, of course, correctly called 'occasional' or tripod tables and it should be noted that modern reproductions, of which numerous examples abound, are usually of considerably lower height than their eighteenth century prototypes.

A rare type of tripod table which was clearly designed as a wine drinking accoutrement, was that made with the edge fretted to allow wine glasses to hang downwards for storage. An example illustrated in plate 234, overleaf, has an additional superstructure which will accommodate twelve decanters in various sizes. Similar to this is a probably unique silver tripod

Plate 234. A very rare mahogany wine table. The slots around the circumference of the top allow glasses to be stored bowl down, while the superstructure will accommodate three large and nine smaller decanters. The tripod base is quite typical of a mid-18th century piece of domestic furniture.

made by the firm of Edward Aldridge in 1760. It holds thirty-one stemless glasses in a pyramidal arrangement of three tiers.

As we have already mentioned, during the closing years of the eighteenth century it became fashionable to seat more people in the dining room than had previously been the practice. Mid-eighteenth century dining tables normally seat six, eight or perhaps ten people at the most whereas by the close of the century dining tables to seat two dozen or more guests were being constructed. At the end of the meal, when the ladies retired the men remained together to drink (a practice which still obtains in some households today). The servants were dismissed at this point so that conversation of a confidential or bawdy nature could be conducted and this meant that the fire which heated the room was no longer tended. The gentlemen would therefore sometimes gather around a 'drinking' table set in front of the chimneypiece to take comfort from the last of the glowing embers. These normally mahogany drinking tables were formed as a

Plate 235. A mahogany horseshoe drinking table of an early date. Such a piece would be accommodated around a fireplace where men would gather to drink after the ladies had left the dining room. The decanters in their coasters were protected from the glare of the fire and rotated along an inner radius. Most tables of this nature date from the 19th century and have turned legs, but this, with its square tapered ones, may date it to the closing years of the 18th century.

semi-circle with the centre section removed. On the inside edge of the table was a track on which ran and pivoted one, or two, coasters. The drinkers would sit on the outside of the table while allowing their wine to coast along the inside. Usually suspended beneath the inside of the table was a net. There are references which suggest that this contained biscuits, but it seems far more likely to have been a safety precaution in the event of one of the decanters accidentally falling over the edge. Although examples of this kind of drinking table are known dating from the 1790s, most commonly they date from the 1820s and 1830s and appear not to have been made very often after the 1840s.

A design by Hepplewhite published in 1793 shows what he describes as a 'Gentleman's Social Table' (see plate 236, overleaf). This appears to be a variation on the theme of the drinking table described above, but it is quite a bit smaller, being 4 feet wide as opposed to 6 feet or more. It has, however, one feature quite unlike the drinking table, an additional piece of furniture which stands in the space normally occupied by the net. Hepplewhite describes it thus — 'a pillar and claw stand in the hollow part, the top of ditto turned to receive five tin bottle cases'. Today it might more accurately be described as a tripod table, the top being formed as a revolving cylinder made of tin or copper and with a mahogany top cut with five holes, each of which contained a metal cylinder to receive a bottle. There seems to be only one known surviving example of this type of furniture which appeared on the market a few years ago and which is illustrated in plate 237. No social or drinking tables seem to have been made after the middle of the nineteenth century, one of the latest being perhaps that at Sherborne Castle, made of oak and varnished to the yellowish colour so fashionable at the time.

Another, but very common, piece of wine furniture is the bottle tray.

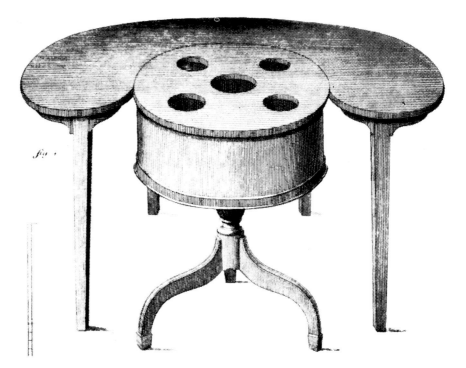

Plate 236. A 'Gentleman's Social Table' — a design by George Hepplewhite for which the following plate appears to be the only known interpretation.

Plate 237. A mahogany table closely based on the design in the previous plate. Artistic and fashionable licence has been taken in the treatment of the legs of both the table and the bottle holder and this is a very rare, if not unique, ensemble.

Plate 238. A horseshoe-shaped drinking table which must be among the very last of its kind to be made. The centre can be filled with the leaf shown on the left and the legs show the Gothic revivalist influence to be found on much furniture of the 1830s and '40s.

Plate 239. Two mahogany bottle holders, one with six divisions, the other with four. The left-hand example has a brass handle and the divisions are fitted with canted sides and are lined with baize. The right-hand example, with its fretted wood handle, has a curious slat formation to hold the bottles and, being made right at the end of the 18th century, is perhaps some twenty years later than the left-hand example.

Plate 240. One of a pair of mahogany bottle holders, each for four bottles, the divisions having canted sides. Plain, dark, rather straight-grained wood was favoured for such pieces.

This, as the name implies, is simply an object made to transport wine from the cellar to the dining or eating room. They survive in quite large numbers, but are much collected. Bottle trays were made to hold an even number of bottles, two, four, six or occasionally even eight. They are rectangular in shape and divided into bottle-sized partitions. The sides are approximately three inches high and shaped at the appropriate end to support the neck of the bottle, when lying horizontally. They have a facility for carrying — a handle, either in brass or mahogany. Some were equipped with blocks to hold the bottles more securely and they were sometimes lined with baize. The addition of mouldings gives quality to the piece. Bottle trays are a remarkably practical accessory because, used with

A BOTTLE TRAY,

£. s. d.

To hold two bottles, a partition acrofs the middle, the ends
cut to receive the neck of the bottles - - - - - - - - 0 3 3

EXTRAS.

If made to hold more than two bottles, each hole - - - -	0	0	4
Fitting in hollow blocks to hold the body of the bottles, each	0	0	9
If with angle blocks, each - - - - - - - - - - - -	0	0	2
An aftragal on the edge of each fide, end, or partition, when ftraight - - - - - - - - - - - - - - -	0	0	1½
Ditto on the edge of the bottom - - - - - - - - - -	0	0	4
Lipping the bottom for cloth - - - - - - - - - - -	0	0	3
Lining ditto with cloth - - - - - - - - - - - - -	0	0	2
Lining each hole - - - - - - - - - - - - - - - -	0	0	3
A plinth round the bottom - - - - - - - - - - - -	0	0	6
Putting on a metal handle - - - - - - - - - - - -	0	0	3
A fingle one to be extra - - - - - - - - - - - - -	0	0	6
Oiling and polifhing - - - - - - - - - - - - - -	0	0	3

A SQUARE BOTTLE CARRIER,

To hold four bottles upright, the edge of the bottom
and rim rounded - - - - - - - - - - - - - - - - 0 3 3

EXTRAS.

Each extra bottle hole - - - - - - - - - - - - - -	0	0	7
Fixing a metal handle - - - - - - - - - - - - - -	0	0	3
Lipping the bottom for cloth - - - - - - - - - - -	0	0	3
Lining ditto with cloth - - - - - - - - - - - - -	0	0	2
A fingle one to be extra - - - - - - - - - - - - -	0	0	6
Oiling and polifhing - - - - - - - - - - - - - -	0	0	3

Plate 241 (left). A page from the 1793 edition of the Cabinet Maker's Book of Prices. It can be seen that this simple item seems cheap, but every small embellishment costs a little more. If for example, the left-hand piece in Plate 239 costs a basic 3/3d., but there is an extra 1/4d for the additional holes, 1/- for six of the angle blocks in each division, 5d for lipping and lining the bottom with cloth, and 3d for the metal handle. Finally a surcharge of 6d for buying a single item. With the additional cost of oiling and polishing, the item could total 7/-.

A SQUARE BOTTLE TRAY, N° 2.

Four inches deep, to hold four bottles upright, the edge
of the bottom and sides rounded, a handle let on - - - - 0 4 6

EXTRAS.

A single one, extra - - - - - - - - - - - - - - -	0	1	0
Two ditto, each - - - - - - - - - - - - - - - - -	0	0	5
Three ditto, ditto - - - - - - - - - - - - - - - -	0	0	3
Four ditto, ditto - - - - - - - - - - - - - - - -	0	0	2
Five ditto, ditto - - - - - - - - - - - - - - - -	0	0	1
Six considered a job.			
Each extra hole more than four - - - - - - - - - -	0	0	8
Lipping the bottom—*See* TABLE, N° 21.			
Astragal or mouldings on the edges or bottom — *See* TABLE *of Mouldings.*			
Lining with cloth, each hole - - - - - - - - - - -	0	0	4
Oiling and polishing, when for four bottles - - - - - -	0	0	3
Ditto, when for six bottles - - - - - - - - - - - -	0	0	3½

Plate 242 (above). Part of a page from the 1813 Cabinet Maker's Book of Prices featuring a 'square bottle tray' with an alternative list of extras.

caution and care, they really do prevent more than minimal disturbance to the sediment in the wine. They rated an entry alongside other items of Georgian furniture in late eighteenth century books of prices and although they were made in many qualities, they were obviously considered to be of importance.

As can be seen from the facsimile of a page from the *London Cabinet Makers' Book of Prices* for 1793 reproduced here, a bottle tray equipped to hold six bottles would have cost approximately seven shillings, but there was an additional surcharge of sixpence if only a single tray was ordered. The same book of prices also mentions a 'Square Bottle Carrier to hold four bottles upright' and this could possibly have also been used for decanters or for bottles containing liquids other than wine which could safely be carried vertically. Following this is a description of a 'Hexagon Bottle Carrier' with a turned pillar in the middle and a brass handle at the top. The authors have never seen a carrier of this shape, but presumably these too were made to hold the bottles upright. A large bottle carrier made in basketwork has been seen in a late eighteenth century engraving, but again apart from modern examples the authors have never encountered one. Split bamboo and wickerwork was very popular around the turn of the nineteenth century and any examples which do survive are more likely to be of this date.

Plate 243. A four-division bottle or decanter holder. As it appears to have been made some time after the 1770s, it seems unlikely that a bottle of the shape and size then fashionable could be accommodated sideways as the front decanters are. Indeed, the cut-outs in the side are curious as decanters are not normally held in this position.

Bottle trays are now very sought after and therefore command high prices. There is however, another very similar object which may be bought relatively cheaply. This is the cutlery tray which is identical, but for its lack of shaping to the top edge to receive the neck of the bottle, and for its smaller interior divisions. Both these omissions can be easily faked and a prospective purchaser of a bottle tray must be very sure that the object offered for sale is not a converted cutlery tray.

Similar to the bottle tray, but not strictly speaking an object which can be described as furniture, is the wooden wine bottle holder. These small, handleless objects are explained in chapter sixteen.

Another item of wine furniture, but one which is peculiarly Irish, is the bottle canterbury. The term 'canterbury' usually refers to an object designed to hold music which was invented at the end of the eighteenth century, but a typical Irish bottle canterbury dates from about 1730 or 1740 and is intended to hold between four and sixteen bottles or decanters in a vertical position. The tray section is usually integral with the stand which is formed of a framework supported on cabriole legs. As is quite normal with Irish furniture of this period, the legs are carved at the knee and where the feet are not of the hairy claw variety they are usually of the faceted pad type which most furniture historians believe came solely from Ireland. The centre of the long rail is often carved with a shell, another peculiarly Irish feature. The upper edges of the tray divisions are usually shaped and scalloped. Most bottle canterburies were made from the dark, purplish-brown mahogany imported from Jamaica.

Plate 244. An Irish bottle canterbury of unusual form. The heavily decorated frieze and carved cabriole legs are typical of English and Irish furniture of the second quarter of the 18th century, but usually such pieces have divisions to hold from eight to a dozen bottles and are rectangular rather than square in plan. A favourite motif for Irish cabinet makers was the shell and, in place of claw and ball feet, faceted pad feet were often employed.

227

Plate 245. Three items of basketwork. The partitioned bottle holder is exceptionally large, the two bottles shown being a magnum and a jeroboam. Basketwork was very fashionable at the end of the 19th century from whence this probably dates. The single bottle cradle would appear to date from the same time, but the bottle-shaped item on the right is nothing to do with wine antiques at all. It is a receptacle for snooker balls! Such baskets are sometimes used for trick shots by professionals.

A very common variety of furniture associated with wine is the butler's tray. Trays of course came in all shapes and sizes and in a variety of media. Some were purely decorative and perhaps intended for display on a sideboard, while others were utilitarian and far more substantial. Butlers' trays, which are either oval or rectangular, can be distinguished from any other variety by their high sides and undecorated utilitarian appearance. Rectangular examples usually have one side of lower height than the other three to facilitate the serving of the tray's contents. Most frequently they have carrying handles fretted into the shorter sides. Better versions will have moulded tops to the sides and de luxe examples, folding sides. The latter is accomplished by brass hinges incorporating a spring so that the tray is only in equilibrium when the sides are either fully lowered or fully raised. The flat surface of the tray may be either plain or panelled. Butlers' trays of oval outline were more expensive and almost invariably had panelled centre sections and hinged sides. Accompanying the tray was a folding X-frame which was prevented from collapsing by webbing. The webbing also supplied the support for the tray when in position. Early frames are quite plain, while later ones have turned or otherwise-decorated legs. A great many butlers' trays have been converted for use as coffee tables during this century by scrapping the original stand and replacing it with a stool-like structure. It should be noted that countless thousands of

Plate 246. A mahogany butler's tray which was made in about 1800. The hinges on each side have springs which retain the sides in the vertical or flat position. This example is unusual in having a reeded edge and a plain, rather than panelled, surface. Many trays of this type have been converted into coffee tables and it is a frequently reproduced form.

reproductions have been made of butlers' trays of oval shape and these now seem to have established themselves as standard items of furniture for a house of good taste.

A rarely encountered piece of furniture is the butler's cabinet. This looks like a chest of drawers or a cabinet with cupboards and is a purpose-made, multi-functional piece. There can be little doubt that these objects were made by cabinet makers to individual requirements and not as furniture to be offered for retail sale from stock. Consequently a set form of definition cannot be undertaken although normally there will be a cellaret drawer or cupboard and provision for cooling the wine and rinsing the glasses. Drawers provide storage space for wine drinking accessories. Most date from the late eighteenth century.

Possibly the final word in wine furniture has to be the gout stool. Popular belief has it that the excessive consumption of port has much to do with this painful affliction. Certainly in the minds of many people, the Georgian imbiber with his rollicking, roistering image suffered awfully from gout. Whatever the truth of this, the gout sufferers of the eighteenth or nineteenth centuries were catered for by the provision of special stools on which to rest the stricken limbs. Simple ones were made of oak while de luxe versions in mahogany were not only upholstered, but also adjusted on one or two ratchets for height and rake.

CHAPTER 14
Punch and its Equipage

Plate 247. An object dating from about 1690 variously referred to as a posset pot, spout pot or caudle cup. George Ravenscroft is known to have made this type of piece at his Savoy glass works and similar forms are encountered in delftware and silver. For a recipe for posset refer to Appendix III.

In even the best regulated cellars mistakes can occur from time to time and the most prudent buyer may choose a vintage subsequently not to his taste or may quite simply drink his wine too late. In these cases it is but a simple matter to flavour the wine with a few spices, sugars and fruits and to dilute it, either with spiritous liquor, or with non-alcoholic beverages, thereby giving it a new lease of life. The resulting concoction can be further enhanced by either chilling or warming.

In Britain one of the earliest forms of concocted drink in which wine was sometimes used as a base was wassail. References to wassail go back to the Norman period and possibly it was drunk even earlier than that. In the seventeenth century a new concocted drink was introduced, known then, as now, as punch. There is much controversy over the origin of the word for while some would say that it derives from an Indian word meaning five,

Plate 248. An engraving by William Hogarth entitled 'A Midnight Modern Conversation' published March 1732/3. Particularly noteworthy are the two stacks of wanded bottles, one on the mantlepiece, the other on the floor, the punch bowl with its chinoiserie decoration, the fruit rind both in the bowl and on the floor, the onion-shaped wine bottles and the shape of the wine glasses. There are of course many other fine details to admire.

Plate 249. *Three items of treen. The largest, a punch bowl (or wassail bowl) has simple astragal moulded bands and an unusually squat stem. Good punch bowls are turned very thinly. The smaller goblet shows a strong resemblance and may even have come from the same workshop. Both date from the early 18th century. The punch ladle has a treen bowl and stem, but the shank and mount to the bowl are both silver. The shape of the punch ladle's antecedent, the dipper, is quite plain from this photograph.*

there being five principal ingredients, wine, brandy, lemon, sugar and spices, others prefer to think that it derives from the word 'puncheon', which was a cask or barrel. Whatever its derivation however, punch enjoyed great popularity during the latter part of the seventeenth and the first half of the eighteenth century, although after that date it seemed to dwindle rather, due to increased consumption of toddy. (This was spiritous liquor which was watered down and sweetened, or not, with sugar). Together with mulled (spiced and warmed) wine, these drinks constituted the larger percentage of concocted beverages and inevitably lead to a special category of objects used in their making and serving. Above all they were convivial drinks, not the sort of beverage to be consumed by a man alone, a fact attested by the large number of satirical works by Thomas Rowlandson, George Cruikshank and others.

The most important object in the punch equipage was the bowl, which was used for both mixing and serving. Punch bowls which pre-date the seventeenth century are exceedingly rare and those which do survive cannot with any certainty be said to be for wassail, punch or any other specific food or drink. Many punch bowls during the seventeenth century were made in turned lignum vitae and although generally no more than twelve to fifteen inches in diameter, some early examples were as much as twenty inches wide. These large, treen bowls are generally described specifically as 'wassail bowls', probably in most cases a misnomer for which we can blame the Victorians, who were wont to attach romantic names to very ordinary objects. It seems far more likely that these large turned wooden bowls were for punch, contemporary as they are with silver punch bowls. They are normally given a stem and a foot and a light form

Colour plate 46. A really magnificent punch bowl formed from turtleshell and silver-mounted by the great silversmith, Paul Crespin, in about 1750. It is in high rococo taste and originally had a matching punch ladle.

of decoration in the form of bands of moulding. The latter also gave them added strength. The grandest bowls had silver mounts and may even have had a tap or spigot. It is likely that many of them were originally fitted with lids, though these seldom survive. The finest bowls were decorated on ornamental lathes with bands of engine-turning and a few were turned of oval cross-section. Turnery was considered a manly pursuit, even a royal one, and many of the great houses of Europe were equipped with a turnery workshop where noblemen and royalty were able to dabble under the guidance of a turning master.

One particular form of seventeenth century wooden bowl which deserves mention is that which has a lid of many components. It will be slightly domed and in the centre will be an enormous finial which is in fact a second

Colour plate 47. 'The Punch Party'. The innkeeper Mr. Hadfield is seen serving punch to a party of well-to-do English gentlemen at his hostelry in Florence, while the faun-like bust on the wall (actually a self-portrait of the artist, Thomas Patch) looks on with disdain. It was painted in 1760.

Plate 250. An engraving of a 'wassail table' and candelabra from Henry Shaw's Specimens of Ancient Furniture, 1836. The engine-turning and the intricacies of the ivory embellishments make this a quite exceptional set. It is now in the Victoria and Albert Museum. Note the four dipper cups.

Plate 251. A fine and rare punch bowl in Lambeth delftware. The curious decoration on the base and the lobed outline are both unusual features.

Plate 252. A George II silver punch bowl made by Edward Vincent in 1731.

cup. This was designed to contain the spices which were added to the punch (see plate 250, page 233). Some punch bowls have three or more turned spindles applied to the lid which accommodated upturned dipper cups. (These are discussed later in this chapter.) Perhaps the grandest of all these treen punch or wassail bowls is that now in the Victoria and Albert Museum which retains not only its lid with spice box and dipper cups, but also its complete equipage of table, pair of torchères and candlesticks. All are en suite, decorated with engine-turning and ivory embellishments.

Inevitably the question arises as to what exactly distinguishes a punch bowl from any other kind. In the late seventeenth and early eighteenth centuries the East India Company and its European counterparts traded extensively with far-flung parts of the world and as we have already mentioned, one of the principal imported products was Oriental porcelain. Naturally many punch bowls were included in this category, some already decorated, either with native designs or with European designs executed under European supervision. Some were left plain and were decorated by English artists on their arrival in Britain. This decoration, and of course their size, varies enormously, and all appear to be within the normal range of porcelain one would expect to find at this date. There can be little doubt that some, and particularly the larger, of these bowls were used for concocted drinks. Today many are used for pot pourri or lavender. The grandest material used for punch bowls was silver. The earliest surviving examples of these date from the 1680s although any which date from before 1700 are very rare indeed. Silver punch bowls inevitably followed the prevailing fashions of design and technique and varied quite considerably in size. Early examples were occasionally fitted with lids and almost all of them had handles until about 1730. Most punch bowls were raised from the ground on a single spreading foot, but occasionally stood on three or more feet. In the chapter on miscellanea we discuss an object known as a

Plate 253. Two glass punch bowls similarly made. The left-hand example has 'nipt diamond waies' decoration on its lower half and stands on a folded trumpet foot. The right-hand example could hardly be plainer. Whereas the left-hand one dates from the closing years of the 17th century, the right-hand one is more of an enigma. While appearing to date from the middle of the 18th century, it might indeed date from the early 19th.

'monteith' or wine glass cooler. It should be said here that many monteiths, like other silver items, were dual purpose objects and sometimes had detachable rims which left a bowl behind intended to be used for punch.

Another material in which one encounters punch bowls is glass. These tend to be of small dimensions and would therefore have been suitable for use when fewer than four people were drinking punch together. Most take the form of enlarged goblets. The earliest date from the 1680s and 1690s and commonly the bowl will have 'nipt diamond waies' decoration on the lower half. By 1730 or 1740 glass punch bowls were shallow and flat-bottomed and had straight, canted sides resting on a trumpet base with folded feet. Few appear to have been made during the middle of the eighteenth century, but towards the end giant-size goblets on plain stems (or stems with minimal decoration) and on low, domed feet were being made in larger numbers. A rare example of around 1800 is illustrated in plate 254, overleaf, where the form is quite clearly derivative of earlier porcelain models.

Many bowls were made during the eighteenth century in pewter and some were large enough to have been used for punch. In general these were simplified forms of silver models. Similar large brass bowls which however, date from the eighteenth century, are more likely to have been made as washbasins. A few punch bowls were made in Cantonese enamel, although these are now a sought-after rarity. This most attractive art form comprises a copper ground overlaid with white opaque glass which was then surface-

Plate 254. *A glass punch bowl of exceptional simplicity and good form. It closely emulates Chinese porcelain and silver punch bowls and, but for its engraving, which appears to be original, it might well be dated to some part of the 18th century. However, the star cartouche and calligraphy indicate a date of about 1800.*

Plate 255. *A group of punch ladles and a toddy ladle. The earliest (the one on the left) dates from 1726, while the complex centre example dates from the mid-1740s. The oval-bowled example on the right-hand side, inset with a sixpence, has a twisted whalebone handle and dates from the 1780s. The small toddy ladle is somewhat later.*

decorated in enamel colours. Objects made in this medium followed Chinese porcelain models.

Having obtained a large bowl for the mixing of the punch, the next item required was a smaller vessel for serving it. The first of these were called dippers, and were small handleless cups which were also used for drinking. They were usually between two and four inches in diameter and had a rounded base. Simple wooden versions would be quite plain, but the more elaborate would be engine-turned to match the punch bowl that they accompanied. In the matching idiom better quality cups would be mounted in silver, very often with a scalloped pattern around the rim. Similar objects were made entirely in silver, though without the engine-turned decoration, and the earliest known example dates from 1636. These are specifically known as tumbler cups. The term 'tumbler' derives from the requirement for the cup to return to a vertical position when placed on its side because of its shape and the dispersal of its weight. Early examples tend to be shorter than later ones and some are known executed in gold.

Dipper and tumbler cups were sometimes made (as were beakers) in sets, graduating in size so that one would sit within the next. A particular variety made in the 1690s was fashioned so that a pair of cups would fit end to end to form a unit of dumb-bell outline. Silver tumbler cups have continued to be made since the seventeenth century, but the dipper cup was largely replaced at the beginning of the eighteenth century by the ladle. It perhaps would be more correct to say that the dipper *developed into* the ladle with the addition of a handle and a reduction in the size of the

236

bowl. Wooden ladles appear to have lost popularity rather rapidly and most extant early punch ladles are in silver. They have a rounded bowl, a shank, and a turned handle, sometimes also in silver, but very often in wood, usually pear or lignum vitae. By the 1730s and 1740s larger, lobed bowls were common, following the late Baroque style, and supporting brackets appeared between the bowl and the shank. During the second half of the eighteenth century punch ladles were frequently made from a crown (i.e. a five shilling piece) which provided an ideal sized blank from which to raise the bowl. The centre of the base of the bowl would be the thinnest area and so very frequently a sixpence, in its perfect state and with its obverse and reverse showing, was inserted. Such punch ladles are seldom hallmarked, if ever, although obviously the date can be gained from reading the date on the sixpence. The defacing of the coinage in this way was possibly not strictly legal, but countless thousands of these items were produced. The most common variety of handle was twisted whalebone, the end sometimes capped with a silver ferrule. Whalebone is a tough and resilient substance which can be bent under heat and pressure into many useful shapes.

Towards the end of the eighteenth century the bowls of punch ladles tended to become elongated ovals of shallower dimensions than previously and frequently resembled miniature sauce or pap boats with a lip for pouring at either end. Bright cut decoration too is found during this period, though with the decline in the popularity of punch, very few examples survive from the nineteenth century.

Punch ladles were also made in porcelain, to match porcelain bowls, and similarly in glass. The latter was on the whole uncommon, although particularly popular during the early years of the nineteenth century. Examples may be either clear or coloured. Other media include paktong, pewter and brass. Some particularly attractive ladles survive with their bowls formed of exotic shells or small coconuts (sometimes chip carved). Coconuts and indeed, coquilla and other rare nuts, of which ladles were also made, were highly prized during the seventeenth and eighteenth centuries. Most were mounted in silver and had either silver or wooden handles.

Towards 1800 stronger concocted drinks were being made, most notably toddy (see page 231). Because of its greater strength a smaller ladle was required and although precisely the same models were made as for punch they are naturally known as toddy ladles.

In the early nineteenth century toddy was also served from a 'toddy lifter'. These were normally made in glass though examples are known in treen and indeed in silver. The toddy lifter looks like a dimunitive decanter, but with a very elongated neck and a small hole drilled in the base of the body. It is operated in the following manner: the lifter is inserted with one hand into the liquid with the thumb placed near the neck

Plate 256. A mid-18th century punch ladle, the bowl formed of a silver-mounted shell. The handle is turned wood and the two are joined by a silver shank. In the 17th and 18th centuries shell was regarded as an exotic acquisition and was highly prized.

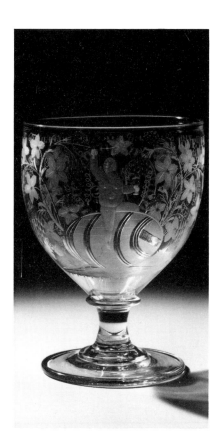

Plate 257. A glass punch bowl of the early 19th century. The ovoid bowl, with a capacity of between one and two pints, is engraved all over with a naïve representation of a sated Bacchus sitting astride a barrel with a glass in either hand. The capacity of such a piece was sufficient for two to four people. Concocted drinks other than punch might have been served from this vessel.

Plate 258. A group of early 19th century glass toddy lifters which have a hole at either end and are used like a pipette. It is thereby possible to serve a standard measure to each drinker. Their increased efficiency made obsolete the punch and toddy ladle.

Plate 259. A most unusual toddy lifter made of silver with an ivory mount. It was made in Edinburgh in 1874.

Plate 260. A silver nutmeg grater/corkscrew combination of about 1745. With the lid screwed on, the upper section resembles an acorn and is just large enough to hold the unground nutmeg. The worm of the corkscrew is steel and is encased in a silver sheath which unscrews. These once popular pieces are now desirable collector's items.

Plate 262. An oval silver strainer (frequently called an orange or lemon strainer). This particular form was popular in Exeter and Edinburgh. This example was made in 1739 by Pentecost Symonds from Plymouth. Below the handle is a small tab which enables the strainer to be latched over the side of the punch bowl while in use.

Plate 261. An 18th century lignum vitae spice grinder which unscrews into many sections. The acorn finial perhaps encloses a nutmeg while the domed lid unscrews to reveal a compartment where spices to be ground are inserted. The bulbous section encloses the grinding mechanism and the base unscrews to allow the removal of the ground spice. The folding handle fits in the upper section when not in use. This charming and pristine piece of treen was made in about 1740.

aperture; once sufficient toddy has entered the lifter from the hole in the bottom, with the thumb covering the uppermost hole, the lifter is raised from the bowl and placed over the drinking vessel. When the thumb is removed the air rushing into the top hole allows the liquid to escape through the bottom. These objects provide a remarkably efficient and drip-free method of serving any concocted drink; the small apertures also filter it.

As mentioned elsewhere in this chapter punch is a mixture of five ingredients, one of which is spice. There were many spices used and most of them had to be grated or ground beforehand. It is perhaps on the periphery of our subject, but a delightful and very collectable antique is the nutmeg grater box. Nutmegs, which are aromatic kernels of the nuts of a tree which grows in the East Indies, were first imported into Britain soon after trading links were established with the Orient. Their medicinal and culinary properties were acknowledged from early on and they were highly prized and consequently carried around by persons of quality in small silver boxes. Seventeenth century examples were very like other small Stuart boxes and were often engraved with tulips or were in the form of a heart. The latter suggests that they were occasionally given as love tokens. In the early eighteenth century they were frequently shaped in the form of acorns and later in the century cylindrical boxes with bright-cut decoration were the norm. The common feature of all nutmeg grater boxes is a small piece of perforated steel fitted in the interior which acted as the grater. Among the most notable as far as we are concerned are those which have a corkscrew attached (see plate 260, page 239). Some fine late eighteenth century examples made by Phipps and Robinson in the form of vases are of this type and cleverly hinge to reveal the grating surface. Nutmeg grater boxes were also made of coquilla nut, sometimes mounted in silver, and no doubt other examples exist in porcelain, enamel and other media.

An important item of punch equipment in an eighteenth century house was a spice grinder. Quite unlike the former article, the spice grinder would be used to grind anything from coffee beans to peppers. Some of the most sought after are those made in treen. Grinders have three essential parts; the upper funnel-shaped receptacle which receives the unground spice, the central grinding mechanism, and the lower chamber which holds the spice when ground. The mechanism was commonly formed from two serrated cones made of cast iron (see plate 261, page 239). In the best examples a unison of design was achieved between the various parts including the lid and handle. The latter may or may not fold and be accommodated within either section when not in use.

Finally, apart from drinking glasses and goblets, the only other item essential for the making and serving of concocted drinks was some form of straining device. All these drinks had liberal quantities of fruit (and

Plate 263. A simple strainer made in London in 1778. Its beaded rim is typical of the period and it represents the last type of strainer to be used for concocted drinks. During the rococo period particularly, many strainers were made with two handles in order that they could rest on the top of the punch bowl. Single handled strainers on the other hand have a tab, as described in the previous plate.

Plate 264. A beaker and a double-ended spice box, both in silver, coming from a travelling canteen. They are engraved in a typically late 17th century style and demonstrate admirably that although an item might be 300 or so years old it need not be worn out. Although other items would have been included in the canteen, these two might well have been used for punch and wassail.

Plate 265. As a postscript to this chapter, a punch drinking scene by Thomas Rowlandson is shown, depicting all the excesses which were attributed to the drinking man. The gouty host, bloated guests and empty bottles are clearly, if somewhat cruelly, shown.

sometimes only coarsely ground spices) which it was clearly desirable to remove before serving. Early punch strainers have simple, circular bowls pierced with holes in a geometrical pattern not unlike a refined version of a kitchen colander (see plate 262, page 239). To the bowl would be attached a handle of circular cross-section. In the seventeenth century these handles tended to be hollow, but by the eighteenth were being made of solid, flat, horizontal section. They were frequently pierced at this date and later cast and chased. As the eighteenth century progressed the simple drilled holes took on a more interesting fretted appearance. Strainers were then made with either single or double handles, in the former case usually with a tab below, which enabled the strainer to be suspended over the side of the punch bowl without falling in. For some reason examples made in both Exeter and Edinburgh tend to be oval and with loop handles. An apparently specialist maker who was working in Plymouth was Pentecost Symonds, although examples by him were actually assayed in Exeter. In trade circles strainers are frequently called 'orange' or 'lemon' strainers and while there are no doubt good grounds for using this nomenclature there can be little question that they were used for a wider variety of purposes.

A small selection of recipes for punch and other concocted drinks can be found in Appendix III.

CHAPTER 15
Miscellanea

There are quite a number of items associated with wine which are not sufficiently numerous to accord a separate chapter. They are so different from one another that it seems appropriate merely to list them one by one.

Wine fountains

In an earlier chapter mention was made of some very grand eighteenth century wine cisterns. Usually these were accompanied by a second piece of silver called a 'wine fountain'. This was not, as one might expect, something from which the wine spurted upwards, but a large vessel with a lid which allowed wine or water to be poured in at the top later releasing it through one or more taps at the bottom. These wine fountains could be more than forty-eight inches high, although most were a good deal smaller, but whatever their size they were ideal for ostentatious display on the sidetable. While they were invariably called wine fountains, there can be little doubt that they were probably more commonly used for dispensing water for rinsing the dining-room plate and glasses. Examples are also known in lignum vitae, a particularly charming form being that in the shape of a barrel covered entirely in ribbed decoration. One famous wine fountain in the collection of the Company of Vintners is in cut glass with silver mounts and dates from about 1745. It too takes the form of a barrel, but is held horizontally and has a capacity substantially less that its earlier silver counterparts. Thomas Betts, the London glass manufacturer, shows a similar wine barrel in his trade card, with a tap and a bung in the form of a gilt metal Bacchus. Many similar barrels, known as tuns, were listed in his inventory at his death in 1765. Other examples of cut glass wine fountains date from the late eighteenth century and are neo-classical in shape. (See plates 266, 267 and 268 overleaf.)

Wine glass coolers

Refrigeration before the twentieth century was achieved by collecting ice in the winter and storing it between layers of straw in specially constructed ice houses for use during the rest of the year. The average ice house (itself now a rarity) was a largely subterranean structure with the roof covered in turf for additional insulation. For obvious reasons they were normally situated near a lake. The ice was of course used for a variety of purposes, more often than not for preservation of food, but it was also required for chilling of wines and other substances before serving. Probably the first type of British wine cooler in which the actual glass, rather than the wine, was cooled, was the monteith. This made its debut shortly after the Restoration of Charles II to the throne in 1660. As mentioned in the

Colour plate 48. Two pieces of glass which may accurately be described as 'Bristol blue' as they are both signed by Isaac Jacobs. Both have gilt decoration deriving from Greek antiquity, while the plate or stand is, in addition, engraved with a crest for the Earl of Verulam. It may be a coaster, but may equally well be used to hold a finger bowl or wine glass cooler. The left-hand object, although it is a finger bowl, is identical to a wine glass cooler, but for the pouring lip on either or both sides.

Colour plate 49. A map covering a wide area of western France by de Witt. Careful searching of the original will reveal the famous vineyards of the Loire and also those of Cognac. Although the colouring is recent, this map dates from the late 17th century.

244

Plate 266. One of a pair of wine cisterns and fountains incorporating much gadrooned decoration and with cast applied handles and spigot. These sets derive from earlier Continental models and were among the most opulent plate of their time. This set was made by David Willaume in 1701.

Plate 267. A cistern and fountain in mahogany, clearly deriving their function from earlier silver examples. The upper section of delicately moulded ogee outline, with its pagoda finial, is lead-lined and fitted with a tap, while the base drawer, which extends into the plinth, is fitted with a removable lead-lined draining box. Such pieces enabled wine glasses and silver plates to be washed in the dining room for immediate re-use.

Plate 268. A unique wine fountain in the possession of the Vintners' Company. The cut glass barrel rotates horizontally and has a spigot in the form of a cockerel. The finial, also in the form of a barrel, has obvious connotations and the curious stand finishes in hoof feet. This piece was made in about 1745 and is known as 'The Shaftesbury'.

Plate 269. *Any early silver monteith engraved with panels of chinoiserie closely resembling those found on Oriental porcelain. The applied, cast border is particularly fine and unusual. A very short-lived fashion for engraving silver with chinoiserie occurred in the late 1680s, mostly during the short reign of James II (1685-1688).*

Plate 270. *A silver monteith of restrained form. The well cast rim allows the glasses to be cooled bowl-inwards, although the notches are shallow and look more ornamental than useful. The rim is detachable so that the bowl may be used for serving punch. It was made in 1701 by Benjamin Pyne.*

Plate 271. *One of a pair of unusually late silver-gilt monteiths of oval outline. Were it not for the fact that it bears English hallmarks, it might be thought to be French. It has the maker's mark 'IK' and the hallmark for the year 1776. It bears the arms of the Earls of Cholmondeley. The stylised wave pattern which forms the rim is called a 'vitruvian scroll'.*

chapter on punch items, it initially took the form of a punch bowl, but with an indented rim. A small proportion were fitted with handles, usually of lion mask and ring form. An often-quoted explanation of the term 'monteith' is the alleged habit of a Scottish gentleman of that name of wearing a cloak with a wavy hemline. By the 1680s the shaped rim was being made detachable, a feature which continued into the eighteenth century. These bowls functioned by being filled with iced water and by having the glasses placed in them bowl-downwards, the stem being held in the notched rim and the feet protruding over the edge. A monteith cooled anything from six to a dozen glasses at once, but by the end of the third

Plate 272. A selection of individual wine glass coolers and one (top right) finger bowl. These demonstrate the various different forms and cutting styles prevailing in the late 18th and early 19th centuries. Individual coolers superseded the communal monteith at the end of the 18th century.

quarter of the century their popularity had waned and it became fashionable thereafter to cool the glasses individually. To this end a single glass bowl with either one, or more commonly two, pouring lips, was placed in front of every diner. This enabled each individual to have one or two glasses cooling in front of him while he ate. In England the practice of cooling wine glasses seems to have dropped from favour altogether by about 1800 and consequently such bowls lost their lips and became finger bowls. It is worth noting that elsewhere in Europe both communal wine glass coolers and rosewater bowls continued in use well into the nineteenth century. The Continental wine glass cooler, usually called a verrière, is typically a short, straight-sided oval tub, also with a notched rim. While occasionally made in brass or silver, many were made of japanned tin or tôle peint. In England many wine glass coolers were made in clear glass, but more attractive are those in blue, amethyst and green, some of the most interesting being those with gilt decoration from the workshop of Isaac Jacobs in Bristol (see colour plate 48, page 244).

Examples in other media are also known. Delftware monteiths were probably at one time fairly common, though few have survived until today. Chinese and European porcelain and European faience examples are known to exist and there are also many recorded examples in salt-glazed stoneware, Sheffield plate, brass, pewter and toleware. The latter three were often of oval, rather than hemi-spherical shape, as shown in colour plate 1, page 19.

Decanter shields

In the chapter on coasters mention is made of coasters with built-in shields. Plate 274, overleaf, illustrates a double coaster of this type with a folding carrying handle. An extreme rarity, based on the same principle,

Plate 273. A wine glass cooler in blue glass, gilded with Greek key pattern. The underside is signed 'Isaac Jacobs, Bristol'.

Plate 274. An early 19th century double coaster with a shield back. Although of well moulded and richly figured mahogany it is curiously cumbersome and most coasters with attached shields are made of a light plywood construction. Between the two decanters is a folding brass handle.

is the independent decanter shield, a pair of which appeared in the exhibition held to mark the centenary of Gilbeys in May and June of 1957. They were illustrated in the catalogue to that event, *The Complete Imbiber*. Each one takes the form of an inverted shield or curved plaque and are made of japanned tin of the type known to have been made at Pontypool.

Bottle holders

There are some people who firmly believe that there are certain wines, like Burgundy, which should not be decanted. Involvement with such a suggestion is outside the scope of this book and besides which, it is largely a matter of personal taste. However, the habit of pouring wine directly from the bottle into the glass has given rise to a particular kind of bottle holder. This comprises a hinging framework with a handle which fits around the bottle. Sometimes there is a form of locking device so that the frame has a stronger grip upon the bottle to prevent it from slipping while the wine is being poured. Many varieties are constructed from a springy metal whereby security is achieved either by tightly clamping the neck alone, or both the neck and the kick-in of the base. Most of these devices seem to be made of silver-plated base metal or electroplated nickel silver (E.P.N.S.) and date from the latter part of the nineteenth century. Many bear registration numbers which would indicate the exact date if investigated. Possibly a unique exception to the rule is one known example which is in unmarked silver and dates from the middle years of the eighteenth century. Apart from the ring which encircles the neck, it looks very much like a scrolled tankard handle which splits in half along its vertical axis, and hinges.

Plate 276. A wine bottle holder. This is not a bottle carrier as there is no handle, but a single bottle is accommodated at an angle of about 30°, the perfect attitude for the withdrawal of the cork. The shaped apron will catch any accidental drips, although this feature is absent in earlier examples.

Plate 275. Two electro-plated bottle holders. In the main these were made after 1860, after the widespread introduction of the gummed paper label, although earlier ones engraved with the name of the wine are known. There are many variations on this theme.

A curious alternative form of bottle holder which dates mostly from the closing years of the eighteenth century — though a few late nineteenth century examples are also known — is that which comprises a mahogany framework designed to hold the bottle at an angle of thirty degrees or thereabouts. This angle is sufficient for the sediment to fall slowly to the optimum position and also happens to be the angle at which a cork is most easily drawn. These are not equipped with handles and therefore cannot be construed as single bottle carriers. Some are quite plain, while others, like that illustrated in plate 276 have a semi-circular apron at the end where the neck of the bottle is accommodated. One can only assume that their function was to hold the bottle while the cork was being extracted and that, once done, the cork could remain for inspection on the apron.

Today basketwork holders are made to hold the bottle on the table at a similar angle, though their efficacy is definitely questionable.

Bottle boot

The demise of the latter form of bottle holder can perhaps be attributed to another aid to cork extraction, the bottle boot. Perhaps the most delightful version of this encountered by the authors is a leather cylinder approximately in the shape of a bottle. Two 'L' shaped pieces of steel are stitched into the leather at right angles to the body at the lower edge. The boot was slipped over the neck of the bottle and the person extracting the cork would stand on the steel lugs to ensure a firm grip.

Plate 277. An interesting leather and iron bottle boot. It is a well crafted if vernacular item in two-tone leather and is very practical.

Wine syphons

A piece of apparatus which might appeal particularly to readers with a mechanical bent is the wine syphon. These strange looking objects were produced from about 1750 until the early years of the nineteenth century and provided an alternative method of decanting to the wine funnel. There are two varieties both comprising a U-shaped tube. One has a pump, not unlike a diminutive version of a bicycle pump, while the other relies on oral suction to instigate the flow of wine from the bottle to the decanter. Both varieties are normally fitted with a tap so that as soon as the dregs and sediment are reached the procedure may be quickly halted. Although other makers are known to have produced them, a substantial percentage of the small number that survive were made by the firm Phipps and Robinson during the closing years of the eighteenth century. Few have more than minimal decoration consisting of applied mouldings to strengthen the various joints, though one or two later examples are known with bright-cut decoration in the bracket strengthening the principal bend.

Decanting machines and bottle tilters

One of the most exciting wine-related antiques from a mechanical point of view is the decanting machine, or decanting cradle or bottle tilter. Indeed, in the Burgandy area of France they sometimes use a decanting machine to pour the wine directly into the glass. It usually consists of a metal framework (of iron, steel or silver) which pivots about a horizontal axis and is controlled by a rod connecting to a rotating worm. The framework, which is raised on a series of columns designed to lift the bottle high enough to function properly, begins to tilt when the worm is turned. Usually it is equipped with either springs or clips, or some other device, which hold the bottle firmly in position. It is the custom, even today, in some Burgundian establishments, whether domestic or commercial, for the decanting machine to sit beside the host, who will then fill each glass and pass it around the table to the appropriate guest. French examples tend to be constructed entirely in steel or cast iron and it is doubtful that any date from before the beginning of the nineteenth century. Portuguese examples are known to exist and it is probably from that part of the world that the idea was first introduced to England. Early English examples are somewhat different and tend to be made of mahogany. At their simplest they comprise a bottle-sized open-topped box with a slot in one end to accommodate the neck and an equally simple frame on which the box pivots. In this case no mechanism is involved. More sophisticated examples, probably of early nineteenth century date, were made in the form of cannon. A mahogany barrel of rather curious proportions and with a wide girth splits in half to accommodate the bottle. This may be tilted either by hand or by a rack-and-pinion mechanism. Other simple and non-mechanical versions are known in toleware, but visually most exciting are

Plate 278. A wine syphon finely engraved with the arms of the Salters' Company. Although it is not properly hallmarked, it is struck with the maker's mark and engraved with the date 1768, together with two inventory numbers. Wine syphons are rare collector's pieces.

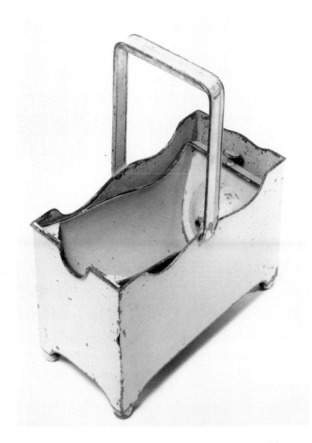

Plate 279. *A manually-operated decanting machine made of blue-painted toleware. The interior receptacle for the bottle has a small knob handle to raise the bottle and is hinged on its front edge. Other examples have been known in red japanned and gilt black chinoiserie-decorated toleware.*

Plate 280. *A fine and elaborate early 19th century decanting machine. The framework and receptacle for the bottle are all made of mahogany with brass mounts. The tilting mechanism is motivated by rotating the flat disc at the top of the machine with its turned brass handle.*

the skeletal frameworks made towards the end of the nineteenth and beginning of the twentieth centuries, mainly in brass, but usually with a steel worm. Farrow and Jackson, a firm who supplied accessories to the wine trade, sold many decanting machines with ivorine plaques containing their name set in the middle of the oval wooden plinth on which the brass framework would stand.

Some years ago, a particularly attractive example of a decanting machine, made of silver-plated brass and with a carrrying handle, was sold in a London auction house for some £2,000, a price which at the time appeared to be quite absurd. This meant that it came to the attention of many people interested in this subject and in recent years many small workshops have begun to reproduce these items in response to sudden demand. These are mostly characterised by a much higher quality than their original counterparts which, due to insufficient understanding of metallurgy, are often found in a very worn condition and are no longer

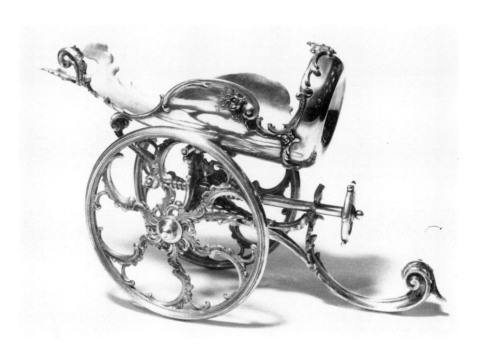

Plate 281. A fine decanting machine in the form of a field gun. The spokes of the wheels and the mouldings at the edge of the bottle holder are Rococo Revival in form.

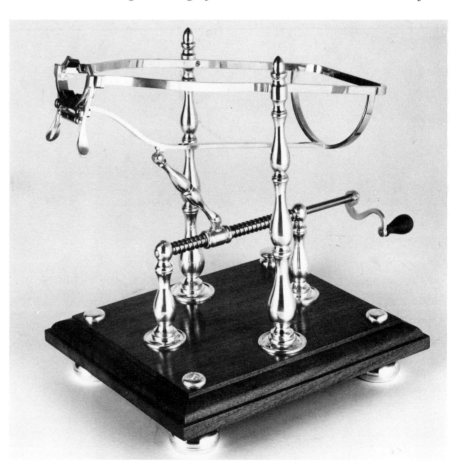

Plate 282. A modern silver decanting machine based on late 19th century models. It has a spring-mounted neck cramp, an adjustable foot to ensure stability on an uneven surface and a stainless steel worm.

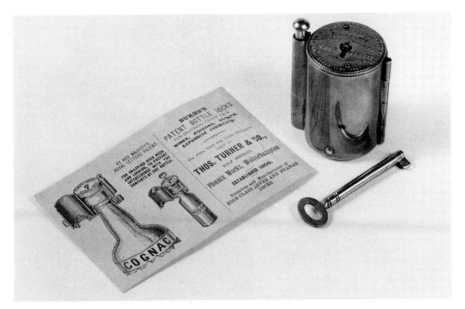

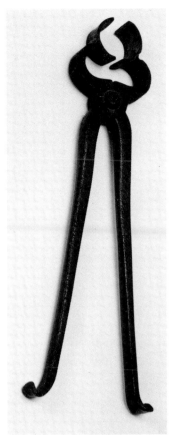

Plate 283. A salesman's trade card showing an advertisement for Burn's patent bottle lock together with the advertised object. These were commonly known as 'butlers' enemies'.

Plate 284. A pair of port tongs of indeterminate date, which are heated in a fire and clamped round the neck of the bottle. This procedure is quickly followed by the application of a cold wet cloth. The rapid change in temperature causes the neck of the bottle to break cleanly away. These can be useful as old corks can crumble very easily when a corkscrew is used.

suited to their original task. A well maintained decanting machine can be a great boon for it will enable a bottle to be tilted so smoothly that the maximum amount of wine can be extracted before the sediment begins to run into the neck. When decanting very expensive wines, particularly for sale in a restaurant, it can have a marked effect on value for money. Some modern machines are sufficiently tall for the entire decanting operation to be accomplished on a table top rather than over its edge. Others are equipped with swivelling candle holders which provide ideal decanting conditions. One version, in solid silver, is equipped with adjustable feet.

Bottle locks

In an earlier chapter the tantalus was described — the lockable framework which enables two or more bottles of spirits to be openly displayed while remaining impenetrable. Late in the nineteenth and early in the twentieth century the same principle was used for securing individual bottles of wine. An advertisement for Burn's Patent Bottle Lock is illustrated here with a photograph of the object offered for sale. Many other similar devices were available, sometimes known as 'butlers' enemies'!

Port tongs

A great problem for a wine connoisseur is how to remove the cork satisfactorily from a very old bottle. A cork of forty years of age or more

253

Plate 285. A most unusual wine tray with long and narrow proportions. There are divisions at either end which will accommodate a pair of decanters as shown. Between this is a thin section designed to hold five wine glasses. The type of mahogany and general outline enable it to be dated to about 1800.

is liable to disintegrate on extraction and there is a strong likelihood that little granules will be scattered over the surface of the wine still inside the bottle. The correct procedure is not to use a corkscrew, but a pair of port tongs. These are merely outsize pliers which are heated until red-hot and then applied to the neck of the bottle, covered with a cold wet cloth and rotated. The result is as dramatic as it is effective; the neck of the bottle breaks cleanly away and the port is left exposed and clean. Port tongs are by their nature utilitarian in appearance and are made in wrought iron or steel. They are not given to turned decoration or any other notable features so are very difficult to date accurately. Although they appear not to feature in any trade lists and references to them do not seem to exist before the beginning of the twentieth century, it is still possible that they were available before 1900.

Trays

Sundry trays are known to exist with clear wine connotations. In Harveys Wine Museum there is a long, mahogany tray with divisions at either end suitable for holding decanters (see plate 285, above). Between these are three long narrow divisions, the base of the central one having a row of five circular depressions presumably for holding glasses. The outer two divisions may possibly be for churchwarden pipes. This piece would appear to be unique.

Along similar lines, in so far as they have depressions suitable for decanters, are papier mâché trays of kidney-shaped outline with raised, moulded rims. On either side of the kidney shape is a further moulded section containing the depression. Some of these trays are quite plain, but examples are known with mother-of-pearl decoration and were probably made by the firm of Jennens & Bettridge in Birmingham.

Plate 286. Two objects, each of which would be used for drying decanters. The left-hand example is made of pewter and the decanter in it demonstrates its use. The right-hand one is designed to be hung on a wall and is one of a pair made in rosewood in about 1825.

Decanter driers

A very unusual item which has only appeared in recent years is a decanter drier composed of a hollow sausage of lint filled with silica gel or some other desiccant. This is hung in the neck of the decanter to absorb the moisture. Previously decanters were merely hung upside-down to dry and usually this was of course done in some remote part of the kitchens. Plate 286 however, illustrates a pair of rosewood brackets, each with two holes of a size perfect for accommodating a pair of decanters. Furthermore, the edges of the holes are bevelled to accord with the shape of a decanter neck of the period between 1820 and 1840 when these pieces were probably made. Also illustrated is a pewter decanter drier, the body shape being not unlike that of a tankard of about 1800, although it bears no touch marks to indicate its provenance. More mundane decanter drying racks, consisting of little more than pine shelves with three to four inch diameter holes drilled along their length, appear particularly in houses in Somerset and Gloucestershire, although presumably in other parts of the country as well. From this it will be seen that it has always been known how important it is to dry decanters. Left wet, they eventually stain. At best, the stain is lime deposited by evaporation of hard water, at worst it is a cloudy etching of the surface by residual acids. The first is readily removed by mild acid such as hydrochloric (Spirit of Salts). This is where these patent remedies come in, such as 'Gran's Denture Cleaner'. The second requires specialised treatment by an expert with buffing or ultra-sonic equipment

Plate 287. A so-called 'brandy' saucepan. Quite typically it is utterly plain with a simple moulded edge, a lip and a treen handle. These vary in capacity from one gill to several pints. This is a very early example made in 1726 by Benjamin Brackley. They surely cannot have been used solely for warming brandy.

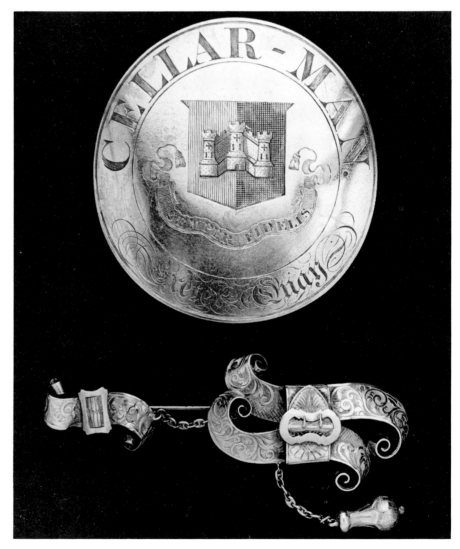

Plate 288. The badges of office of a cellarman at Exeter Quay engraved with the city's coat of arms and motto. It was made by Joseph Hicks in 1823.

to remove a minute layer of the interior surface. Hydrofluoric acid is sometimes used with very mixed results. The old suggestion of lead shot or sand should be strenuously avoided.

Brandy saucepans

An often encountered eighteenth or early nineteenth century silver, or occasionally silver-gilt, item is the so-called 'brandy saucepan'. Eighteenth century examples typically have a squat, baluster-shaped body with a hollow, cylindrical shank accommodating a turned wooden handle. At right angles to the handle is a pouring lip. They vary in size from one and a half inches in diameter to seven or eight inches and later examples are fitted with lids. The earliest appear to date from the very beginning of the eighteenth century. While it may have been the habit of gentlemen to heat brandy over a flame, it seems likely that these were general purpose saucepans — literally pans for making and serving sauce.

Badges of office

Until the beginning of the nineteenth century the senior servants of large and grand households and of livery companies and civic bodies were required to wear a badge of office. The practice continues in the latter case today. At its grandest this might have been an enamelled jewel suspended from an elaborate chain, but more frequently it was of silver and was worn on the upper sleeve. A particularly attractive example in the Exeter Museum was designed to be worn by cellarmen at Exeter Quay and is accordingly engraved. It bears the maker's mark of Joseph Hicks and the hallmarks for Exeter for 1823-24.

An apparently unique object possibly loosely related to the badge of office, but in any case one which cannot be categorised, is the charming antique illustrated in plate 289. Its purpose is uncertain, though it is said to have connections with the Company of Vintners as a staff of office. Made entirely of boxwood, the upper section is clearly turned in the shape of a barrel, while the lower part is in the form of a trumpet-bowled wine glass. The two end pieces are separated by a third section which could be described as an inverted goblet but is basically of spherical outline. Around this are three wooden rings which cannot be removed, although they are free to rattle and revolve. The whole piece is only three inches long and in style both the barrel and the wine glass would appear to date from just before the middle of the eighteenth century. It is quite possible that this piece had no purpose, but in fact was made merely as an exercise in turning.

Wager or milkmaid cups

Another item possibly associated originally with the Vintners' Company is the 'milkmaid' or wager cup. A silver example dating from 1680 is in the Company's collection and a number of other examples based on this

Plate 289. A most unusual object, about 3ins. long, made of boxwood. The lower section is quite obviously a goblet and the top one a barrel, but its precise purpose and origins have yet to be explained. Perhaps a reader can oblige?

have survived dated 1827. A few are known in treen (mostly pearwood) with silver mounts. Either type are in the form of a woman in seventeenth century costume with a wide, hollow skirt. A small milk pail cup swings between her uplifted arms. Both the inverted skirt and the swinging pail were filled with wine and, on admission to the Company, each Liveryman was required to drink from both cups, in turn without spilling a drop. Very rarely examples are seen in the form of a man.

Masonic pieces

Another category of wine antiques to which consideration must be given is that comprising Masonic drinking vessels. These consist principally of large, engraved glass punch goblets and similarly-made drinking and toasting glasses. Unlike these large later pieces, in general eighteenth century decanters and glasses are small and quite rare. Most are engraved, although enamelled examples exist. These are naïve and are not considered to have come from the Beilby workshop. Gilded Masonic decanters date from about 1770 which would seem to be the earliest period for the use of these emblems on glass. By the late eighteenth century and throughout the nineteenth, vessels of all types with elaborate Masonic decoration were made in considerable quantity, and they are easily identified by set

Plate 290. A silver wager cup which was made in Dublin in 1706. Wager cups were almost invariably formed as a swivelling cup held aloft by a girl wearing a broad skirt. Both the skirt and the cup would be filled and the wager was won by drinking the contents of both cups without spilling a drop before it was put down.

Plate 291. Three pieces of Masonic glass, two large goblets and a beaker. All three are engraved in the late 18th or early 19th century style and incorporate emblems and symbols of freemasonry. The two goblets have what are known as 'lemon squeezer' bases.

258

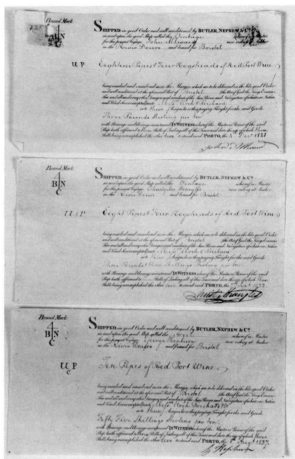

Plate 292. A map of the Medoc by the cartographer Bleau. Maps such as these went to many editions, the first being 1631. It is perhaps interesting to see how many names hold prominence today and how many great chateaux are absent.

Plate 293. Three bills of lading dating from 1828 to 1837. They indicate the brand marks to be found on imported casks and provide an interesting insight into the early workings of a wine merchant.

squares, dividers, pillars, crescent moons, stars and the rest of the vocabulary of Masonic symbolism.

Books, maps and memorabilia

It seems extraordinary that a substantial volume has recently been published on a subject which should clearly come within the scope of this book, yet here is allocated only a short paragraph. The subject is 'books about wine' and the publication in question an annotated bibliography of the many and various books available on the subject in the English language (see Bibliography). It would be invidious to single out any of the volumes listed and guidance to collectors is best given by antiquarian and other specialist booksellers. Perhaps more easily included here is a brief description, or explanation, of wine-related maps. Until the nineteenth century individual maps were not intended to be displayed as pictures, but were issued as part of an atlas. The great age of map making was the sixteenth and seventeenth centuries when maps were published in black and white and may, or may not have been, hand-coloured. Strangely it is not regarded as untoward in the 20th century to colour an earlier and originally monochrome map or print. For modern purposes the most obvious shortcoming of many early maps is their lack of roads and, as far as those recording wine producing areas are concerned, their shortage of relevant names. The Ortelius map of Burgundy, for example, which dates from the 1580s, fails to show such towns as Mersault, Beaune, Pommard, Nuits St. George or Gevrey Chambertin, although it does record Santenay and Chagny. Presumably the former were hamlets at that date. During the seventeenth century maps covering many of the wine-producing areas of today were executed by the great Dutch cartographers Janssen and Bleau, and later in the century by De Witt (see colour plate 49, page 244), but it was not until the nineteenth century that maps specifically relating to wine-making were produced. Perhaps the most obvious of these are the town plans of Bordeaux, which show the headquarters of the various wine-producing firms. Again collectors are advised to seek the help of specialist mapsellers.

No chapter on the miscellanea of wine objects would be complete without reference to wine memorabilia. Many wine merchants of long standing like to advertise their history to visitors by hanging on their walls old cellar books, decorative bills or invoices, (perhaps for a pipe of port, once considered a perfect christening present for a baby boy), an ancient passport stamped frequently for Portugal, prizes or medals for the production of fine wines, or personal keepsakes of the vintner. Although the majority of these are collected by wine sellers, cellar books and bills in particular are of more general interest and can give a good idea of the types of wine preferred at any one date.

CHAPTER 16
Wine Antiques Today

Perhaps the most cogent reason for an interest in wine related antiques is that many of them enhance the enjoyment of wine today. In the following pages we discuss the relevance of the various objects one by one and hopefully, by pointing out some of the many pitfalls that may be encountered, give some sound advice to those who would like to assemble an antique wine equipage for modern use.

There are few people today who buy their wine by the cask and therefore need sealed bottles in which to keep it, though such bottles may be used for decanted sherry. There are of course many who collect old wine bottles simply because they are attractive and most try hard to acquire a bottle of every type and from every decade in which they were once used. Very large bottles may be used to good effect as the bases of table lamps and provided they are not drilled to take an electrical cable, there can surely be no harm in putting them to such use. Unfortunately the price of good, and particularly sealed, early wine bottles has reached very high levels compared with that of other glass because of the attention of a few collectors and the recent trend for a small number of wine merchants to give their offices and retail premises a period atmosphere by displaying past tools of their trade. For similar reasons there are few uses for bin labels today, although for those with a large cellar, and for those who buy and sell wine, bin numbers are as relevant now as when they were first made.

Corkscrews on the other hand are more useful. A large number are still thoroughly practical, particularly perhaps those of T-configuration and some of the nineteenth century mechanical types. Care must be taken when using an old corkscrew to ensure that the point is still sharp and that the worm has not deviated from its original pattern. Should anyone be tempted to employ a defective corkscrew, then the problem will only become worse with use. A corkscrew which has lost its tip, or which has been otherwise mutilated, will foul the cork or will be likely to dislodge a piece of cork into the wine itself. It should particularly be remembered that some antique screws have now acquired a very substantial value owing to the growing attentions of corkscrew addicts. The utilisation of any antique exposes it to possible damage and the greater the value, the greater the care that should be taken to protect it from breakage. At the time of writing this, corkscrews do not on the whole warrant the cost of reproduction (with the exception perhaps of the Vulcan which makes no pretence at antiquity), but it seems likely that this situation will not obtain for long. Buyers should be aware of the possibility of rebrushed handles, sharpened points and evidence of worn parts having been reshaped.

Colour plate 50. An arrangement of wine antiques. Apart from the cinnamon sticks, fruit and sugar used for making punch, there is a punch bowl, ladle and strainer, a 'Newcastle' goblet and a plain example, a finely engraved silver beaker, a nutmeg grater and box, a corkscrew dating from 1710 and a blue glass decanter with a magnificent label for sherry.

A wine taster, or *tastevin,* has always been a tool of the professional. However, before serving wine at a dinner party many men like to ensure that the wine from their cellar is not too old, too young, tainted or simply bad, and for this reason they take the precaution of having a small tasting before the guests arrive. One might use a wine glass, but if a taster is available, then it may well be used instead. Indeed, with its many indentations and bright lustre, it can show the colour of the wine very well and give the owner a preview of its taste with great satisfaction.

Tastes vary as to where one might decant red wines. Some, who have tables in their cellars, prefer to do it there. Others may perform the operation over the kitchen sink, while yet more prefer to do it in the dining room. Those who prefer to decant their wines upstairs might well use a bottle carrier to bring the bottles up from the cellar, thereby keeping them undisturbed and in a horizontal position. A Georgian bottle carrier is ideal for this purpose. For those who decant their wine in the cellar the decanters

Plate 294. A great many people feel that all antiques should be revered and that somehow age mysteriously bestows merit. It doesn't. This is a bad corkscrew; apart from being boringly simple, it will no longer work properly because the tip has been broken from the worm and the final curve of it is straightened. Any endeavour to use it would result in a crumbled cork that would send pieces of debris into the wine. It is rusty, battered and frankly worthless.

too may be brought to the dining room in an upright carrier. In any event, a funnel, particularly one made in silver (see Chapter 8), and a decanter are as useful now as they have ever been and eighteenth century funnel design has not been improved upon. Decanting machines can, of course, also be used to spectacular and sensible effect.

From the practical point of view a Georgian decanter, particularly one dating from the late eighteenth century, is to be preferred. The lack of sharp angles at the shoulders makes for easy pouring, the neck rings allow one to get a good grip and the restrained decoration allows one to see clearly the colour and clarity of the wine. It is for the latter reason, as already stated elsewhere, that the drinking man prefers his glass to be plain, while glass collectors generally prefer theirs to be decorated. The only drawback to the use of Georgian decanters today is their escalating cost, and great care should be taken when making a purchase that it is the genuine article. A Georgian decanter should at least have a contemporary stopper; it is unfortunately difficult to prove that it is original unless both the stopper and the body are numbered or have some peculiarity of design common to both.

Many decanters made in the twentieth century in Georgian style, while not intended to be fakes, are so good that at first glance one may think them to be original. One method of detecting a copy is to examine the neck rings. In the late eighteenth century, these were formed of applied annulets

Plate 295. Pieces from a suite of glass that at first sight might appear to be Georgian, or more precisely, early 19th century. The decanter and claret jug look quite convincing, as does the beaker. The variously sized glasses are less convincing, but the real give-away is the straight-sided finger bowl in its stand. This is not a Georgian pattern and proves beyond peradventure that the entire suite is a copy. Imagine what one would think of the decanter by itself though.

of glass. Later, in high quality glass, they could be produced by cutting the decanter neck back, leaving the rings proud. While some twentieth century copies have applied neck rings, others were machine pressed into a mould which included the neck rings. In this case, the interior surface follows the exterior and one can feel the negative indentations inside the neck. The presence of this feature is a certain indication of modern manufacture. Naturally a small number of twentieth century decanters *are* intended to deceive and one should guard against, for example, replicas of so-called ship's decanters which have had their bottoms scratched and abraded to simulate wear and tear. (Those engraved with ships and inscribed OUTWARD BOUND and HOMEWARD BOUND are invariably twentieth century). The same can be said of outsize decanters which now command a premium.

Recently decanter prices have reached a level at which it is considered worth executing repairs. The broken lip of a decanter for instance, might be ground down and the neck of another substituted in its place and glued in position with modern adhesives. It is not always easy to detect such a repair as, if done well, it will correspond with some form of horizontal decoration, be it a neck ring or step cutting. Again, investigation of the inside of the neck will disclose this type of repair since new and old will seldom match in diameter. Although many repairs are quite acceptable, an item which has been over-restored seldom merits the attentions of the serious collector. Any glass object with a handle should be very carefully checked at the union of the handle with the body, as this is the one point

Plate 296. During the 19th century large houses employed more and more servants and the need was felt for greater security concerning the contents of the cellar. This bottle carrier, made of maroon-painted steel with a pretty turned wood handle, is fitted with a door which may be padlocked, and makes an interesting alternative to the standard bottle carrier.

Plate 297. A delftware plate of the late 17th century. As indicated it is the third plate of a longer series (only three of which survive in this case). When the plates are put together the verse reads as follows: 1. A friendly Feast. 2. ? 3. Good Wine and Beere. 4. And Wholesome Cheese. Does any reader know the remaining lines? Plates from two other series are known.

where damage most frequently occurs. It is quite normal to find on the widest part of decanters some very tiny star cracks, a form of damage easily occasioned when two decanters knock together. Such a crack will not render a decanter useless, but its monetary value will be substantially reduced. Such a piece may make an excellent acquisition though, for someone who wishes to use a decanter daily.

How many readers have not been to an hotel or restaurant and witnessed white wine being chilled in a metal bucket beside the table before being served? Though eighteenth century silver table coolers are no less efficient, it has to be confessed that they are beyond the means of most people being reckoned in tens of thousands of pounds for pairs of good examples. Silver plate and other examples can still be found however, for far less cost. Recently double-skin clear plastic coolers have been introduced which obviously cannot compare aesthetically with eighteenth and nineteenth century pieces, but nevertheless are a considerable improvement on some of the modern metal buckets.

Larger wine coolers, which are of course pieces of furniture, can be most attractive. Although modern refrigeration and insulation techniques enable wine to be chilled without being plunged into iced water and dried

265

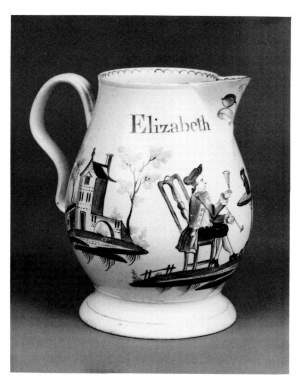

Plate 298. A Leeds creamware jug which is inscribed 'Elizabeth Knight'. It is decorated with red and black enamels and, apart from the houses with their rather Chinese-looking roofs, the principal scene is two seated men smoking and drinking.

Plate 299. A silver jug in the form of a head of Bacchus, clearly indicating that it was intended for wine. The head was moulded during the 19th century from an earlier, plain, 17th century tankard and the present handle and upper section were also added at that time. The original silver bears the hallmarks for 1759 and the maker's mark for Thomas Cooke & Richard Gurney but because the additions are not marked, this is not a legal silver object and it would be unlawful to attempt to sell it.

with unsightly towels, the vision of an antique cooler brimming with chilled bottles may present a veritable cornucopia of generosity and constitute a magnificent method of getting a party in a good mood. Coolers are often used to display plants and it is an easy matter to remove the greenery temporarily and replace it with ice. It is sad that so many wine coolers end their days in polite drawing rooms as receptacles for undarned socks or other items which their owners prefer not to display!

A well-designed wine cooler should be made in fine materials and fine carving and good workmanship will always reflect this. It is now very seldom that the original lead lining of a cooler survives intact and does not leak. However, it is a straightforward matter to re-line an old piece with a thin sheet of lead obtained from a builder's merchants and thereby renew its useful life.

Any well-equipped dining room should also be fitted with a sideboard, but seldom, if ever, does one encounter the wine cooler drawer of a sideboard being used for its original purpose. They are though, frequently used as cellarets and the top surface of the sideboard is the perfect place

Plate 300. Although the photograph appears to show a book, it is in fact a brandy flask, leather bound and entitled appropriately 'Paradise Regained'.

Plate 301. In the days before hot water bottles, beds would be warmed with warming pans. During the 19th century these were normally plain and in copper, but 17th century examples exist with brass lids, often amusingly embossed and engraved. This example bears the legend 'The Vintners Armes' and the date '1630'. The centre has a crude representation of the arms of the Vintners' Company.

to keep the decanted wines and port prior to bringing them to the table. Butlers' trays are often also encountered, but generally in quite the wrong context. Whereas they were made to be stored and brought out by the butler for temporary use, today they make an ideal stand for the battery of bottles which are often produced for pre- and post-prandial drinks in the drawing room.

One cannot pretend that wine labels can be put to much use today except perhaps on the rare occasions when two different wines of a similar appearance may be served at one sitting. However, many houses have a table whereon is placed a group of decanters or a tantalus containing spirits or sherry and to have a label on these indicating their contents is most desirable. When buying a wine label care should be taken to ensure that the name of the wine coincides correctly with the date of the label. There was no demand for example, for an eighteenth century label for 'Whisky' for, although it was available, it was not a socially acceptable drink for those who could afford silver wine labels. Silver labels should always be checked by the 'blowing' procedure (see page 274), before purchase as it is not uncommon for a label with a frequently encountered name such as 'Madeira' to be re-engraved with a rare name or one which is in greater demand, such as 'Port' or 'Claret'. With plated labels there is a difference in value between Sheffield and electroplate examples, the former being more expensive than the latter. An item loses its value if it is re-plated.

Plate 302. Two rather attractive, if simple, pairs of wine label rings, one pair dating from 1796 and the other from 1801. What a pity it is that some people choose to wear these as bracelets and wear them out unnecessarily quickly.

On the other hand (to paraphrase a popular expression from *1066 and All That*), a coaster is 'a good thing'. Any decanter put on a polished surface should be placed in a coaster, particularly when there is more than one decanter on the table. Coasters will prevent the two from chipping if they accidentally touch. Double coasters in the form of jollyboats or decanter wagons are perhaps rather 'over the top' for a domestic dining table, but certainly look magnificent at a grand banquet or official function. Wooden based silver or silver plated examples may be preferred, though it cannot be denied that papier mâché coasters are very attractive. However, if any wine is spilt on to the latter, it should immediately be wiped away as it can soon destroy the structure of the paper. Sheffield plated coasters can be identified by a vertical seam somewhere on their sides, while electroplate examples do not exhibit this feature.

Antique drinking glasses constitute one area where modern design has a distinct edge over the antique counterpart. One very attractive feature of wine is its smell — its 'nose' or 'bouquet'. It is not merely an affectation when some wine buffs roll the wine around in their glass and take a deep intake of breath through their noses to assess the subtle nuances of the bouquet. Professionals, and some amateurs as well, can tell much about a vintage or grape variety from its nose alone. To make the most of this feature a wine glass should be in-curved at the top and the glass of sufficient size that it need be filled only a third full or less. The practice of using small glasses and filling them to the rim dispels the bouquet. A

Plate 303. A claret jug made entirely of silver. At first sight this might be thought to date from the late 18th century, but the attenuated neck and surface decoration differentiate it from the prototype which can be seen in plate 144, page 149. It has a well-cast and chiselled handle and was made in 1886 by Charles Boyton & Sons.

rich, full-bodied red wine will be more aromatic than a light table red, which in turn will probably have less to offer the nose than a white wine. Consequently they should be served in ever decreasing sizes of glass. A white wine is furthermore served in a smaller glass because it should correctly be drunk cold. It is better to let the bottle remain in the cooler and only a small amount warm up in the glass than to allow a lot of wine to warm and spoil.

Though there are some who drink an evening glass of sherry or port from an eighteenth century wine glass, the majority of glasses are too small for sensible use and only goblets compare favourably in size with today's wine glass. In the chapter on drinking glasses it was explained that most early glasses had funnel- or trumpet-shaped bowls. The trumpet shape, while being visually attractive, is perhaps the antithesis of the ideal. The only eighteenth century glasses one can commend for wine are those with ovoid bowls, or the so-called 'mead' glasses with their cup-shaped bowls. One certainly cannot recommend late nineteenth and early twentieth century champagne glasses for consumption of that drink. Most champagne glasses made between about 1880 and 1950 were in the form of a shallow saucer atop a thin stem (possibly reflecting the *tazza* form popularised by the Renaissance revival) and nothing could be more ill-suited for enjoying that king of wines. Champagne should correctly be drunk from a tall flute glass. Flutes were made in large numbers during

Colour plate 51. A group of objects which we feel constitutes the basic kit required for the present day drinker. It includes two antique decanters and a magnum carafe, a modern plastic wine cooler, a 'Screwpull' corkscrew, an antique taster, coaster and funnel and four different sized wine glasses, two antique and two modern. Note the considerably thicker feet of the two older examples. The modern examples incidentally, although of an ideal shape, can be bought very cheaply, for less than £1.00 at today's prices.

the second and third decades of the nineteenth century and indeed ale glasses of the eighteenth century were of flute shape. By contrast, many eighteenth and early nineteenth century tumblers are ideal for the consumption of spirits and nineteenth century utilitarian rummers provide excellent drinking vessels for today. Their coarseness perhaps prevents them from being advocated for use on a smart dinner table, but for a daily tipple they are excellent. The long sets of glasses made during the nineteenth century can be extremely elegant and prettily decorated and, although perhaps not all of them can be used, they present a delightful finishing touch to a well-set table. However, while many many antique glasses are not the perfect vessels for the consumption of wine, the utilisation of any beautiful object always constitutes a great joy to the user.

Collecting drinking glasses is principally an area for the specialist. Unless an example is of an unusually rare type, one should avoid glasses with chips on either the foot or the rim. Very small chips can be ground out and then polished and detection can be very difficult. It is, therefore, a good idea when considering a purchase to hold the bowl in one hand and to run the forefinger of the other hand around the base of the glass. By doing so one will probably detect any irregularity in the once completely circular foot. When looking at the rim of a glass, hold it into the light against a plain background and observe how the glass marginally swells at its lip. This is because the glass was hand finished when hot. If the glass does not swell at its very edge, it must have been ground into shape, a technique not practised on eighteenth century drinking glasses. Also consider the colour and clarity of the material itself; pieces of poorer quality such as, for example, a rummer made for use in a nineteenth century tavern, are likely to be blown from glass containing imperfections and will probably also be of a poor colour.

Consideration must be given to items used in the making and serving of punch. Although this drink has generally lost favour and old recipes are seldom used, various concoctions are still encountered at parties, and punch bowls, ladles and toddy lifters can still satisfactorily be utilised today, particularly at Christmas time when mulled wine seems to be appropriate.

An item not discussed in the previous chapters, but which nevertheless is an important feature of the modern domestic cellar, is the wine rack. These provide the most sensible method of storage for wine intended for imminent drinking as a single bottle can be removed without disturbing its neighbours. Whether wine racks were made before the middle of the nineteenth century is open to conjecture, but, being utilitarian objects, they are difficult to date.

Most serious wine enthusiasts keep records of their cellar's contents in a cellar book. This will indicate its current and past contents, when each wine was purchased, from whom and for how much. It may even record

Plate 305. Six various unexceptional drinking glasses. The earliest was made in the 1740s and the latest at the end of the same century. All, apart from the small opaque twist stem glass, are eminently suitable for a glass of sherry or port, but none has any exciting characteristics which would elevate it to the status of a collector's prize possession. Such glasses are still today within the means of a modest collector.

the occasions on which the various wines were served and note with whom, with what food and in what quantities they were consumed. The more ambitious will give tasting notes and possibly comparisons with other wines consumed at the same time. Such records provide a fascinating document to pass on to successive generations of one's family.

To conclude, a word or two about price; there seems never to have been a period when it has not been fashionable to condemn the current pricing of antiques and prices today are higher than they have ever been. Anyone searching for antiques hopes that one day they will chance across a bargain. The lucky ones occasionally do, but it must be remembered that there are many professionals who scour the market place day in and day out for pieces to add to their collections and their stock, and if an amateur buys a piece for apparently little money, the chances are that there will be something wrong with it. It is far better to face the facts and be prepared to pay a reasonable sum of money to acquire precisely the object for which one is looking. It is always worth paying a premium for an object in excellent condition and the idea that because an object has been around for a couple of hundred years it can be excused for being in bad condition must be considered invalid. Condition and quality, of workmanship, materials and design, are of prime importance.

As with all antiques, the moment a collecting mania takes off, the price of the object rockets and as soon as the price of the antique overtakes the price of the modern replica, it is liable to attract the attentions of the forger or 'improver'. However fakes are often betrayed by a magnificent concept crudely executed or by perfection of materials and workmanship combined

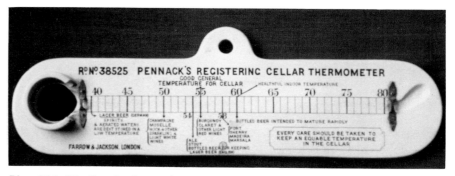

Plate 306. Ideally wine is stored at a constant temperature of 14° centigrade. However constancy of temperature is more important than a low one. Special thermometers were made for cellars; this example is by Farrow and Jackson who were a major supplier of accessories to the wine trade until very recently, and shows the backplate. The thermometer itself has unfortunately not survived!

with unsatisfactory design. In any case many deceptions can be detected by a close study of the technology employed in their making. A comparison between an eighteenth and a twentieth century glass, for example, will by and large show a marked difference in colour; it will also betray the use of different tools. Comparison can make recognition easy, but of course when an object is viewed individually, much practice and experience is required to identify the truth.

When buying any silver item later additions and alterations can often be detected by breathing on the surface and then examining the object in a good light. Most imperfections will immediately become apparent. The effects of blowing may be enhanced if the piece is first cooled in a refrigerator for a short period. Every piece of silver should be thoroughly checked in this manner before purchase as any defect should be reflected in the price. When trying to differentiate between Sheffield and electroplate pieces, blowing will reveal a seam or join on the former, but not on the latter. Sometimes the two can also be identified by examination of surface wear, because the pure deposit left on the base metal during electrolysis is easily abraided, whereas the Sheffield plate and the silver has a more resistant skin of silver alloy, being of the sterling standard.

Reading this last chapter of the book, the novice collector may be tempted into thinking that the acquisition of any antique is a daunting task and that the art market is peopled by sharks. This is just not so. Much good advice can be gained from museums and books, and indeed, from reputable dealers, who, despite rumours to the contrary, exist in large numbers

In conclusion then, the acquisition of a collection of wine-related antiques can be of interest and value, not only financially, but in practical terms too. The authors hope that they have traced the evolution of the various objects comprehensively, but if they have failed to include some aspect of the subject, they will be only too pleased to receive further information so that the shortcomings can be rectified in any subsequent edition. It only remains to wish every reader much happiness in the drinking of fine wines and great enjoyment in the use of the appropriate accessories to accompany them.

APPENDIX I
The Making of Wine

Most books on wine will give an outline of the methods employed in its making; here we intend to give only a simple explanation of what wine is.

As everyone knows wine is made from grapes. When crushed, the grape produces a sweet, fruity juice whilst the skins provide yeasts, pigment and tannins. If left alone the mixture will begin to ferment, that is, the yeasts will convert the sugar content of the grape into alcohol. This is however a self-destructive process as when the alcohol content reaches about 15% the yeast is killed and fermentation ceases. Everyone knows that some grapes are sweeter than others, but few are sweet enough to have any residual sweetness after the 15% strength has been attained through natural fermentation. In fact, the sugar in most wine will have been used up long before that level has been reached. It is quite possible to halt fermentation by adding sulphur, which will inhibit yeast (thus fermentation activity), or by simply adding alcohol. Alternatively with todays modern methods it is possible to remove all yeasts before they have finished their work using a centrifruge.

The juice of all grapes is pale in colour and could produce white wine whether the grapes were green or dark-skinned. Red wine is achieved by leaving the fermented juice in contact with the red skins for some time and rosé by leaving it in contact for only a short time. Champagne and its related imitators are bottled before fermentation is complete, but the majority of wines are put into large barrels or casks to mature. Modern methods dictate that stainless steel vats are mostly used in place of the older wooden types, though some fine wines continue to be made in the traditional manner.

There are three principal ways in which wines differ from one another. First, there is the variety of grape used. It is interesting to note that in England in the 1760s fifty-seven varieties of vine are recorded as being planted. Today thousands of varieties are planted around the world, each intended to produce a different flavour. Second, there is the flavour imparted by the soil in which the vine is grown and this may vary from one tiny patch of ground to another, even within the same vineyard. Third, there is the climate, which varies not only from place to place but, as we all know, from year to year. It is this latter factor which has of course produced one of the most interesting aspects of wine, the variance of vintages. The Romans were aware that some years produced better wines than others and although it is obvious that some great years of Hungarian Tokay were known at the beginning of the seventeenth century, it appears not to have been until the nineteenth that commercial advantage was generally taken of this fact with some of the famous wines of Bordeaux.

A much higher alcoholic content can be achieved by distilling wine, a procedure producing brandy. In turn the addition of brandy to wine will produce a much higher alcohol content than is present in the wine itself, but less than in pure brandy. Common examples of these so-called 'fortified' wines are port, sherry and Madeira.

APPENDIX II
Bottle Sizes

The capacity of a bottle is dictated by a number of factors. Within reasonable limits, the larger the bottle, the better the lasting qualities of the wine inside. The two varieties of wine which keep better than any other are claret and to a lesser extent burgundy and so, if wine is to be bought with a long term interest, it is as well to buy a bottle of large capacity, provided, that is, that one is sure of an occasion at which such a volume can be consumed at one sitting. Not much point one might say, in buying a magnum of fine claret to drink on one's own over a number of days as it will have spoiled after only a number of hours.

Tradition has a part to play in bottle size as well. Hungarian tokay, for example, is normally sold by the half litre, although the substantial majority of wine is sold in bottles of three quarters of a litre (i.e. 75 cl.) or 26⅔ fluid ounces. Burgundy and champagne bottles used to be of a somewhat larger size. During recent years, probably in an attempt to gain a competitive edge in price, many bottles have been made with a capacity of 70 cl. European legislation appears now to be standardising all bottles to three quarters of a litre, though it may take many years for this to be universally adopted.

While very fine wines may be enhanced by bottling in large sizes, inexpensive wines too are now similarly bottled purely for convenience for mass consumption at parties and elsewhere. Large volumes of wine can now be bought in cardboard boxes lined with plastic bags. At the other extreme very small quantities (⅓ or ¼ litre) can be purchased in cans. Many wines are of course available in half bottles (i.e. 37.5 cl. capacity). A few are bottled in a magnum, an almost universal name for the double or 1½ litre bottle.

Champagne has for a long time been bottled in capacities of up to twenty bottles. The names given to the various sizes are taken from biblical characters: four bottles, Jeroboam; six bottles, Rehoboam; eight bottles, Methuselah; twelve bottles, Salmanazar; sixteen bottles, Balthazar; and twenty bottles, Nebuchadnezzar.

Clarets and red burgundies are not bottled larger than an eight bottle size because anything larger would be almost impossible to decant. The larger sizes are as follows: three bottles, marie-jeanne; four bottles, double magnum; six bottles, jeroboam; eight bottles, imperial(e). It is perhaps confusing that a jeroboam can have two different values and that burgundy is sometimes for historical reasons referred to in champagne rather than claret measures.

It has been noted recently that some fine wines from Italy and Spain are being bottled in large bottles, most of which appear to be in multiples of litres and which so far have not been accorded particular names. During the eighteenth and nineteenth centuries very large bottles for wine were called carboys, apparently regardless of their exact size.

During the 1820s a substantial endeavour was made to standardise all measurements throughout the land; the ounce, the yard and the gallon were to be the same in Plymouth as in Aberdeen and to this end every major city corporation ordered standard measures whereby tradesmen and merchants could check their weights and measures. A quite common series of measures runs from a gill through a pint, quart, gallon and so on up to a bushel or more. All these will be stamped wih proof marks signifying that they have been tested to an accepted degree of accuracy. However, just as there is a separate unit of weight for measuring precious metals, the troy ounce as opposed to the avoirdupois ounce, so there was a different measure pertaining to wine to that used elsewhere. It is only very rarely that one encounters an official standard wine measure.

APPENDIX III
Recipes for Concocted Drinks

As has been explained in the chapter on the history of wine drinking, even in classical times it was normal procedure to enhance (or disguise) the natural flavour of wine with a variety of herbs, spices and other additives. Of course few wines were matured, as a satisfactory method of stoppering wine containers was not universally used and additional flavouring was more of a necessity than a pleasant option. The custom however prevailed long after proper methods of corkage were adopted towards the end of the seventeenth century.

While negus and punch seem to have been the mainstay of the eighteenth century wine imbiber, there were many other popular concocted drinks. A large number of recipes for these concoctions were published during the nineteenth century in various handbooks for servants and a small selection follows here.

Flip: While a quart of ale is warming on the fire, beat 3 or 4 eggs with 4 ozs. moist sugar, a teaspoon of grated ginger or nutmeg, and a quart of good old rum or brandy. When the ale is near boiling, pour it into one pitcher, the eggs and rum into another, and turn it from one pitcher to the other, until smooth as cream. Anne Cobbett, *The English Housekeeper*, 1842

To mull wine: Boil the quantity you choose, of cinnamon, nutmeg grated, cloves or mace, in a ¼ pint of water; add a pint of port, and sugar to taste, boil it up, and serve, with thin slices of toast.

Anne Cobbett, *The English Housekeeper*, 1842

To make punch: Put 40 grains of citric acid, 7 full drops of essence of lemon, 7 ozs. of lump sugar, in a quart mug; pour over 1 pint of boiling water, when the sugar is melted, stir; then add ½ pint of rum, and ¼ pint of brandy.   Samuel and Sarah Adams, *The Complete Servant*, 1825

Shrub: To 1 quart of strained orange juice, put 2lb. loaf sugar, and 9 pints of rum or brandy; also the peels of half the oranges. Let it stand one night, then strain, pour into a cask, and shake it four times a day for four days. Let it stand till fine, then bottle it.

Anne Cobbett, *The English Housekeeper*, 1842

Wine posset: Boil some slices of white bread in a quart of milk; when soft, take it off the fire, grate in half a nutmeg, and a little sugar. Pour it out, put in a pint of sweet wine by degrees, and serve it with toasted bread.

The Housekeepers Receipt Book, 1813

APPENDIX IV
Alphabetical List of Names on Wine Labels

The following list of wines is largely composed of names noted on wine labels by members of the Wine Label Circle. In drawing up this list we have discarded names which are obviously grain spirits, but it is quite probable that a substantial number of non-wine names remain as we have been unable to check with certainty the nature of every item. In addition we have by and large deleted variations of spelling, though a few, such as that for claret, have been left. A great many names are spelt in more than a dozen ways and generally we have retained the common form.

Adega
Aguardente
Alba
Albaflora
Alchermes
Alicante
Alize
Almade
Almeida
Aloque
Aminta
Amontillado
Amorosa
Angelique
Anjou
Apricot
Arbois
Argostola
Arinto
Armagnac
Artimina
Assmanshauser
Asti
Athalie
Avalon
Avignon
Ay

Bakano
Banyuls
Barolo
Barossa
Barsac
Beaujolais
Beaume
Beaune
Benicarlo
Benrig
Berne
Bernis
Bochet
Bordeaux
Bordeos
Bounce
Bouquet Du Roi
Bourgogne
Bourguille
Brandewyn
Brandy
Brandy Shrub
Brescia
British
Bronte
Brown Bang
Bual
Bucellas
Buchanans Royal Household
Buda

Budock
Burdeos
Burgundy
Burntisland
Bushby

C.A.
Cacao
Cahors
Calabre
Calamity Water
Calcavella
Calliste
Canary
Cannella
Caore
Cap Breton Rouge
Cap De Bonne Espèrance
Cape
Cape (Red)
Capillaire
Capo Buona Speranza
Capri
Captain White's
Capt. Master R.M.
Carlo Witz
Carton
Catalan
Caveza
Cavo
C. De M
C. De Rose
C.E.
Celia
Centurin
Cérons
Chablis
Chagny Blanc
Chamberry
Chambertin
Chambolle
Champagne
Chareck
Chateau Grillée
Chateau Lagrange
Chateau Larose
Chateau Margaux
Chateau Y'Quem
Cherac
Cherry Bounce
Cherry Ratifia
Chetna
Chianti
Chiches
China
Ch. Lafue
Chusclan
Chypre

Cider
Cipro
Claret
Clairret
Clarete
Clarett
Clarret
Clart
No 1 Claret
No 2 Claret
Claret 2
Claret 66
After Dinner Claret
Australian Claret
Best Claret
Dinner Claret
E. Claret
English Claret
F. Claret
French Claret
Light Claret
Old Claret
Premier Claret
Rioja Claret
Clary
Clos Veugeot
Clynelish
Cockagee
Cocktail
Cognac
Coldinghame
Colenso
Coleraine
Collares
Coltsfoot
Commandaria
Como
Condrieux
Constantia
Convent
Corremilla
Corton
Cos D'Estournel
Côte Rôte
Coulanges
Country
Cowslip
Crèma Di Vino
Creole
Currant Wine
Cylinh
Cyprus

Dalmatia
Damascene
Dantzic
Davidson
De. La. Côte

Derdesheimer
D'Madras
D'Oeil De Perdrix
Donald
D'Orgeat
Draagenstein
Dry
Duke
Dunville
Durhin

Elder
Elderberry Wine
Elie
English
English Wine
Ennishowen
Erlaure
Escubancy
Espagne
Esparin
Espiritu Santo
Essence
Este-Este
Etna
Extra Preserve

Facel
Falerian
Faro
Flore
Florence
Fontenoy
Foyolle
French Wine
Frontiniac

Gamelrom
Garachio
Garus
Gilka
Giscours
Gloria Mundi
Grande Maison
Graves
Grayes Wine
Green Grape
Grenache

Hautbrion
Hay
Hermitage
Hippocras
Hocheimer
Hock
Home-made
Home Made Wine
Hungary

Ideal
Imperial
India
Indian Sherry
Ionia
Ischia
Italian

Jerez
Johannisburg
Jurancon

La Côte
La Fille
Lafite
Lamalgue
Lanalque
Langon
Languedoc Rouge
Lavradio
Leagus
Le de Non
Lentolaccio
Leoville
Lillet
Lisbon
Lissa
Lombock
Lunel
Lutomer

Macabor
Macon
Madiera
Majorca
Malaga
Malmsey
Malt Wine
Mandarinette
Maneater
Manzanilla
Maraschino
Marc
Marcella
Marcobrunner
Margraviat
Marsala
Medina
Medoc
Melniek
Melomel
Mendia
Messina
Methelgin
Methuen
Mirabolante
Mischianza
Monrose
Monte Catini
Monte Pulciano
Montesquieue
Montferrato
Montrachet
Morat
Moselle
Mothers Ruin
Mountain
Mourache
Moyeau
Mr. Allsopp
Mr. Hendrie
Mr. Snodgrass

Mr. Tarratt
Mrs. M. Whylock
Mrs. Travers
MS.
Mulseau
Muratore
Muron
Murseault Blanc
Muscat
Muscatel
Musigny
Muskatvin
M Wine

Native
Nectarine
Nector
Negus
Nelson
Neuchatel
Newtonia
Nice
Nig
Noiset
Norfolk
Noussa
Nuits
N. Punch

Obermmel
O.D.V.
Ofner
Old J.
Old Tom
Olliver Rily
Oloroso
Orange Wine
Ovile
O.W.
Oyras

Pagarès
Paid
Pake
Palme
Palmella
Palmer, Cht
Pando
Parfait Amour
Partners
Pass The Bottle
Pasto
Patras
Paxarete
Peau D'Espagne
Pedro Jimenez
Peralta
Père Kerman
Perignan
Persicoa
Persico
Picolito
Pisco
Pomard
Pomerans
Pomino
Pontac
Pontet Canet
Popt
Port
Portaport
Porto see also Oporto

Porto Seabra
Portugal
Poturon
Priosato
Prunelle
Ptissane Royale
Punch
Pyment

Quinta De Ponta

Rack
Raisin
Ralph James & Robert
Rancio
Ransford
Rare Old Fank
Raspail
Rat
Ratafia
Ratzersdorf
Rauzan
Redemptine
Refosco Del Année
Regent
Reignac
Renadt
Reno
Rhenish
Rhone
Rob Roy
Rocamadora
Rodego
Romanee
Rosa
Roster
Rota & Rotta see also Tent
Roublon
Roussillon
Roquemare
Royal
R.S.
Rudesheimer
Rustenberg

Sack
St. Estephe
Saint George
St. Joseph
St. Julian
St. Laurent
St. Lorent Du Rein
St. Perez
Samos
San Loranp
Santenay
Santo
Santo-Nero
Santoria
Santornei
Santo Vin
Saumur
Sauterne
Schiraz
Scopoli
Segus
Sercial
Setges
Setubal De Portugal
Sévé
Sherry
Shrub

Sicily
Sillery
Skydam
Sloe Wine
Smyrna
Solera
Solferino
Southern
Spanish
Spruce
Stein
Steinberg
Stisted
Strong White Wine
Sultana
Sweet
Syracuse

Tanazon
Tarragona
Tavel
Teneriffe
Tent
Termo
The Abbots Bottle
The Duke 1812
The Old
Thera
Thompson's Grand
Tokay
Tonnert
Torino
Touriga
Tours
Trappistine
Tria Juncta In Uno
T. Stevens
Turanfon Blanc
Touriga

Valedpénas
Vallena
Valmur
Valpolicella
Vandegrave
Van De Purll
Van Der Horn
Verdelho
Vergun
Versenet
Verveine
Vespetro
Vho Romano
Vidonia
Vin
Volnay
Vosne

Walporzheim
Webber
White

Xaloque
Xérès

Yvorne
Yap

Zantera
"Zq"
Zeltingen

GLOSSARY

Amphora: a large Graeco-Roman or Egyptian pottery storage vessel usually with two handles and a pointed base.

Archimedean screw: a bladed spiral screw with a central core (see chapter on corkscrews).

Art nouveau: a late 19th/early 20th century stylistic movement characterised by sinuous curves, stylised flowers and leaves and a tendency towards asymmetry.

Arts and Crafts: a late 19th century decorative movement emphasising handicrafts and good design inspired by the works of John Ruskin and William Morris.

Astragal: a moulding with its cross-section composed of a rectangle surmounted by a semi-circle.

Augur: a bladed spiral screw (see chapter on corkscrews).

Baroque: a late 17th/early 18th century art form originating in Italy and characterised by exuberant decoration and symmetrical curvilinear lines, particularly the G-scroll.

Bead: a repetitive moulding comprising a sequence of conjoined hemispheres of small size.

Bead and reel: a classical repetitive moulding comprising lengths of beading (q.v.) separated by oblong reels.

Bellarmine: a Rhenish stoneware flask with a moulded mask of a bearded man opposite the handle. Made from about the 15th century onwards and later named after the Counter-Reformationist, Cardinal Roberto Bellarmino.

Binning: the method of stacking bottles on their sides in pigeon holes in a cellar.

Bright cut: a form of engraving, particularly on silver, whereby minute slivers of metal are removed with a graver leaving a glistening surface.

Cabriole leg: a leg curving outwards at the top or knee and tapering in an elongated 'S' towards the foot. Originated in China and popular in England from the early 18th century onwards.

Cartouche: a tablet, normally in the form of a curling scroll or shield to accommodate an inscription or armorial device.

Casting: a method of construction using a mould.

Champfer: (or bevel). An angle cut at the edge of a flat surface.

Chasing: the tooling of a metal object from its outer surface to produce a raised pattern.

Chinoiserie: the Western imitation of Oriental art. Late 17th century onwards.

Creamware: a variety of 18th century lead glaze pottery with a cream-coloured body containing flint.

Cross-banded: veneered decoration on the edge of furniture and panelling where the wood grain is at a right angle to the edge.

Delftware: English tin-glaze earthenware made from the 16th century onwards emulating similar earthenware products from the Dutch town of Delft.

Die-stamping: a method of decorating and piercing metal by compressing and puncturing it in a heavy press.

Earthenware: (pottery). All types of wares made from clay.

Egg and dart (egg and tongue): a repetitive classical pattern consisting of alternating ovals and arrow heads. It signifies Life and Death.

Embossing: generic term for relief decoration on metal.

Enamelling: a form of decoration in which a layer of glass is fused to a metal base.

Engraving (on metal and glass): a method of decorating a surface by inscribing the required pattern with a rotating abrasive wheel or a sharp tool (diamond point or steel graver).

E.P.N.S. (Electro-plated Nickel Silver): electro-plate wares (usually nickel though sometimes silver) were coated with silver by the process of electrolysis. Process patented in 1840.

Escutcheon: originally a shield bearing a coat of arms, but also a decorative Greek plaque. (In addition a metal plate protecting a keyhole on furniture.)

Etching: the process of decorating metal by the application of acids.

Faience: French name for tin-glazed pottery.

Feather-edge: a form of bright cut (q.v.) chased, fluted decoration used as a border on silver, especially spoons and forks.

Fluting: ornamentation of close-set, concave semi-circular, vertical grooves.

Gadrooned: a decorative moulding of convex curves, usually used as an edging.

Garrya husks: classical decoration of stylised bell-flowers.

Gilding: decorating with a very thin layer of gold leaf.

Gothic: an art form characterised by pointed arches, trefoils, quatrefoils etc. Originated in France in the 12th century and was revived (in a modified form) in Britain in the 18th and 19th centuries.

Hobnail: a variety of glass cutting whereby a grid of Vs cut in the surface leaves an upstanding pattern of squares.

Ivorine: a 20th century plastic imitation of ivory.

Japanning: the Western imitation of Oriental lacquer work.

Knop: a decorative swelling on the stem of a glass object.

Lead glass: glass containing a percentage of lead oxide. Often called lead crystal, thereby confusing it with rock crystal which is naturally occurring.

Lignum vitae: a very hard and dense wood from South America; often used for turned treen and said to have life-giving properties, hence its name.

Lunar slices: a variety of late 18th century glass cutting, particularly favoured in Ireland, comprising the removal of shallow, crescent-shaped slices.

Lustreware: pottery fired with an iridescent metallic glaze.

Mannerism: a development of the Renaissance style, characterised by elongated forms.

Marvering: the finishing of glass by rolling the still-hot melt on a 'marvering' table (see Introduction).

Metal: in the context of this book, the substance or composition of glass.

Must: the residue left after juice has been pressed from the grapes, stalks etc.

Neo-classicism: a style which emerged in the 1750s characterised by symmetry, simple geometric forms and the use of classical Greek and Roman architectural ornament.

Nipt diamond waies: a form of glass decoration dating from about 1660-90 in which trails of applied glass are pincered while still molten to form a trellis pattern. Particularly associated with George Ravenscroft.

Ogee (double ogee): an elongated 'S' shape (repeated).

Paktong: an alloy of copper, zinc and nickel invented for Imperial Chinese use. Used in the 18th century in England as an economic alternative to silver.

Papier mâché: a moulded composition of layered or pulped paper and glue. Commonly lacquered or japanned.

Patera (plural paterae): an oval or occasionally circular medallion frequently incorporating a stylised flower head.

Pennyweight: one twentieth of a troy ounce.

Pontil rod: a solid iron rod used in a glasshouse for handling glass during making.

Pricking: a form of decoration found on 16th and 17th century silver consisting of numerous tiny dots executed by needlepoint.

Prunt: a small blob of glass applied to the main body of a piece for the purpose of decoration.

Raising: a silversmithing operation whereby a flat sheet of metal is hammered over a block to produce a hollow shape.

Reeding: a form of simple convex moulding comprising two or more closely spaced parallel grooves.

Repoussé: the projecting decoration on metal achieved by hammering from the underside.

Renaissance: a sophisticated cultural and artistic movement based on Ancient Roman ideals which began in Italy in the 14th century and spread throughout Europe. Decorative motifs were based on classical orders of architecture and ornament found on Roman sarcophagi.

Romanesque: a pre-Mediaeval art form characterised largely by rounded arches and chevron decoration.

Salt glaze: a glaze applied to stoneware and formed by the addition of salt during firing in the furnace which produces a distinctive speckled and pitted surface.

Silesian: a square or polygonal tapered stem found on glassware.

Silver standards: Sterling: an alloy of silver and other metals where the silver content is 925 parts per thousand; **Britannia:** The same but with the silver content 958.4 parts per thousand.

Soda glass: glass in which sodium carbonate replaces potash as the flux.

Hard/soft soldering: the joining of two pieces of metal by melting lead (soft) or silver (hard) with a flux.

Strapwork: a form of (originally Renaissance) decoration characterised by symmetrical arrangements of simulated leather straps or carved fretwork.

Strawberry cutting: a variety of glass cutting consisting of hobnails (q.v.) with additional hatching.

Tazza: originally a shallow saucer on a stem and foot. Often incorrectly used to describe salvers on feet.

Tigerware: a type of late 16th and early 17th century stoneware with a heavily mottled brown salt glaze producing an appearance not unlike that of the skin of a leopard.

Tin glaze: an opaque white glaze applied to earthenware and made from oxides of lead, tin and silicate of potash.

Toleware: originally a term used to describe American japanned metalwares, but more recently used in reference to similar British wares. Derived from the French name for the same, 'tôle peint'.

Treen: literally 'wooden', but generally used to describe domestic utensils made of wood and most particularly for items made on a lathe.

Ullage: seepage or loss of wine from a bottle or cask in its stored state through an apparently firm stopper.

Wirework: decoration formed of silver mouldings (often rims). Wire is the general term for metal (particularly silver) mouldings of almost any cross-section.

Wrigglework: a form of engraving upon silver whereby the graver is wriggled from side to side producing a wavy or zig-zag line.

BIBLIOGRAPHY

Note: A great many general books on English furniture, silver and glass will yield some information. Serious students are recommended to refer to the journals of the Furniture History Society, the Silver Society and, in particular, the Wine Label Circle.

General

Butler, Noel G., *The Philoenic Antiquary,* catalogue of the British Antique Dealers Association Exhibition of Period Accessories for the Wine Drinker, 1978.

Clayton, Michael, *The Collector's Dictionary of the Silver and Gold of Great Britain and North America,* second edition, Antique Collectors' Club, 1985.

Fleming, John, and Honour, Hugh, *The Penguin Dictionary of Decorative Arts,* Penguin, 1977.

Gabler, James, *Wine into Words,* Bacchus Press, 1985. (A bibliography of wine books.)

Loyen, Frances, *The Thames and Hudson Manual of Silversmithing,* Thames and Hudson, 1980.

Pinto, Edward H., *Treen and Other Wooden Bygones,* Bell and Hyman, 1969.

Simon, André, *Bottlescrew Days,* Duckworth, 1926.

Taylor, Gerald, *Silver,* Penguin, 1963.

Weinhold, Rudolf, *Vivat Bacchus,* Argus Books, 1978.

Witt, Cleo, Weeden, Cyril, and Palmer Schwind, Arlene, *Bristol Glass,* Redcliffe Press Ltd., 1984.

Younger, William, *Gods, Men and Wine,* Wine and Food Society in conjunction with Michael Joseph, 1966.

The Compleat Imbiber, catalogue of the Gilbey Centenary Exhibition, 1957.

The Goldsmith and the Grape: Silver in the service of Wine, catalogue of a Goldsmiths' Company exhibition, 1983.

The International Wine Trades Loan Exhibition Catalogue, 1933.

Wine and the Artist, 104 prints and drawings from the Christian Brothers Collection at the Wine Museum of San Francisco, Dover Publications, 1979.

History

Johnson, Hugh, Janson, Dora Jane, and McFadden, David Revere, *Wine: Celebration and Ceremony,* Cooper-Hewitt Museum, New York, and the Smithsonian Institute, 1985.

Allen, Herbert Warner, *A History of Wine,* Faber, 1961.

Bottles

Dumbrell, Roger, *Understanding Antique Wine Bottles,* Antique Collectors' Club, 1983.

Ruggles-Brise, Sheelah, *Sealed Bottles,* Country Life, 1949.

The English Glass Bottle, catalogue of the exhibition at the Country Museum, Truro, 1976.

Corkscrews

Perry, Evan, *Corkscrews and Bottle Openers,* Shire Publications, 1980.

Watney, Bernard M., and Babbidge, Homer D., *Corkscrews: for Collectors,* Sotheby Parke-Bernet, 1981.

Tasters

Mazenot, René, *Le Tastevin,* Éditions des 4 Seigneurs, 1973.

Decanters

Davis, Derek C., *English Bottles and Decanters 1650-1900,* Charles Letts & Co. Ltd., 1972.

Hollingsworth, Jane, *Collecting Decanters,* Studio Vista, 1980. (Covers chiefly 19th century decanters.)

Labels

Penzer, N.M., *The Book of the Wine Label,* White Lion Publishers, 1974.

Glasses

Bickerton, L.M., *Eighteenth Century English Drinking Glasses: an Illustrated Guide,* Antique Collectors' Club, 1986.

The Baluster Family of English Drinking Glases, exhibition catalogue of Delomosne and Son Ltd., 1985.

100 British Glasses, exhibition catalogue, Asprey and Company plc, 1985.

Furniture

Edwards, Ralph, *The Dictionary of English Furniture,* second edition, Country Life, 1954, Antique Collectors' Club, 1983.

INDEX

Osierwork (see also Bottles, wanded), 64, 132, 133
Osterley Park, 217
Ostrich egg, 215

Pad feet, 227
Paktong, 176, 185, 237, 281
Palace of the Bishops of Ely, 38
Papier mâché, 25, 28, 177, 183, 185, 187, 188, 189, 254, 268, 281
Parchment, 71, 79, 160
Paterae, 112, 116, 139, 155, 281
Patch, Thomas, 233
Paw feet, 119
Paxaretta, 75
Peak family, 70
Pearwood, 24, 27, 131, 237, 258
Pemberton, Samuel, 94
Penrose of Waterford, 156, 158
Penzer, Dr. Norman, 160, 173
Pepys, Samuel, 70, 216
'Perfect', 90, 91
Pewter, 105, 130, 176, 185, 186, 235, 236, 237, 247, 253, 255
Phipps and Robinson, 240, 250
Phylloxera, 47
Pier tables, 217
Pilgrim bottle, 26, 149, 151, 152
Pinotage, 172
'Pinopage', 172
Pinto Collection, Birmingham, 185
Pitch, 30, 79
Plaster, 30, 79
Platel, Jean, 102
Plymouth, 239, 242, 276
Pommard, 260
Pontypool, 28, 248
Porcelain, 27, 63, 98, 102, 120, 122, 123, 130, 154, 164, 172, 234, 235, 237, 240, 246, 247
Port, 40, 44, 46, 47, 48, 68, 74, 146, 163, 164, 169, 173, 229, 253, 254, 264, 275
Port Sunlight, 186
Posca, 37
Posset, 230
Posset pot, (see also Spout pot and Caudle cup), 230
Posset recipe, 277
Pottery, 29, 30, 33, 38, 62, 64, 71, 72, 78, 123, 133, 160, 164, 186
Prince of Wales feathers, 199, 208
Prunt, 60, 64, 69, 135
Punch, 44, 47, 167, 230-242, 246, 262
  recipe for, 277
Punch bowls (see also Wassail bowl), 14, 19, 42, 153, 230-242, 246, 262, 272
Punch dippers, 231, 233, 234
Punch ladles, 14, 33, 35, 231, 232, 236, 237, 262, 272
Puncheon, 231
Pyne, Benjamin, 246

Rack, 80, 86, 89, 90
Ravenet, 162, 164, 165
Ravenscroft, George, 63, 133, 134, 135, 192, 212, 230

Rawlinson, Mr., 70
Regency, 16, 116, 118, 122, 173, 179
Rehoboam, 276
Renaissance, 15, 16, 191, 280
Renaissance Revival, 270
Resin, 30, 31
Restoration of Charles II, 243
Rhineland, 59, 61, 196
Rhyton, 31, 33
Ricketts & Co., 66, 67, 68, 70
Robinson, Michael, 100
Robinson and Rhodes, 23
Rococo, 16, 17, 154, 155, 163, 164, 165, 175, 185, 205, 232, 241
Rococo Revival, 177, 252
Rodgers & Son, 87, 92
Rodney, Admiral, 147
Rolfe, T., 72
Rolled paperwork, 186
Roman period, 15, 34, 35, 51, 59, 72, 79, 126, 150, 164, 167, 184, 191
Rosewood, 85, 90, 93, 178, 255
Rothschild, Baron Philippe, 71, 76
Rousden, 70
Rowlandson, Thomas, 43, 231, 242
'Royal Club', 90
Royal Society, 39
Rum, 44, 147
Rundell, Bridge and Rundell, 176, 178
Rustenberg, 172

Saccus, 35
Sack, 38, 39, 65
St. Dunstan, 22
St. Eustacius, 40
Saintsbury Club, 45
Salmanazar, 276
Salters' Company, 250
Salvers, 177
Santenay, 260
Sarcophagus, 116
Savoy Glass Works, 230
Scales, 56
Scandinavia, 146
Schofield, John, 187
Scolia, 32
Scotin, Gerard Jean-Baptiste II, 111
Scott, Digby, 171, 176, 178
Scottish influence, 128, 129, 160, 167, 173, 207, 246
Screw-on bottle top, 61, 79
'Screwpull', 91, 93, 271
Seal, 55, 58, 62, 67, 68, 69, 70, 83, 84, 85
Sealers, 79, 81, 83, 85, 86, 88, 89, 90, 92, 94, 95, 96, 97
Sediment, 226, 249, 250, 253
Sercial, 163
'Shaftesbury, The', 245
Shaw, Henry, 233
Sheffield, 22, 87, 92, 96, 157
Sheffield plate, 122, 161, 163, 176, 177, 178, 179, 183, 185, 186, 187, 188, 189, 247, 267, 268, 274
Shell, 237

Sheraton, Thomas, 219, 220
Sherborne Castle, 223
Sherry, 47, 48, 53, 64, 74, 75, 77, 169, 261, 267, 275
Shrub, 147, 277
Sicily, 34
Sideboard, 218, 219, 220, 221, 266
Side table, 217, 221
Sieburg jug, 62
Silber, A.M. (catalogue), 82
Silber and Flemming (catalogue), 83
Silesia, 196, 198
Silver manufacture, 18-23
Simon, André, 153
Sissons, W.G., of Sheffield, 157
Skinner and Rook of Nottingham, 84
Slate, 71
Slipware, 72
Smith, Benjamin, 171, 173, 176, 178, 181
Somerset, 255
Sotades, 31
South Africa, 172
Southwark, 27
Specimens of Ancient Furniture, 233
Spice box and grinder, 39, 216, 234, 239, 240, 241
Spigot, 52, 232, 245
Spirits, 169, 173, 267, 272
Spode pottery, 72
Spout pot (see also Posset pot and Caudle cup), 230
Spratt patent, 96
Staffordshire, 27, 164, 165
Sterling standard, 20, 21, 22
Stockwell, E.H., of London, 159
Stoneware, 63
Stopper, 135, 138, 139, 142, 143, 169, 182, 263
  disc, 142
  globe, 148
  heart, 146
  mushroom, 142, 144, 152
  ovoid, 145
  pear, 133, 134, 139, 141, 145, 146, 152
  shapes, 142, 143
  spire/steeple, 134, 137, 155
  targets/bullseyes, 142, 158, 187
  tasting, 151, 153
Storr, Paul, 123, 171, 176, 178
Stourbridge glass, 156, 191, 204
Strainers, 33, 35, 124, 160, 239, 241, 242, 262
Stringing, 109, 115, 185
Stuart National Anthem, 205, 206
Sussex, 72
Sweden, 148
Sycamore, 27
Symonds, Pentecost, 239, 242
Symposium, 31

Table, 182, 216, 218, 224, 234, 237
Tankard, 266
Tantalus, 148, 267·
Tap, (see also Spigot), 52, 232, 245, 250

Tasters (tastevin), 14, 52, 98-104, 131, 212, 262, 271
Tasting, 262
Tasting book, 58
Tavern, 35, 69, 96, 272
Taylor, Joseph, 92
Tazza, 270, 280
Thatched House Club, 43
The Complete Imbiber, 248
The Complete Servant, 277
The English Housekeeper, 277
The History of English Plate, 103
The Housekeeper Receipt Book, 277
The Mysterie of Vintners, 39
The Practical Cabinet Maker, 117
The Principles of Decorative Design, 17, 18
Thermometer, 55, 58, 274
Thomason, Edward, 86, 88
'Thief', 52
Tigers' claws, 170, 171
Tigerware, 16, 62, 150, 151, 281
Toast, 41, 43, 195, 207
Toddy, 231, 240
Toddy ladle, 236, 237, 238
Toddy lifter, 237, 238, 240, 272
Tokay, 275, 276
Tole peint verrière, 19
Toleware, 27, 247, 250, 251, 281
Tongs, 58
Torchères, 234
Turtleshell and tortoiseshell, 110, 232
Townsend, William, 100
Trade card, 132, 253
Trays, 177, 254
  bottle, 223, 226, 227
  butlers', 228, 229, 267
  wine, 254
Treen, 19, 24, 27, 54, 130, 180, 185, 216, 231, 234, 239, 240, 256, 258, 281
Tripod tables, 221
Trocar, 93
Truro Museum, 69
Tuns, 243
Turkey, 34
Twisden, Francis, 83

Ullage, 52
Unton, Sir Henry, 32
Urbino, 105
Urns, 218, 221

Vans de Purll, 172
Venetian, 134, 191, 192, 193, 195, 196, 202, 211
Verrière, 247
Vertue, George, 111
Verulam, Earl of, 184, 244
Verzelini, Giacomo, 191, 192
Vessels, 212, 214, 216, 258, 272
Victoria, Queen, 22, 47, 70, 167
Victoria and Albert Museum, 105, 233, 234
Victorian, 16, 17, 47, 62, 92, 145, 168, 169, 171, 231
Vidonia, 75
Vincent, Edward, 234
Vines, 49, 50, 177

285

ANTIQUE COLLECTORS' CLUB

The Antique Collectors' Club was formed in 1966 and now has a five figure membership spread throughout the world. It publishes the only independently run monthly antiques magazine, *Antique Collecting*, which caters for those collectors who are interested in widening their knowledge of antiques, both by greater awareness of quality and by discussion of the factors which influence the price that is likely to be asked. The Antique Collectors' Club pioneered the provision of information on prices for collectors and the magazine still leads in the provision of detailed articles on a variety of subjects.

It was in response to the enormous demand for information on 'what to pay' that the price guide series was introduced in 1968 with the first edition of *The Price Guide to Antique Furniture* (completely revised 1978 and 1989), a book which broke new ground by illustrating the more common types of antique furniture, the sort that collectors could buy in shops and at auctions rather than the rare museum pieces which had previously been used (and still to a large extent are used) to make up the limited amount of illustrations in books published by commercial publishers. Many other price guides have followed, all copiously illustrated, and greatly appreciated by collectors for the valuable information they contain, quite apart from prices. The Antique Collectors' Club also publishes other books on antiques (including horology and art), garden history and architecture, and a full book list is available.

Club membership, open to all collectors, costs little. Members receive free of charge *Antique Collecting*, the Club's magazine (published ten times a year), which contains well-illustrated articles dealing with the practical aspects of collecting not normally dealt with by magazines. Prices, features of value, investment potential, fakes and forgeries are all given prominence in the magazine.

Among other facilities available to members are private buying and selling facilities, the longest list of 'For Sales' of any antiques magazine, an annual ceramics conference and the opportunity to meet other collectors at their local antique collectors' clubs. There are over eighty in Britain and more than a dozen overseas. Members may also buy the Club's publications at special pre-publication prices.

As its motto implies, the Club is an organisation designed to help collectors get the most out of their hobby: it is informal and friendly and gives enormous enjoyment to all concerned.

For Collectors — By Collectors — About Collecting

The Antique Collectors' Club, 5 Church Street, Woodbridge, Suffolk IP12 1DS